POWER
AND
INSECURITY

POWER
AND
INSECURITY

═══════════

Beijing,
Moscow, and
Washington,
1949–1988

Harvey W. Nelsen

Lynne Rienner Publishers ▪ Boulder & London

Published in the United States of America in 1989 by
Lynne Rienner Publishers, Inc.
1800 30th Street, Boulder, Colorado 80301

and in the United Kingdom by
Lynne Rienner Publishers, Inc.
3 Henrietta Street, Covent Garden, London WC2E 8LU

Library of Congress Cataloging-in-Publication Data
Nelsen, Harvey W.
    Power and insecurity: Beijing, Moscow, and Washington, 1949-1988.
    Bibliography: p.
    Includes index.
    ISBN: 1-55587-161-5
    ISBN: 1-55587-162-3(pbk)
    1. Soviet Union—Foreign relations—China. 2. China—Foreign
relations—Soviet Union. 3. China—Foreign relations—1949-
4. United States—Foreign relations—1945- 5. Soviet Union—Foreign
relations—1945- I. Title.
DK68.7.C5N45   1989
327.47051—dc19   89-3634
                                                        CIP

British Cataloguing in Publication Data
A Cataloguing in Publication record for this book
is available from the British Library.

Printed and bound in the United States of America

The paper used in this publication meets the requirements
of the American National Standard for Permanence of
Paper for Printed Library Materials Z39.48-1984.

Contents

Foreword

We are now entering a fourth phase of Sino-Soviet relations in the postwar era. In the 1950s, the Soviet Union and China were in an alliance against the United States. In the 1960s, there was the historic split between the two communist giants, but China remained hostile to the United States. In the late 1970s, it seemed as if China and the United States were entering into a united front against the Soviet Union. Now, as the 1990s approach, a normalization of relations between the Soviet Union and China is taking place for the first time in thirty years. Mikhail Gorbachev and Deng Xiaoping are to meet early in 1989, and a settlement of the border issue and a mutual withdrawal of forces from the border region may take place in the next several years, particularly if there is a compromise settlement of the Cambodian issue. The Soviet Union and China have powerful motives for wanting to improve relations with each other. Both are preoccupied with domestic reform and modernization, and both want a stable international environment while they concentrate on their domestic priorities.

In this thorough, well-documented, and wide-ranging account of Sino-Soviet relations since the 1950s alliance, Harvey Nelsen provides the essential background for understanding the latest phase in the relationship and its potential implications for the West. In his incisive analysis, he puts particular stress on the national security policies and threat perceptions of the two great communist powers. His book will be a valuable contribution to the study of one of the most crucial aspects of postwar international relations.

Donald S. Zagoria

Preface

We can never feel secure so long as the United States feels itself insecure.
—Mikhail Gorbachev

This book is an explanation of the Sino-Soviet dispute—from its origins through its militarization to the current phase of detente between Beijing and Moscow. It is an attempt to systematically interpret the history of the dispute in national security terms. The subtitle includes Washington, D.C., because the United States has been at the center of the security concerns of both the major communist powers.

A number of books have been written on the national security perspectives of Moscow and of Beijing. There are many volumes on the topic from a US perspective. This study integrates the viewpoints of the three nations to show how they inter-related and affected one another. The lead-in quotation from General Secretary Gorbachev was chosen because the interplay of threats and security constitutes the analytical theme of the study.

The late 1980s seemed an appropriate time to reconsider Sino-Soviet relations, since the dispute had largely run its course and the danger of an Asian war between China and the Soviet Union appeared less threatening than at any time since the early 1960s. The relations between Moscow and Beijing were not much worse than might be expected between two powers that were not part of the same alliance system. Bilateral relations went from "as close as lips and teeth" in the mid-1950s to the brink of war in 1969. They stabilized in the 1970s, but at a high level of military confrontation. The eventual development of Sino-Soviet détente coincided with (and was partially prompted by) the Reagan Presidency in the 1980s. Tangible progress was made in 1988 on the remaining obstacles to "normalized" relations between Beijing and Moscow.[1]

This book developed from an effort to decipher the twists and turns in Sino-Soviet relations. Issues transformed, disappeared, or even switched sides as the dispute worsened during the first half of its three-decade span and, even though new issues arose in the 1970s, lessened over the past decade. Neither ideology nor economics served as consistent guides to understanding the changes—it was national security perceptions that emerged as the best road map. At every turn, US policies intruded on my attempts to fathom Sino-Soviet bilateral relations. Thus, the book became a triangular analysis.

The chronology uses the last four decades as natural breaking points. By coincidence, watershed developments occurred at the end of each of those ten year periods, so the choice was not based on mathematical neatness. The analytical technique portrays the security and defense policies of Moscow, followed by a parallel exposition for China. Conclusions are drawn from the comparison and contrast. The disadvantage is that a number of specific subjects (for example, nuclear weapons, Afghanistan, and Vietnam) are revisited in different chapters, thus reducing the topical continuity and causing some repetition. I concluded, however, that because the national security perceptions of the actors are so crucial to the course of events, it was most important to provide sustained viewpoints from each capital.

In terms of global power politics, this particular triangle still commands attention. China provides a key variable in superpower relations because it is large, powerful, has nuclear weapons, and does not fall under the hegemony of either superpower. It has been an independent global actor since 1958, when Beijing decided to separate its nuclear development from any form of Soviet command and control. That same year saw Mao Zedong initiate the "Taiwan Straits crisis," which effectively announced the independence of Chinese foreign and national security policies from Soviet leadership. Thus, the People's Republic of China (PRC) has for over thirty years influenced Asian, global, and nuclear politics as an independent actor. Few nations, other than the two superpowers, can make similar claims.[2] By looking at the triangular relations among the US, USSR, and PRC, it is possible to isolate themes of "power and insecurity" that are central to international relations today.

Fundamental questions addressed in the book include why the Sino-Soviet dispute grew so rapidly to dangerous proportions, why it cooled off in the 1980s, and how far the current Sino-Soviet détente might proceed. The role of US foreign policy is systematically explored, but only those aspects that have had a direct impact on the USSR and the PRC. An unexpected discovery was the importance of nuclear weapons in the 1950s and 1960s to the policy processes of all three of the actors. The impact of US nuclear superiority during most of that time period has not been sufficiently appreciated.

The efforts to identify coercion, threats, and threat perceptions in Moscow, Washington, and Beijing carry the study into the slippery area of attributing motives. Memoirs and other accounts by persons involved have been used where available. However, in many cases intentions are intuited on the basis of probability and the known facts. That method will not arrive at the truth in every instance. The alternative would be to omit intentions where they cannot be clearly documented, but history is then reduced to a tedious chronology of events. Domestic politics, of course, weigh heavily on the development of foreign and defense policies. Those factors have been taken into consideration while avoiding too much treatment of the "Kremlinology" literature and its Chinese equivalent. However, the domestic dimensions of US foreign policies are not considered herein. There is an immense literature on that subject and it would draw this study away from its central focus on international power and security concerns. The cut-off for the inclusion of substantial new materials was the end of December, 1988.

The romanization used is pin-yin, a PRC system that has recently been widely adopted in the West. Taiwanese and Mongolian geographic names remain in the "traditional" Wade-Giles system, for example Taipei rather than Taibei.

Funded writing time was made available by the University of South Florida and its International Studies Program, where I hold a professorship. Draft versions of this manuscript benefitted immensely from the expertise of my colleagues in the International Studies Program—Susan Stoudinger, Darrell Slider, and Ambassador John O. Bell. Two historians, John Belohlavek and Gary Mormino, converted much of my tortured prose and opaque analysis into lucid narrative. Rajan Menon of Lehigh University generously offered his expertise in Soviet Asian policy. Lynne Rienner Publishers functions as an academic press by using anonymous experts to review manuscripts prior to publication. Those comments contributed much to refining the study. The deficiencies that remain are mine alone, or the detritus from an imperfect universe.

Notes

1. It is, however, not altogether clear what constitutes "normal" relations between these two giant Asian neighbors.

2. France is still tied to NATO even while maintaining an independent nuclear arsenal and not participating in the joint command structure of the alliance. India, while testing an atomic "device" in 1974, waited until the late 1980s to develop a nuclear arsenal.

Harvey W. Nelsen

Acronyms

AAA	anti-aircraft artillery
ABM	anti-ballistic missile
APSR	*The American Political Science Review*
CCP	Chinese Communist Party
CENTO	The Central Treaty Organization (US founded)
COMECON	The Council for Mutual Economic Assistance (Soviet founded)
CPSU	The Communist Party of the Soviet Union
CQ	*The China Quarterly*
FEER	*The Far Eastern Economic Review*
GLF	The Great Leap Forward (China, 1961-1968)
GNP	gross national product
GPCR	The Great Proletarian Cultural Revolution (China)
ICBM	intercontinental ballistic missile
IRBM	intermediate-range ballistic missile (1,200 to 3,500 miles)
MBFR	Mutually Balance Force Reduction negotiations (NATO-Warsaw Pact)
MPR	The Mongolian People's Republic
MRBM	medium-range ballistic missile (300 to 1,200 miles)
NATO	North Atlantic Treaty Organization (the "Western alliance")
NLF	The National Liberation Front (SRV-dominated political arm in South Vietnam, 1960 to 1975)
NSC	The National Security Council (US)
PLA	People's Liberation Army (China; refers to all armed forces)
PLAAF	People's Liberation Army Air Force
PLAN	People's Liberation Army Navy
PRC	People's Republic of China
PWNL	people's wars of national liberation
ROC	Republic of China (Taiwan)
SDI	Strategic Defense Initiative

SEATO	Southeast Asia Treaty Organization (US founded)
SLBM	submarine-launched ballistic missile
SRV	Socialist Republic of Vietnam (For consistency, the abbreviation is also used for the period between 1954 and 1975 when communist Vietnam was formally a "Democratic Republic.")
UN	The United Nations
US	United States of America
USSR	Union of Soviet Socialist Republics

PART 1

THE FIRST DECADE: ALLIANCE TO ANIMOSITY, 1950–1960

1

Stalin: From the Strategies of Survival to the Manipulation of an Empire

This introductory chapter and the one that follows will begin the exploration of continuity and change in the national security policies and threat perceptions of the USSR. The emphasis is on continuity until the thermonuclear era begins in 1953. Some anonymous scholarly wag averred that the most difficult thing to explain about the Sino-Soviet dispute is why the two powers ever formed an alliance in the first place. This chapter deals with the historical roots of the ill-fated pact from the Soviet perspective. Chapter 3 briefly revisits the topic from the standpoint of the Chinese Communist Party (CCP) leadership.

Historical Background

Two fundamental continuities dominated the career of Joseph Stalin—his tyranny over the Soviet body politic and his pursuit of Soviet national power and security in an extremely threatening and hostile international arena. Until recent times, the foreign policy of the USSR has been synonymous with efforts to ensure national survival. A brief summary of early Soviet national security policies is needed to introduce Moscow's objectives in the cold-war era.

Between 1926 and 1927, Stalin continued the Lenin-initiated program in China of supporting a political alliance between the CCP and the larger, more popular based, Nationalist Party (the Guomindang). A weak China could be used as a launching platform from which such powerful enemies as Japan and Great Britain might harass the Soviets in Central Asia and Siberia. A strengthened China could reduce or eliminate Western and Japanese imperialist presence. Moscow also hoped to gain influence over the leadership and direction of the Nationalist Party. In 1927, the commander of the Nationalist military forces, Generalissimo Chiang Kai-shek,[1] ruined that hope when he ended the Nationalist/Communist alliance in a bloodbath that left the CCP reeling.

Despite the costs to the CCP, the minimal objective was furthered, if not attained. China became more or less reunified under an anti-imperialist government, the Nationalists. The danger that major powers would threaten the USSR from semicolonial holdings in China was much less in 1930 that it had been in 1925. Of course, the anti-imperialism of the Nationalists made no exception for Soviet imperialism, especially as manifested in Moscow's control of the east-west rail link in Manchuria, a part of the Trans-Siberian Railroad. In 1929, Chiang Kai-shek attempted to seize control of that Manchurian segment, but the Red Army easily rebuffed his efforts. Unfortunately for Stalin, the Japanese army saw an impending extension of Nationalist political influence into Manchuria and decided to protect its vested interests through a military takeover of the region. The conquest was completed between 1931 and 1932.

For the remainder of the decade, Stalin moved to protect his Siberian flank by implementing three courses of action. First, he sold the east-west Manchurian rail link to Japan while building a long rail loop that skirted Manchuria to Vladivostok. This removed a potential bone of contention between Tokyo and Moscow. Second, he strengthened Soviet troop strength in the region. This force was tested by the Japanese—most seriously in 1939—and proved capable of defending itself in a large-scale border clash. Third, Stalin normalized relations with the US and Nationalist governments while attempting to interest both in containing Japanese expansionism.

These developments in East Asia were unwanted distractions to Stalin, who was primarily concerned with the European sector. It was widely recognized then, as now, that Germany held the key to the balance of power in Europe. For the halcyon years between 1922 and 1925, the USSR had Germany on its side. Since both nations had been victimized by the Versailles Peace Treaty of 1919, they signed a pact of mutual support known as the Treaty of Rapallo (1922). The British Foreign Office led a drive to reduce punitive war reparations imposed on Germany and to bring that nation back into the Western community. The strategy culminated in the 1925 Treaty of Locarno, which guaranteed Germany's western borders but noted nothing of its eastern frontiers. Great Britain had launched a strategy of aiming German power and future expansionism through Eastern Europe against the USSR. In the words of British Foreign Secretary Austin Chamberlain: "The Polish border is not worth the bones of a single British grenadier."[2] With Adolph Hitler's rise to power in 1933, the strategy assumed alarming proportions. The Berlin-Tokyo Anti-Comintern Pact of 1936 made it likely that Stalin would soon face a two-front war wherein German legions would penetrate the USSR as far as the Ural Mountains while Japan occupied Siberia and Central Asia.

To the delight of Stalin, Prime Minister Neville Chamberlain destroyed the fifteen-year-old British strategy in March 1939. After Hitler ignored his earlier pledge regarding Czech sovereignty by invading Prague, Chamberlain unilaterally guaranteed the Polish border. Any efforts by Hitler to invade the USSR through Poland, the only militarily feasible avenue of approach, would automatically mean war with Britain and her ally France. The groundwork was thereby prepared for the Soviet-German Non-Aggression Pact of August 1939. Stalin and Hitler agreed to divide Poland between them. Stalin could then sit on a hill and watch the tigers fight. This series of events also ended any chance of a Japanese invasion of Siberia, since Tokyo would not have the advantage of catching the USSR in a two-front war. A Soviet-Japanese neutrality pact soon followed, enabling Tokyo to concentrate on its conquest of China without fear for its vulnerable rear areas in Manchuria. The timing could not have been better for Stalin, since Hitler launched his ill-conceived invasion of the USSR in June 1941.

China reentered Stalin's power calculus no later than 1936. Chiang Kai-shek and his Nationalist government might help protect the USSR from the Japanese wing of the Anti-Comintern Pact. Thus, when a renegade general kidnapped Chiang in 1936 and invited the CCP to participate in deciding his fate, Stalin telegraphed urgent orders to obtain Chiang's release. In 1937, the two nations signed a secret alliance, when Japan invaded North China in July, Stalin began a large-scale military assistance program to keep Chiang from surrendering. The help continued even after the Russo-Japanese Neutrality Pact had been signed, ended only with the German invasion of the USSR in June 1941. Stalin's best hope for the security of his eastern frontiers was a prolonged and costly war for Japan in China.

There is no need here to chronicle the events of World War II, but the peace arrangements are important to understanding the 1950 Sino-Soviet Alliance. The February 1945 Yalta summit meeting determined the timing and objectives of the Soviet Union's entry into the war against Japan. Specifically, the USSR pledged to declare war within two or three months of Germany's surrender and had the responsibility of capturing Manchuria and the northern portion of the Korean Peninsula from the Japanese occupation forces. Chiang Kai-shek was not initially informed of the decision due to fears of a security leak, but a few months after the summit meeting, the United States urged the Nationalist government to undertake treaty negotiations with Moscow.

The US-Soviet agreements placed Chiang Kai-shek in a terrible predicament. His government and military forces were bottled up by the Japanese in southwestern China. He could do nothing to prevent a Soviet occupation of Manchuria. The most he could hope for was a Soviet pledge to return the territory to China, and Chiang paid dearly for that concession. Stalin obtained the entire Manchurian rail network, a long-term lease on a naval base and harbor (Lushun and Dalian, also known as Port Arthur and Darien), significant mining rights related to the railroad lease, and, for the first time, Chinese recognition of the "independence" of the Mongolian People's Republic. The latter required China to renounce any claims of suzerainty and accept Mongolia's de facto status as a Soviet satellite nation. The August 1945 Sino-Soviet Treaty was an unmitigated triumph for Joseph Stalin. The Manchurian ports were virtually icefree, unlike any other Soviet outlet to the Pacific Ocean, and they had easy access to the Trans-Siberian Railroad. Czarist Russia had been in pursuit of hegemony in Manchuria even before the Russo-Japanese war o 1904-1905, a war that was largely fought over Manchuria. Stalin had seemingly achieved a goal that his modern predecessors could not.

From Moscow's perspective, East Asia must have looked rosy indeed in the autumn of 1945. Soviet armed forces occupied Manchuria, northern Korea, parts of North China, all of Sakhalin Island, and the Kurile chain. Hegemony over Mongolia was affirmed and, in northwestern China, a Soviet-dominated East Turkestan Republic controlled a large portion of Xinjiang. Virtually the only cloud on the horizon was the US insistence on excluding the USSR (and all other allies as well) from having a meaningful voice in the occupation of Japan. A considerable US military presence still remained in North and East China, but every indication pointed to an early withdrawal.

Most of Stalin's China diplomacy between 1945 and 1949 was intended to protect and consolidate the extraordinary gains won at Yalta and in the August 1945 treaty with Chiang. The CCP, which has barely deserved mention up to this point, began to play a significant role in Stalin's calculation. Mao Zedong had benefited immensely from the Japanese occupation of China and the resultant geographic isolation of the Nationalist government. From a poorly equipped force of 30,000 men in early 1937 holding a few counties in northwestern China, the People's Liberation Army (PLA) had expanded by war's end to over a million strong, operating in the countryside throughout North China and with smaller guerrilla units as far south as Hainan Island. Mao felt ready to challenge Chiang for national supremacy and prepared for a civil war in the wake of Japan's surrender.

Stalin viewed things quite differently. He did not believe that Mao could win; moreover, a civil war might jeopardize his treaty with Chiang. Furthermore, such a conflict might lead to direct US involvement and extend US military presence in North China. Finally, Stalin had little reason to trust Mao, who was not one of the Moscow-trained lackies whom Stalin had earlier dispatched to China to take charge of the CCP. Stalin therefore invoked "proletarian internationalism"[3] and ordered Mao to negotiate a coalition government with Chiang under US sponsorship. He also reportedly suggested that Mao disband the PLA—seemingly a highly unlikely course of action, unless one considers that Stalin, in the same time period, did order the French and Italian communist parties to lay down their arms. Mao reluctantly agreed to pursue negotiations, but he certainly did not disband the PLA.

Meanwhile, Stalin maximized his options. When the Red Army invaded Manchuria, it brought along an old CCP rival of Mao's, Li Lisan. Local provisional governments were set up in Manchuria under Li's titular leadership. If Stalin could find a way to prevent or interminably delay returning Manchuria to the Nationalists, a Soviet-dominated puppet was ready to perform a legitimizing role for the perpetuation of Moscow's control over the region. Stalin soon gave up on that idea, possibly in return for Mao's agreement to negotiate with Chiang. Stalin also allowed the PLA to infiltrate Manchuria and provided it with considerable stores of captured arms. Finally, he stripped Manchuria of Japanese-installed industrial equipment—worth about $1 billion. However, Stalin refrained from doing the same thing in North Korea. Manchuria was systematically robbed of its machinery and rolling stock because, if it were to revert to full Nationalist control, it was important that the region not serve as an industrial bastion for a revitalized China. Even if Mao was eventually able to control the region, it would still be necessary to ensure CCP economic dependence on the USSR. In the Korean case, the Soviet puppet government there was already fully dependent on Moscow due to the artificial division of the peninsula at 38 degrees North. If North Korean industry had been removed, it would have endangered its political survivability in the face of the US-supported rival government in the South.[4]

By the spring of 1946, Stalin was ready to withdraw his forces from Manchuria in order to ensure a US pullout from North China. Chiang's forces had to fight their way into Manchuria against the entrenched PLA. Stalin no longer importuned Mao to avoid a civil war. As long as the Soviets had "plausible deniability" regarding their support for the CCP, no harm could come from a military test of strength.

Stalin also ventured into the Chinese political arena by offering to mediate the civil war following the collapse of the first US efforts to obtain a coalition government in the spring of 1946. He renewed the mediation offer in December 1947 after General George Marshall had also failed to achieve a government of national unity.

Stalin had at least two objectives in proffering his good offices: to reduce the US influence in China, and to revise the economic clauses of the August 1945 treaty (e.g., allowing more Soviet mining rights in Manchuria). In February 1947, the CCP proclaimed nonrecognition of all treaties made by the Nationalists after January 1946, but doing so did not stop Stalin from seeking further deals with Chiang. During the precipitous collapse of the Nationalist armies in 1948 and 1949, Stalin offered a Soviet guaranteed divided China, using the Yangtze River as the boundary between the CCP- and Nationalist-controlled territories. Such an arrangement would have guaranteed a weak China and perpetuated CCP dependence on the USSR. Chiang's government did not respond favorably, and the rapid advance of PLA units into southern China soon outdated the offer. In April 1949, shortly before Mao's forces penetrated the extreme northwest region of Xinjiang, the Soviet consul in the capital of Ulumuqi approached the top Nationalist general there and offered to obtain an order preventing the CCP from occupying the region. In return, the general was to proclaim the area an independent republic, which the USSR would recognize and support. The general refused this quisling role, preferring to see the region remain Chinese.[5] Clearly, Stalin's imperial ambitions in China were not dampened by the prospect of having a "fraternal" party in charge of the nation.

Indeed, Stalin almost overplayed his hand. He was very late in abandoning the Nationalist government, and the Soviet press treated Chiang Kai-shek gently through most of the civil-war period. Only Soviet diplomats followed Chiang's government when it fled the capital of Nanjing and moved to Guangzhou (Canton) in 1949. It was not until July 1949 that an official Soviet military mission flew to communist-held Beijing. In the same month, Stalin invited the CCP chief in Manchuria, Gao Gang, to negotiate a Soviet-Manchurian economic agreement. This was accomplished only two months prior to the official establishment of the PRC on October 1, 1949. Meanwhile, there was a rising tide within the CCP against aligning the "new China" with Moscow. A group led by Zhou Enlai favored a neutral posture for the PRC. However, this threat was averted (see Chapter 3), and Stalin was able to invite Mao to negotiate a treaty.

The Sino-Soviet Alliance of 1950

When Mao journeyed to Moscow at the end of 1949, Stalin did not deign to greet him at the train station. In the weeks of negotiations that followed, Mao was so often ignored that he threatened to return to China. Stalin's neglect of his state visitor may well have been a negotiating tactic, but the Soviet leader also had other priorities. He faced very serious problems on the European front and was not about to devote a major portion of Soviet foreign policy resources to the PRC. Consider for a moment the difficulties facing Stalin in 1949: the reindustrialization and political reconstruction of West Germany, the failure of the Berlin Blockade, the success and extension of the Marshall Plan for European economic recovery, the failure and isolation of the hard-line French and Italian communist parties, the formation of the North Atlantic Treaty Organization (NATO), the growth of the US defense budget and the Strategic Air Command, the reindustrialization plans for Japan, and the defection of Tito's Yugoslavia from the communist bloc. Small wonder that Stalin molded his relationship with the PRC in such a way that China would provide immediate assistance to the USSR while minimizing Soviet investment costs.

Stalin's initial concern was to prevent the PRC from following the Yugoslav road. In 1948, Joseph Broz Tito refused to subordinate his country to Soviet demands and needs. Nationalistic socialism threatened proletarian internationalism. Stalin reacted with a bloody purge of Eastern European communist leaders who had established national reputations in resistance movements against the Nazi occupation. Since the Red Army was in firm control of the entire region (excepting Yugoslavia and Albania), Stalin had little difficulty in carrying out his purge. But if Mao Zedong should opt out of the bloc, Stalin had no means to prevent it, nor any effective method to punish the Chinese leadership for their apostasy. He dealt with this potential threat first by consolidating his special politicoeconomic relationship with Manchuria in the treaty signed with Gao Gang in July 1949 and in the 1950 alliance that stipulated that no third-country citizens would be allowed to live in either Manchuria or Xinjiang. He also tried unsuccessfully to extend the Sino-Soviet joint stock companies into a wider range of industrial, mining, transport, and communications enterprises in the PRC, thereby weakening Chinese economic sovereignty.

On balance, the 1950 Sino-Soviet treaty favored Moscow's interests over those of Beijing, but it entailed real costs to the USSR that the one-sided treaty of August 1945 did not. In the eleven years during which the treaty was active, the USSR committed $1.56 billion in aid to the PRC, including thousands of scientists and technicians (then in short supply in Russia).[6] The most exploitative aspects of the 1950 treaty—the Manchurian railroad, the naval base in Dalian, and the "joint stock" companies (used for the purposes of extractive industry)—lasted only five years. The 1945 Sino-Soviet treaty with the Nationalists had simply exploited a weak China. The 1950 treaty was less exploitive and cost Moscow more because the treaty also incorporated conditions clearly aimed at ensuring PRC dependency on the USSR. For example, all credits provided were in rubles, a non-convertible currency. Chinese repayments took the form of raw-material exports, which were undervalued in the exchange. This effort to subordinate the PRC to the Soviet economy was to fail within a few years of Stalin's death, but the Soviet costs for maintaining the alliance went up during the 1950s. In retrospect, the USSR would have been better off both strategically and economically if Stalin had been able to keep his 1945 treaty with the Nationalist government and the CCP had never come to power.

A case can also be made that Stalin intentionally prevented China from developing wider international contacts. If the PRC obtained general diplomatic recognition from the West, the resulting economic and political options would reduce Beijing's dependency on the USSR. The Soviet boycott of the UN Security Council, begun in January 1950, has been singled out as the

most important strategy Stalin devised to keep China isolated. The UN secretary general at that time, Trygvie Lie, told Soviet Foreign Minister
Vyacheslov Molotov that the boycott was counterproductive and that there
was a good chance the PRC would be admitted to the UN at a very early date
if the boycott were dropped. Molotov "merely smiled."[7]

The Korean War

Whatever Titoist potential the PRC might have had was temporarily averted
by the outbreak of the Korean War. By definition, an alliance extends beyond
bilateral relations. It is supposed to condition a coordinated mutual response
to an external threat or military opportunity. Korea was the first international
test of the newly formed Sino-Soviet alliance. The origins of the conflict are
shrouded in mystery, and it is impossible to determine the priorities that
molded Stalin's decision. Stalin almost certainly authorized the conflict; he
provided North Korean leader Kim Il-sung with the military capability to
launch the attack on South Korea.

Stalin probably considered several factors in his decision to support the
invasion. First, both Secretary of State Dean Acheson and General Douglas
MacArthur considered South Korea (and Taiwan) to be outside the US
defense perimeter in East Asia. All US occupation forces had been withdrawn in June 1949. Vulnerable and expendable, South Korea stood alone.
Second, the United States had reversed its earlier position of keeping Japan
disarmed. What eventually became the Japanese Self Defense Force was in
the planning stages during the early part of 1950. Concomitantly, the United
States announced that US forces and bases would be retained in Japan rather
than be terminated with the signing of a peace treaty with Tokyo. Stalin may
have felt that Soviet bases at the southern tip of Korea would serve to offset
the US presence and provide better defenses for Siberia and the key port of
Vladivostok.

Third, given the 1949 birth of the NATO Alliance, a military consolidation of the Soviet Union's eastern flank may have seemed more important
than before. A consolidation was needed since South Korean President
Syngman Rhee was threatening to invade the North, though his military
might did not match his jingoist rhetoric. Finally, Kim Il-sung and Mao
Zedong probably influenced Stalin's decision. Mao was in Moscow negotiating the alliance when Kim arrived. According to Nikita Khrushchev's memoirs, Mao helped overcome doubts about possible US intervention, thus leading Stalin to provide the military wherewithal for the invasion.[8]

Like most revolutionaries newly come to power, Mao was eager to challenge enemies on his borders and to consolidate his revolution through military strength. Mao's targets included the western salient in Korea, the

Nationalists on Taiwan, and the French in Indochina.

> This put the Russians in a painful dilemma; even if they preferred to be cautious, which is by no means clear, they would lose whatever influence they hoped to exercise over the Chinese revolution and, specifically, would lose their dominant position in North Korea.[9]

Stalin reduced the risk of retaliation against the USSR by withdrawing all Soviet military advisors from North Korea prior to the invasion.

President Harry Truman reacted to the June 25, 1950, invasion of South Korea by immediately committing US air and naval support, followed shortly thereafter by US troops. He also "neutralized" the Taiwan Straits by presidential proclamation and obtained a UN Security Council decision to provide military assistance through the creation of a UN "police action." Apparently, neither Stalin nor Mao had anticipated those countermoves. The Soviet boycott of the UN Security Council (due to its failure to seat the PRC) cost the Soviet Union its opportunity to exercise veto power over the UN military intervention.

The Taiwan Straits neutralization represented the most important long-term consequence of the Korean War since it evolved into a Washington-Taipei defense pact. Truman issued the pronouncement because he was concerned that the attack on South Korea might be part of a larger communist strategy to encircle Japan. The United States had ample intelligence information regarding the planned PRC invasion of Taiwan scheduled for July or August 1950. In communist hands, Taiwan could serve as a springboard for attacks futher north up the Ryukyu Islands chain toward Japan proper. Thus, a declaration stating that the United States would oppose military actions in the Taiwan Straits seemed a simple and cheap insurance policy. Mao's invasion fleet consisted mostly of junks and small merchant vessels, so the threat of Seventh Fleet warships forced the PRC to cancel its invasion plans.

The North Korean surprise attack in late June succeeded in capturing most of the South. However, General MacArthur's brilliant amphibious landing at Inchon encircled the communist forces from the rear, sending them into a pell-mell retreat. In September, President Truman ordered UN forces to cross the 38th parallel and sweep toward the Chinese and Soviet borders with North Korea.[10] Beijing made a vain attempt to shore up the crumbling North Korean army by sending new units from Manchuria that had been raised from the local Korean population. The numbers were insufficient to stop the rout. If a communist regime were to continue in North Korea, direct military intervention by China or the USSR would be necessary.

Why did President Truman convert what began as a war of resistance into a war of conquest? Mere containment of the North Korean attack, in Truman's view, would encourage future aggression on the peninsula or elsewhere. Moscow would believe that the worst possible outcome of communist aggression was the eventual reestablishment of the status quo antebellum.[11]

Moscow initially reacted to the stunning battlefield reverses by offering a major diplomatic concession—free elections for the entire peninsula to be supervised by the UN. Apparently, Stalin felt he could live with a noncommunist Korea, especially since the communist party there was still strong enough to wield influence and might eventually regain control. This proposal was rejected by the United States, and the Soviets withdrew the offer following the invasion of North Korea.

As is well known, after repeated warnings, the PLA intervened as UN forces drew near the Yalu River boundary. Somewhat less well known was the initial objective of the intervention. It began with a three- to five-day offensive in October that was directed only at South Korean troop units. A lull lasting almost a month followed, during which the PRC made a new peace proposal to the UN via the Polish delegation. It called for the withdrawal of Chinese troops from Korea in return for the creation of a North-Korean-controlled buffer zone below the Yalu. In addition, the PRC called for the withdrawal of US recognition and support of the Nationalist government on Taiwan.[12] Unfortunately, this "limited application of force" was misread by Douglas MacArthur, who declared it showed the critical weakness of PLA logistics—Chinese units could not fight for more than a few days. He prepared for the "final offensive," the tragic result being two-and-a-half more years of mounting bloodshed.

Stalin initially objected to the Chinese decision to intervene. He feared the war might widen. Mao insisted that the intervention was necessary, and Stalin eventually gave him support.[13] However, all of the Soviet materiel used by the PLA in the conflict was charged to China's account, payable within ten years following the end of the conflict. The debt amounted to about $2 billion.[14] The Korean War cost the USSR remarkably little in treasure or lives lost. Yet, according to US intelligence estimates in the autumn of 1951, the Soviets had about 27,000 troops in North Korea and adjacent territories in Manchuria. These were primarily air force, anti-aircraft artillery, engineering, and medical units.[15] Thus, Moscow's degree of direct commitment was higher than often assumed.

Considering the fact that the PRC paid (albeit on credit) for all Soviet-supplied beans and bullets, Stalin remained remarkably parsimonious in handing out material—at least until 1952. Only about 7 percent of the communist weapons captured between February and March 1951 were of Soviet manufacture.[16] As the PLA's need for more and better equipment became painfully obvious in the spring and summer of 1951, Stalin used Beijing's military needs to further control his junior partner, Mao Zedong.

From November 1949 through most of 1951, the Chinese claimed that the Maoist revolutionary model combining protracted guerrilla war with a united front of four social classes (workers, peasantry, petite bourgeoisie and national bourgeoisie) constituted a new contribution to the legacy of Marxism and held special relevance to Asian countries struggling against colonialism and imperialism. Since this implicitly challenged Stalin's one-man leadership of the entire communist bloc, the Soviets chafed against the claim.[17] It was partly the increasing PRC military dependence on Moscow that caused China to drop references to "Mao's road" after November 1951, and the flow of heavy equipment, artillery, aircraft, and naval vessels rose markedly thereafter. This was the first occasion in which Moscow used Beijing's national security dependence to obtain ideological concessions. It would not be the last.

Stalin also used his leverage to extend Soviet presence in Manchuria. The rail lines were returned to Chinese control as stipulated in the 1950 treaty, but Soviet naval rights at Dalian and Lushun were continued until a peace treaty with Japan could be concluded—an indefinite extension. This concession may not have been very difficult to wrest from the PRC since Soviet presence in Manchuria helped deter the United States from bombing beyond the Yalu River.[18]

Also in 1952, Stalin agreed to allow the construction of a rail line from Beijing to Ulan Bator, the capital of the Mongolian People's Republic. The line connected to another rail line that leads north into the USSR. This marked a significant concession by Stalin. Prior to this time, he had adamant-ly opposed any Chinese political and economic influence in Mongolia. Stalin had finally become convinced that the PRC was a reliable partner. Mao summed up the impact of the war on Sino-Soviet relations some eight years later:

> When our revolution succeeded, Stalin said it was a fake. We did not argue
> with him, and as soon as we fought the war to resist America and aid Korea,
> our revolution became a genuine one (in his eyes).[19]

The Sino-Soviet alliance had been sealed in the blood of the Chinese and North Koreans and the Korean war results favored Soviet interests. China stood as a condemned "aggressor" nation by the UN, cut off from the West politically and economically. Prior to the outbreak of the war, Secretary of State Dean Acheson planned for an early diplomatic recognition of the PRC following the expected conquest of Taiwan. That potential US opening was relegated to the ash heap of history for over two decades. Of course, there were serious costs to Moscow, but they were mostly in Europe, where NATO took on real muscle as a result of the demonstrated willingness of the USSR to use military means to extend its empire.

As early as mid-1951, it had become apparent to Stalin that there was nothing further to be gained by the continuation of the Korean conflict. He had several good reasons to see the war ended. It was becoming more costly in terms of Soviet resource allocations. Stalin was probably reluctant to continuously build up China's military power without any means of control over the PLA. The war provoked NATO to the point where there was a serious threat that West Germany would rearm and enter the alliance. Finally, there existed the danger of escalation. Both Truman and Eisenhower had threatened to use nuclear weapons.[20] There remained the problem of how to end the war.

Following the initial success of the PRC intervention, the communist bloc in the UN put forward highly ambitious peace terms. All foreign forces must leave Korea, the United States must stop supporting and defending Taiwan, and the PRC must become the sole representative of the Chinese people in the UN. When the war once again stalemated following Chinese defeats and retreats, those terms were changed into a simple armistice proposal that enabled the prolonged process of peace talks to begin. The major impasse remained prisoner repatriation. The PRC insisted that all prisoners of war be returned to their country of origin. Immediately after Stalin's death on March 5, 1953, Zhou Enlai proposed a compromise that came close to the UN position—prisoners who did not wish to return to their home country were not forced to do so. The USSR endorsed the compromise a few days later, an action that was a reversal of usual Soviet procedure. Prior to that time, the Soviets took the lead and China followed.[21] With Stalin gone, China better controlled the reins of its own destiny. The armistice was finally signed on July 27, 1953. Chinese forces had lost 400,000 men.[22] The United States had lost just over 50,000 men, the bulk of the losses suffered by the "UN Police Action" force. Figures are not available for North Korean and Soviet losses.

Stalin's foreign policy succeeded in East Asia. Beijing accepted its dependent economic and security relationship with the USSR. Unlike Eastern Europe, where workers' riots and instability wracked East Germany, the Chinese revolution was quickly consolidated and seemed congruent with Soviet interests in East Asia. Stalin's fears regarding the "Titoist" potential of Mao Zedong had not been realized. Sino-Soviet relations appeared to have a solid foundation, and the alliance promised to benefit Moscow for many years to come. Stalin's successors were to learn otherwise.

Notes

1. Jiang Jieshi in pin-yin and Chiang K'ai-shek the traditional Wade-Giles romanization of the Cantonese pronunciation.

2. Lionel Kochan, *The Struggle for Germany*, 1914-1945, p. 45.

3. Discipline was enforced in the Communist International, or "Comintern," on

the principle that all communist parties must defend the best interests of international communism. That, in turn, was defined as the defense of the USSR, the only communist nation in the world at that time.

4. Charles Maclane, *Soviet Policy and the Chinese Communists, 1931-1946*, pp. 239-240.

5. Allen Whiting, *Sinkiang, Pawn or Pivot*, p. 117.

6. Geoffrey Jukes, *The Soviet Union in Asia*, p. 269.

7. Robert Simmons, *The Strained Alliance: Peking, Moscow and Politics of the Korean War*, pp. 90-92.

8. Strobe Talbott, ed., *Krushchev Remembers*, pp. 367-368.

9. Marshall Shulman, *Stalin's Foreign Policy Reappraised*, p. 141.

10. The initial orders called for no US forces to approach the Yalu River or the Soviet boundary with North Korea. Only South Korean troops would be allowed in the northern portions of North Korea. See University Publications of America, *Documents of the National Security Council*, 1947-77, NSC 81, Sept. 1, 1950, reel 2. Truman was later convinced by MacArthur to rescind that restraining order.

11. William Stueck, *The Road to Confrontation: American Policy Toward China and Korea*, 1947-50, p. 174.

12. Stueck, *Road to Confrontation*, p. 248.

13. Huang Hua speech in *Issues and Studies*, Jan. 1978, p. 113.

14. Joseph Camilleri, *Chinese Foreign Policy: The Maoist Era and Its Aftermath*, pp. 52-53.

15. Simmons, *Strained Alliance*, p. 202.

16. Camilleri, *Chinese Foreign Policy*, pp. 180-181.

17. Philip Bridgham, Arthur Cohen, and Leonard Jaffe, "Mao's Road and Sino-Soviet Relations: A View From Washington, 1953," *The China Quarterly*, London, No. 52, Oct.-Dec. 1972, pp. 670-695.

18. Harold Hinton, *China's Turbulent Quest*, p. 55.

19. Stuart Schram, *Chairman Mao Talks to the People*, pp. 101-103.

20. See Chapter 3 for more details.

21. Simmons, *Strained Alliance*, p. 234.

22. The 400,000 figure was provided in a Deng Xiaoping speech to communist countries at the Moscow Conference of 1960. The term "casualties" is used in the English version of the translation from the Russian; the original Chinese term is not available. Presumably, Deng's reference was actually to "fatalities" since Western estimates of the number of Chinese killed in Korea run as high as one million. University Publications of America, *CIA Research Reports, USSR*, reel 3, frame 401.

2

Khrushchev and the Development of the Sino-Soviet Rift

The Moscow-Beijing alliance, which had seemed so firm and valuable to both parties at the end of Stalin's lifetime, was to come apart within the seven years following Stalin's death. Continuing to explore the Soviet perspective, this chapter examines how China lost its value and credibility as an ally.

The Malenkov-Khrushchev Rivalry

Following Stalin's death, Georgi Malenkov had the first opportunity to take the reins of leadership. A mere five days after Stalin's death, Pravda ran a doctored photo showing Malenkov with Stalin and Mao Zedong.[1] The PRC had become the most important ally in the Soviet bloc, and the symbolism of Mao and the Chinese revolution could be manipulated to advantage in Kremlin politics.

Malenkov was confirmed as premier and began liberalized economic policies that emphasized consumer-goods production for the first time since the 1920s. Party Secretary Nikita Khrushchev mounted his ultimately successful challenge against Malenkov by taking the Stalinist orthodox position that capital goods should continue to receive first priority. In foreign policy, Malenkov argued for a dialogue with the West in order to avoid the destruction of world civilization he claimed would result from a nuclear war. Khrushchev, on the other hand, alleged that a nuclear war would destroy capitalism rather than world civilization. He stressed the aggressive intentions of imperialism in a reprise of the Stalinist "two camp" theory of East-West confrontation.[2] In resource allocation, Khrushchev's first priority was the modernization of the defense establishment for use in the nuclear age.[3]

When Khrushchev headed a Soviet delegation to Beijing in the autumn of 1954, Mao warmly seconded his policies. The PRC relied on Moscow's armed forces to offset the growing US encirclement of China. Military might depends upon capital-goods production. Mao also knew that China would be risking war with the United States in the foreseeable future over Taiwan, so the Malenkov-led war-avoidance strategy could well be at the expense of China's revanchism. Unfortunately for the Chinese leadership, they could not know that Khrushchev's policy positions were partly tactical. Following the ouster of Malenkov from his premiership in 1955, Khrushchev quickly changed his tune and adopted peaceful coexistence as his own policy. He also reduced the size of the Red Army, though he did continue to modernize strategic forces. Mao felt betrayed, and the origins of the personalized distrust between Mao and Khrushchev date from that period.

Khrushchev's ability to shoulder Malenkov aside during 1954 and 1955 resulted from both the patronage power inherent in the post of party secretary general and the policies Khrushchev advocated. It was Malenkov who took the risky new policy initiatives against the entrenched interests of his comrades on the Politburo and in the Central Committee. The entire economic system was geared to heavy industry. Since 1947, no one had dared to explore mutual interests with the United States for fear of being accused of capitulationism or worse. Why, then, did Malenkov adopt such high-risk policies, and why did Khrushchev embrace most of them immediately after Malenkov was deposed?

The US Role

Peaceful coexistence had become a necessity for Moscow. A technological breakthrough had altered the nature of war. Between 1945 and 1952, the atomic bomb posed the greatest strategic threat, but there were not enough of them in US and Soviet inventories for the two countries to threaten each other with national extinction. Soviet conventional military power facing Western Europe was enough to counter the West's advantage in atomic bombs and delivery systems. That situation changed in the 1952-1954 time period when both the United States and the USSR developed and deployed the hydrogen bomb, i.e., thermonuclear weapons. The United States had the means of delivery. The B-36 bombers of the Strategic Air Command could strike targets deep within the USSR and return to their bases in the United States. More numerous were the B-47 medium bombers based in Western Europe. While they carried fewer nuclear weapons, the warning time of an air attack would have been much less from Western Europe than from the United States.

The Soviets, however, did not have any heavy bombers until 1954 and they were thereafter produced only in small numbers. While a few could undoubtedly have reached their targets in the United States, they could not have crippled the US war-making potential, even if thermonuclear weapons were used. Soviet bombers could easily reach targets in Western Europe and

Japan, but such an attack would prompt an overwhelming retaliation from the United States.

The Eisenhower administration sought to convert its superior striking power into an international political gain. In January 1954, Secretary of State John Foster Dulles formally announced the doctrine of "massive retaliation," which threatened the USSR with national destruction if the United States defined an action of the Soviets as aggression, be it conventional or nuclear. Dulles also initiated a confrontational crisis-management style to accompany the new strategic doctrine. He added a new word to the dictionary of the English language—brinksmanship, best defined as a game of nuclear "chicken." The opposing players threaten each other with thermonuclear weapons until the weaker party backs down. The Soviets were guaranteed to be the weaker party. As long as Washington could count on rational behavior from Moscow, the strategy could not lose. General Curtis LeMay, father of the Strategic Air Command, is reputed to have said: "Communism is best handled from 50,000 feet."

Stalinist national security policies were inadequate to meet this new and unparalleled US threat. Conventional forces became much less important, and holding Western Europe as hostage to the Red Army was too dangerous. It might provoke the very attack it was intended to deter. The safest course of action was to mollify the United States while increasing Soviet strategic striking capability. Khrushchev showed great political skill by initially appealing to the vested interests of the entrenched Stalinists. However, after Malenkov's defeat, Khrushchev was forced to adopt his rival's foreign policy.

It was also important to maximize Soviet nuclear capabilities in the eyes of the United States. During the 1955 Moscow air show, Khrushchev arranged to have one squadron of a new heavy bomber (the Bison) make a wide circle and repeatedly overfly the central reviewing stand so that this embryonic force would appear much larger.[4] The ruse worked only too well. It caused the United States to speed up production of existing aircraft and to hasten the development of the B-52 bomber.

Despite the "bomber gap," the US leadership knew that it still maintained an overwhelming superiority in strategic weapons, especially considering the bombers and the new medium-range ballistic missiles (MRBMs) deployed in Europe. In early 1956, the National Security Council (NSC) concluded that the United States had achieved a preemptive nuclear-attack capability against the USSR.[5] A preemptive, or "first strike," capability was defined as an attack so devastating that no retaliation would be possible, or one by which the Soviet polity would be reduced to chaos.

Also in 1956, U-2 reconnaissance aircraft began overflying the USSR in order to locate military airfields and missile bases (Moscow began testing MRBMs in 1955 and 1956). Soviet radars immediately identified the U-2s, but no weapons were then available to down the aircraft. A few years later,

Khrushchev publicly responded to the US aerial reconnaissance:

> Information about the locations of missile bases can be of importance not
> for a country concerned with its defense requirements, but solely for a state
> which contemplates aggression and intends to strike the first blow and
> therefore wants to destroy the missile bases so as to avoid retaliation after
> an attack.[6]

The United States had the capacity to carry out a first strike, and was rapidly
developing the intelligence needed to make such a strike feasible. Peaceful
coexistence increasingly seemed a necessity to ensure the survival of the
USSR.

The Abbreviated Honeymoon in Sino-Soviet Relations

Khrushchev's sharp reversal regarding foreign policies (adopting those of his
predecessor Malenkov) did not become fully apparent until 1956. Thus, 1954
to 1955 constituted the apogee of Sino-Soviet amity. The Soviet leadership
curried favor with the PRC, and Beijing looked to Moscow to support its
ambitious First Five Year Plan of economic development. Both Malenkov
and Khrushchev were eager to enhance the bonds linking the two nations and
to remove potential sources of friction. The Soviet state visit to the PRC in
September and October 1954 constituted one of the highest ranking delega-
tions ever to visit a fraternal country. No longer was Mao kept waiting in
Kremlin antechambers. The Soviets now offered tribute at the Gate of
Heavenly Peace.

In the diplomatic exchanges during and immediately following the
Khrushchev mission to Beijing, the USSR gave up its naval base in
Manchuria, returned Soviet shares in the joint stock companies to China
(though not without compensation), offered $130 million in new credits, and
pledged aid for the construction of fifteen new large-scale industrial enterprises while increasing the pace of 141 other installations already receiving
Soviet assistance. Moscow and Beijing agreed on the construction of a rail
line connecting the two nations through China's northwestern provinces and
the Xinjiang Autonomous Region. Also, Moscow granted greater Chinese
access to Mongolia. Chinese immigration up to a level of 10,000 annually
was permitted, and Ulan Bator accepted a grant-in-aid of $40 million from
the PRC.[7]

On the international front, Beijing and Moscow successfully coordinated
their strategies at the 1954 Geneva Conference on Indochina. The
Vietnamese communist movement led by Ho Chi Minh had successfully

defeated the French forces and anticipated a complete diplomatic triumph at this great-power conference. Instead, Ho had to settle for less than half a loaf. Vietnam was "temporarily" divided at the 17th parallel, and Laos and Cambodia were created as neutral states. Ho was left in undisputed control over only the northern half of Vietnam.

The Soviet Union supported this settlement as part of a face-saving trade-off for France. In return, French President Mendez-France made less than a concerted effort to obtain National Assembly approval of the European Defense Community.[8] If passed, the West Germans would then have been rearmed. Fortunately for Moscow, it was not necessary for the USSR to take the lead in depriving Ho Chi Minh of the victor's spoils.

Zhou Enlai, leading the PRC delegation, pressed the Vietnamese to settle for the compromise that was eventually agreed upon. Since the Vietminh (Ho's communist-led political party) was then dependent on Chinese military and economic assistance, Zhou had ample leverage. Soviet Foreign Minister Vyacheslav Molotov took a backseat, letting Zhou do most of the bargaining for the socialist bloc. A divided, and thus weakened, Indochina suited China well, as long as it did not serve as a power vacuum to be filled by the United States. Three aspects of the Geneva Accords seemed to assure that the United States would not extend its military presence into the region—the neutrality guarantees for both Cambodia and Laos, the limits on foreign military advisors, and the US pledge to do nothing to violate the agreements (even though Secretary of State John Foster Dulles refused to sign the final documents). If the PRC and USSR had demanded the full measure of conquest for the Vietminh, the United States might well have intervened militarily, perhaps with nuclear weapons.

The Geneva Accords thus found parallelism in the policies of Moscow and Beijing while strengthening Chinese status in the international arena. The final agreement also had the advantage of keeping the Vietminh dependent on the PRC. Twenty-five years later, the Vietnamese leadership publicly attacked the PRC for denying them the fruits of victory.[9] In its polemics, Hanoi conveniently ignored Soviet collaboration with the PRC in Geneva.

In 1955, Khrushchev undertook a wide-ranging diplomatic offensive. He pulled Soviet occupation forces out of Austria in return for a neutrality pledge, began a détente with Tito, and made a trip to East and South Asia, a trip that resulted in the first Soviet economic assistance to India. Throughout the year, he reiterated the theme of peaceful coexistence with the West. The peace offensive was not a total success. Germany was included in NATO in October 1954, overriding French objections, and Moscow felt compelled to respond by creating the Warsaw Pact the following year. No effort was made to involve China in that European-oriented defense arrangement.

The 20th Party Congress and Its Aftermath

The Sino-Soviet alliance might have endured some years longer if it weren't for priorities and decisions made by Khrushchev in 1956. China was still considered an important partner, but other political and international problems overshadowed the connection with Beijing and caused Khrushchev to ignore and override the interests of the PRC. The 20th Congress of the Communist Party of the Soviet Union (CPSU) was completely Khrushchev's show. But it was not the performance of a man secure in his position of leadership. Most of the proposals and propositions he put forward were intended to strengthen his position at home, to resolve problems in Eastern Europe, and to reduce East-West tensions.

If Khrushchev was to carry out his ideas for the economic and political development of the USSR, he had to eliminate the Stalinist legacy and remove many of the conservative old guard of the CPSU. He therefore made a surprise speech at a closed session of the 20th Congress in which he denounced Stalin, primarily for his crimes against the Soviet populace and CPSU. He also attacked rule by cult of personality and called for collective leadership as the proper communist model.

In his public presentation to the Congress, Khrushchev offered an unprecedented freedom of action for "fraternal" communist parties. He announced that there were many roads to socialism. The Soviet model need not be replicated when other cultural and political conditions reduced its relevance.

Implicit in this thesis was relief for Eastern Europe from Moscow's iron-fisted control. The combined effects of economic exploitation and imperial dominance were causing restiveness. This had first surfaced in the Berlin riots of 1953. Workers' unrest in Poland followed hard on the heels of the 20th Congress. The ultimate nightmare for Khrushchev was a general uprising in an Eastern European nation that would overthrow the communist leadership and then receive military support from the United States. This might easily create a domino effect, thereby causing the USSR to lose all it had gained as a result of World War II. The scenario was made more plausible by the Yugoslav example and by US policy that called for a "rollback" of communism in Europe rather than the "containment" policy of the Truman administration. It was vital that the Eastern European communist parties gain legitimacy and authority, a goal that required much more political and economic latitude for the indigenous leaderships.

Finally, Khrushchev needed to reduce the size of the Red Army and emphasize strategic forces rather than infantry in order to overcome a national labor shortage. But it would take years for his modernization of strategic forces to take effect. Thus, he strongly emphasized peaceful coexistence and added the important theme that war was not inevitable between capitalist and communist systems. The economic strengths of the Marxian systems would prove the innate superiority of socialism, and the democratic institutions of the West would enable a peaceful transformation to a worldwide socialist order. Khrushchev had adopted a long-term strategy of conflict avoidance.

The Chinese, and particularly Mao Zedong, had difficulty accommodating to this sea change in Soviet policies. Beijing had little problem with a critical reevaluation of Stalin's career. Granted, it was embarrassed because its delegation to the congress had made all the appropriate obsequious noises about Stalin's greatness prior to Khrushchev's "secret" speech late in the proceedings. That was a minor problem, though, and the PRC leadership owed no debt of gratitude to the deceased tyrant. It was only in the 1960s that the PRC revived the issue of Stalin's merits as one more arrow in the quiver of Sino-Soviet disputation.

The denunciation of the cult of personality and the emphasis on collective leadership did perturb Mao. Many of the charges leveled by Khrushchev against Stalin could apply to Mao as well. Through the publication of his collected works, Mao glorified his historical role and the originality of his ideological contributions in applying Marxism-Leninism to Chinese conditions and as an international model for all nations struggling against colonialism and imperialism. Khrushchev's timing was especially damaging to Mao since the PRC leadership had been locked in a domestic political struggle over the pace of agricultural collectivization. When the 8th Congress of the CCP convened seven months after the Moscow congress, Mao's opponents were strengthened by Khrushchev's pronouncements against personality cults and one-man rule. They removed the thoughts of Mao Zedong from the list of Marxian canonical writings. Also introduced was the concept of the first and second lines of leadership. Ideologists and theoreticians (e.g., Mao), were relegated to the second line as opposed to those in the first line who handled the day-to-day affairs of the party and state.

Regarding East-West relations, Khrushchev's definition and application of peaceful coexistence differed sharply from that of the PRC. China applied the concept primarily to Third World nations. Still worse from Beijing's viewpoint was the noninevitability of war precept and its concurrent conflict-avoidance foreign policy. The PRC still had a civil war awaiting resolution. The only solution to the Taiwan problem appeared to be military conquest. Moreover, if Khrushchev set a high priority on avoiding confrontations with the United States, it followed that he had less interest in defending China against the tightening circle of US-led alliances.

The PRC immediately supported the "many roads to socialism" idea since it promised tolerance of variations from the Stalinist model of national development. Trouble was to come from the unforeseen crises in Eastern Europe. The Polish problem began with workers' riots, which spread quickly to most of the major cities. Old-line Stalinist leader Edward Gierek had died in March 1956 while still in Moscow following the 20th Congress. Khrushchev personally flew to Warsaw to help choose his successor, Edward Ochab. However, with the spread of the riots in June, the armed forces showed signs of mutinous behavior when called upon to suppress the workers.

The Polish leadership needed a popular figure who could combine the support of the citizenry, military, and the party apparatchiks. Wladyslaw Gomulka, a war hero and nationalist whom Stalin had purged as a potential Tito, was the clear choice. Khrushchev protested the unprecedented action of the Poles in selecting a national leader without Soviet approval. The crisis sharpened when the Polish leadership demanded the removal of Marshal Konstantin Rokossovsky, a Soviet military leader who had been installed as Poland's defense minister in 1949. Over the ensuing weeks, the Poles persisted while Khrushchev blustered and eventually threatened Soviet military intervention. He backed down after Warsaw threatened to mobilize a mass national resistance to any Soviet invasion. The fact that the PRC strongly supported Warsaw throughout the crisis may also have encouraged Khrushchev to capitulate, and a face-to-face meeting between Gomulka and Khrushchev certainly helped resolve the crisis. Beijing was polite enough not to use the public media for its support of Poland. The appearance of bloc solidarity was still deemed important to the PRC.

The subsequent Hungarian crisis developed before the Polish affair was peacefully resolved. The party ousted its Stalinist leader, Mathias Rakosi, leading to the emergence of "Hungary's Gomulka," Imre Nagy. As in the Polish case, popular grievances were deep and had been pent up for years, resulting in demonstrations and riots. By late October, Soviet units stationed in Hungary were fighting ineffectually to contain the violence. The new government included noncommunists, and the tide of popular revolt forced Nagy to move still further away from Marxist-Leninist orthodoxy. He pledged to end one-party rule and to withdraw Hungary from the Warsaw Pact. On November 1, 1956, large-scale Soviet reinforcements entered Hungary and crushed the uprising in a brief but bloody war. China firmly backed Khrushchev's invasion, reaffirming Soviet leadership of the socialist bloc and the vital importance of suppressing counterrevolutions threatening all within the Marxian camp. In January 1957, Zhou Enlai visited Moscow, Warsaw, and Budapest to show support for Soviet foreign policy in Eastern Europe. The crisis had passed. China had struck a blow for autonomy within the bloc while defining the limits of permissibility.

During the first six months of 1957, Khrushchev did a good deal of backtracking. After the 20th Congress, he had warmly embraced President Tito as an example of effective Eastern European leadership. Though the rift between the USSR and Yugoslavia was blamed entirely on Stalin, Tito was not about to reenter the bloc. He retained his independent foreign policy and continued to defend his market socialism as superior to the Soviet centralized-command economy. After the crises in Poland and Hungary, Tito's usefulness to Khrushchev declined, especially since the Yugoslavs provided only a delayed and highly qualified support for the Soviet intervention in Hungary. Khrushchev began to describe Yugoslav revisionism and Stalinist dogmatism as equal threats to the correct party line. De-Stalinization was relegated to the back burner. Those ideological retreats suited the PRC and may have been partially prompted by Beijing. In 1957, it seemed that Sino-Soviet harmony had recovered from the strains imposed by the 20th Party Congress and its aftermath.

Nuclear Sharing: 1957 to 1959

Mao Zedong made his second and final trip to the USSR in 1957 on the occasion of the fortieth anniversary of the Bolshevik Revolution. In a major public speech, Mao proclaimed that there can be but one leader of the socialist bloc, and that leader was the USSR. Earlier in the year, a secret deal was struck between Mao and Khrushchev in which the latter offered to provide nuclear weapons technology to the PRC. Over the next two years, the Soviets began construction of a gaseous diffusion plant capable of producing bomb-grade uranium; they provided a sample medium-range ballistic missile (MRBM), minus its atomic warhead, and a G-Class ballistic missile submarine (without its missiles). Khrushchev also sold TU-16 Badger bombers to the PRC, and Chinese nuclear scientists were trained at Soviet atomic-research institutes. The deal included a sample atomic bomb, complete with assembly instructions, although the delivery was eventually canceled for reasons discussed below. In 1956, Beijing began the construction of its first MRBM rocket-assembly factory,[10] presumably built with Moscow's approval, if not direct Soviet technical assistance.

It was nothing short of extraordinary for the Soviets to share with the PRC such an extensive nuclear capability, complete with delivery systems. Why would the Soviets turn over technology of ultimate destruction to another country, much less one they had no way of controlling? Moscow has never offered to share those secrets with any members of the Warsaw Pact, where Soviet military presence and integrated command structures would provide security against misuse. Nothing in the written record from the USSR helps to solve this mystery.

The conventional wisdom in Western scholarship holds that the nuclear-sharing decision was a quid pro quo. The Chinese supported Soviet bloc leadership and in return received nuclear weapons technology.[11] This explanation will not suffice. The PRC had publicly supported Soviet bloc leadership since January 1957 when Zhou Enlai made his trip to Russia and Eastern Europe. Why give the Chinese such a dangerous gift for services already provided? Why reward the PRC at all for protecting bloc unity when that was in Beijing's own interest?

US-Soviet nuclear negotiations at the time made the Soviet decision even harder to explain. By 1956, Moscow sought a test-ban treaty with the United States in order to inhibit US efforts to miniaturize warheads and develop mobile nuclear weapons of limited yields and reduced radiation. Even at this early stage, differences emerged between Moscow and Beijing. The PRC objected to separating a test ban from the broader issue of nuclear disarmament.[12] There is little use in preventing a shark from growing new teeth if he keeps all of his old ones, especially if you happen to be a small fish, like Beijing, with no nuclear teeth at all. Khrushchev disregarded the PRC concerns, and the atmosphere was conducive to a test-ban agreement with the United States within a few years. So why risk this important strategic understanding by providing the PRC with such highly visible assistance as a nuclear gaseous diffusion plant and a missile-firing submarine? Once the United States learned of the Soviet nuclear proliferation, the negotiations would probably fail. Moreover, the discovery of Soviet nuclear sharing would greatly increase the chances that West Germany would acquire nuclear weapons from the United States, a Soviet fear at the time.

Only one Western scholar, Walter Clemens, explored this problem in depth. He posited five hypotheses to explain Khrushchev's nuclear-sharing arrangement with the PRC. First, the technology might have been offered in order to obtain an eastern Warsaw Pact that would include Soviet operational control over the PLA. The Chinese later claimed that the USSR made "unreasonable demands to put China under Soviet military control." However, the CCP Politburo and Central Military Commission decided in the summer of 1958 to have their own totally independent nuclear weapons program. Yet direct Soviet assistance continued until June 1959, with Chinese nuclear scientists receiving training in the USSR on into the early 1960s. Thus, this first hypothesis did not convince Clemens. If control was the objective, Khrushchev would first have demanded command integration and then provided the nuclear reward rather than the other way around.

The second possibility had Khrushchev attempting to "buy" Chinese adherence to a test-ban treaty with the United States. Clemens dismissed this as obviously false. Why would the PRC start a nuclear program only to cripple it in its infancy? Advanced nuclear weapons require testing. There is, however, evidence supporting this hypothesis. On March 31, 1958, Khrushchev announced a unilateral suspension of Soviet nuclear weapons tests and called upon the United States and Great Britain to do the same. While the moratorium was in effect, further efforts were made to reach a formal test-ban treaty. Moscow's initiative failed. Britain and the United States proceeded with scheduled tests. However, as Adam Ulam points out, had that effort succeeded Beijing would have been under great pressure to enter into a comprehensive test-ban arrangement.[13]

The third hypothesis posited a complex "double game" being played by Khrushchev: nuclear sharing would be used to obtain PRC support for Soviet bloc leadership. Failure to assist China would not prevent its eventual development of nuclear weapons; it would merely delay it. More rapid, Soviet-assisted arms development would add to the overall strength of bloc forces and would not endanger the USSR in the foreseeable future. Finally, if the USSR did negotiate a test-ban treaty, the Soviets might obtain Beijing's signature to the agreement and thus not have to worry about an independent PRC nuclear force. This explanation is flawed in that Moscow already had Beijing's support for bloc leadership. However, the hypothesis is supported by a 1956 PRC policy debate over whether to develop independent nuclear forces or to continue to rely on the Soviet nuclear umbrella. Failure to provide strategic weapons technology would probably cause the PRC to take the independent course, which it did anyway. However, Khrushchev could not have predicted that 1958 Chinese decision.

A fourth possibility was that a deeply divided Soviet leadership was bidding for Mao's support. This is easily dismissed since Khrushchev had defeated his major political rivals in a showdown just four months prior to the nuclear-sharing agreement.

The final hypothesis had Khrushchev simply muddling through attempting to balance the contradictory demands inherent in East-West nuclear diplomacy and the great power aspirations of the PRC. Clemens considered this last explanation to be the most probable.[14]

Though excellent, Clemens' analysis was limited to Moscow and Beijing. It would be wise, however, to look at Washington, D.C., as well. The late 1950s were the heyday of the Eisenhower administration. Massive retaliation and brinksmanship were entrenched doctrines, backed up by the awesome new B-52 bombers. Even more frightening, MRBMs and IRBMs threatened the USSR from Western Europe and Turkey. The Soviet strategic force was pitifully weak; two heavy bomber types, the turbo-prop Bear and the jet Bison. The former was slow, and the latter performed so badly that only a few were produced through 1957. Still worse, deceptive efforts on the part of the Soviets to make their small bomber fleet look large had failed by the beginning of 1957.[15] The "bomber gap" had disappeared from the anxiety closet of the Eisenhower administration. Finally, as earlier noted, the United States had achieved a true preemptive strike capability in 1956. Though 1957 saw the Soviets test the world's first intercontinental ballistic missile (ICBM), it was years away from being a deployable weapons system. Firing preparations required days, and the fuel could be stored only for short periods since cryogenic materials were used. Meanwhile, the Soviets remained without a credible nuclear deterrent against the continental United States.

Perhaps the best explanation for Khruschev's nuclear-sharing arrangement with the PRC is the simplest. Moscow entered into that agreement because it feared a preemptive first strike by the United States. Once China had an arsenal of its own, the Sino-Soviet alliance would be transformed into an additional nuclear deterrent against US attack. For the first time, the communist bloc would be able to hold most of continental Southeast Asia and Taiwan nuclear hostages. PRC nuclear forces would also strengthen Soviet striking power against Japan and South Korea. Finally, a Chinese nuclear arsenal would immensely complicate US nuclear targeting and would reduce by one-third or more the number of missiles and bombers that could be allocated to attacking the USSR.[16]

Khrushchev may well have determined that the dangers inherent in nuclear sharing without joint controls were less hazardous than pitting the Soviet arsenal alone and unaided against those of the United States and Great Britain. In 1957, Khrushchev could not foresee the collapse of the Sino-Soviet alliance, much less its devolution into a military confrontation. Foreign policy differences had thus far been relatively minor; the PRC had just completed a highly successful First Five Year Plan of economic development in conjunction with Soviet assistance. It seemed Beijing had no choice but to continue with its Soviet ally. The PRC was subject to a Western economic embargo and a policy of diplomatic nonrecognition since being branded an aggressor nation during the Korean War. Until this time, the USSR had to carry the nuclear umbrella for China while receiving few strategic benefits in return. From that 1957 perspective, nuclear sharing would enhance Soviet security.

Cessation of the Soviet nuclear assistance to China in June 1959 is better documented and more easily explained than its initiation. In the second volume of Khrushchev's memoirs, he referred to his last-minute decision to halt the shipment of the sample atomic bomb to China (which was already crated for delivery). He found himself on the horns of a dilemma. Relations with the PRC were bad and he no longer trusted the Chinese, especially regarding nuclear weapons. Yet failure to deliver the bomb as promised would worsen relations still further. The latter option seemed the lesser of the two evils.[17]

The Missile Gap: 1957 to 1960

The time period that saw Soviet nuclear sharing with China also saw momentous developments in East-West nuclear security. On August 27, 1957, the Soviets announced the world's first successful test of an ICBM. Less than two months later, the Soviets launched the first man-made satellite. Those events were extensively celebrated during the fortieth anniversary of the USSR. Mao proclaimed Soviet technological superiority over the United

States and announced in Moscow that "the east wind now prevails over the west wind" (Marxist socialism prevails over capitalism). As will be explored in the next chapter, Mao drew quite different policy conclusions from this assessment than did the Soviet leader, but the differences were not immediately apparent.

Following the triumph of the fortieth anniversary celebrations, Khrushchev began boasting of Soviet missile capabilities. In 1959, he claimed one factory was capable of producing 250 ICBMs annually.[18] Those lies were believed in the West until about 1960, when accumulated intelligence information began to cast doubt on the Soviet claims. U-2 reconnaissance aircraft failed to find any deployed ICBMs. In 1961, the British spy in the Kremlin, Colonel Oleg Penkovsky, documented the fact that the USSR had deployed no missiles until the previous year and that the current total of ICBMs was only six to nine.[19] The first-generation missile was too unreliable and inaccurate to be a usable weapon system. The so-called missile gap disappeared from the Western lexicon until the end of the 1970s.

In 1958 and 1959, Khrushchev's bluff succeeded in inflating the official US "national intelligence estimates" on Soviet strategic forces. However, President Eisenhower refused to be stampeded by the alleged missile gap. Chief of the General Staff Nathan Twining, told the Senate Foreign Relations Committee in secret session that the number of Soviet ICBMs were more than offset by the large number of US IRBMs deployed in Italy and England.[20] Ironically, it was the Kennedy administration that deployed new solid-fuel ICBMs in unprecedented numbers, even though the missile gap was then known to be nonexistent. Khrushchev's nuclear blustering may well have contributed to the later US decision to deploy an overwhelming force. The early 1960s found the Soviets more vulnerable to nuclear attack than ever before.

Why did Khrushchev launch the big lie campaign between 1957 and 1960? Once again, motives must be inferred since there is little hard evidence. Khrushchev may have attempted to maximize the effectiveness of the Soviet nuclear umbrella without paying for a general military buildup. Also, the stronger the USSR, the less need for an independent Chinese nuclear program. However, that motive must have diminished sharply after August 1958 when the PRC opted for an independent strategic weapons program.

Perhaps the most important motive for Khrushchev's nuclear bluff was Germany. There were two aspects to the problem, the first being the threat potential of West Germany, especially if it were armed with nuclear weapons. The second was the viability of East Germany. To deal with the first aspect, the USSR proposed in October 1957 a nuclear-free zone for Central Europe. Specifically, both Germanies, Poland, and Czechoslovakia would have no nuclear weapons stationed within their borders and would be removed from the nuclear target lists of the great powers. The United States immediately rejected the offer. Washington believed that Khrushchev's plan was intended to neutralize NATO's intermediate-range nuclear forces, thereby strengthening the value of the supposed Soviet ICBM lead.[21]

As to the viability of East Germany, it was dying from loss of blood. The open artery was West Berlin, through which hundreds of thousands of highly skilled workers were fleeing to the Federal Republic of Germany. On November 27, 1958, the USSR sent an ultimatum to the United States, Great Britain, and France. Reach an agreement on the German problem within six months or access to West Berlin would be turned over to the control of East Germany, which would then presumably isolate the city. The note went on to suggest a comprehensive solution: the neutralization and disarmament of both West and East Germanies as well as Berlin. This would achieve the other key objective of preventing West Germany from obtaining nuclear weapons via NATO.

The 1958 ultimatum helps explain why Khrushchev perpetuated the "missile gap" myth. In that period of brinksmanship in US foreign policy, Khrushchev would have to convince the West that the USSR could win any strategic confrontation in order to make credible his six-month German ultimatum. The Eisenhower administration was not intimidated; more than six months passed without any crisis unfolding. In August 1959, CIA Director Allen Dulles analyzed Khrushchev's fizzled ultimatum as indicative of continued US strategic nuclear superiority. However, he was of the opinion that Khrushchev believed time was on his side and could therefore afford to wait.[22]

Although the timing is unclear, it seems that Khrushchev tried to sweeten the deal he was demanding from the West. Prior to the June 1959 decision to cut off nuclear sharing with China, Khrushchev apparently sought to obtain a pledge from Beijing that the PRC would refrain from producing nuclear weapons if the United States would make a similar pledge for West Germany. The PRC apparently refused and, from that time forward, no Soviet leader was able to speak for China.[23]

Khrushchev's nuclear bluff was called. Specious Soviet striking power did not deliver a German settlement, and apparent Soviet strength could not sustain bloc unity. If the USSR were the world's strongest military power, why should it place concerns regarding a relatively weak and divided old enemy (the Germans) over the strategic growth of its most important bloc partner? Khrushchev's claimed strategic superiority ranks as a foreign-policy mistake of the same magnitude as his nuclear sharing with the PRC. The sham was abandoned in the first half of 1960. Khrushchev no longer asserted that Soviet casualties in a nuclear war would be far less than those of the West. In July he stated: "If we start war to settle disputes between states . . . we shall destroy our Noah's Ark, the earth."[24]

This relatively neglected chapter in Soviet diplomatic history encapsulates the most important single cause for the opening of the Sino-Soviet rift. To Khrushchev (and his successors), national security concerns relating to the United States and Western Europe outweighed considerations relative to China. From mid-1959 on, as bilateral relations worsened, Khrushchev was ever more inclined to sacrifice China on the altar of improved relations with others. Even India came to outweigh China on the scales of relative importance to Moscow. This was a self-perpetuating process, since worsened relations diminished the inherent value of the 1950 alliance and China became increasingly expendable. The 1958 to 1959 effort to obtain a German settlement began the slide down the slippery slope. Both Beijing and Moscow date from 1959 their differences in terms of dealing with the West. Beijing then came to realize that Moscow was willing to use the PRC as a pawn in the great power game. However, it was not until Khrushchev and Eisenhower concluded their historic initial meeting that Mao realized the full extent to which China might be sacrificed in superpower politics.

The Spirit of Camp David

In September 1959, the first US-Soviet summit meeting since the advent of the cold war took place at the presidential retreat known as Camp David. Eisenhower agreed in principle to Khrushchev's proposal of a summit meeting of the "big four"—France, Great Britain, the United States, and the USSR—concerning the German question. More important, there was a tangible thaw in the frozen atmosphere of mutual distrust and confrontation. For the first time since the end of World War II, there was a feeling that the United States and the USSR could engage in mutually beneficial diplomatic negotiations. If that atmosphere was to be retained, China could not threaten the newfound amity.

Khrushchev traveled to Beijing immediately after his US visit. He suggested the PRC accept a "two Chinas" solution to the Taiwan problem, thus eliminating the major issue between Washington and Beijing. The United States could force the Nationalists to renounce aspirations of reconquering the mainland and give up claims to represent China as a whole. The PRC in return would recognize the Nationalist rule over the island of Taiwan. This had about as much appeal to Mao Zedong as would an equivalent proposal to Abraham Lincoln in 1861—recognize the confederacy but restrict its control to the southern states. The Mao-Khrushchev meeting was reportedly short and stormy. If the previous proposal linking Germany and China in nuclear nonproliferation was injurious to China, Khrushchev's new proposal was downright insulting.

The PRC prepared to break publicly with the USSR. On April 16, 1960, the authoritative party journal Red Flag published the famous lengthy editorial entitled "Long Live Leninism." That blast at the USSR (thinly veiled by the use of Yugoslavia as a surrogate target) may have been personally written by Mao. The only restraint in its vilification of Moscow was that it was couched as an ideological attack and thus did not reveal all the skeletons in the closet of Sino-Soviet relations. Three months later, Khrushchev broke economic relations with the PRC by suddenly ordering all Soviet advisors and technicians in China back home. The Sino-Soviet alliance had endured for just over a decade.

As a result of reading this chapter, one might conclude that the root cause of the Sino-Soviet dispute was US nuclear superiority. It was the fear of potential nuclear attack that made the Soviet leadership ignore Chinese interests in favor of détente with the West. The same fear first initiated and later terminated the Sino-Soviet nuclear-sharing agreement.[25] The next chapter traces the evolution of Chinese national security policy and finds additional causes that contributed to the rift, but no single cause was more important than the US strategic threat.

Notes

1. Robert Conquest, *Power and Policy in the USSR: The Struggle for Stalin's Succession*, pp. 202-203.

2. Merle Fainsod, "What happened to Collective Leadership?" Abraham Brumberg, ed., *Russia Under Krushchev*, p. 102.

3. George Breslaur, *Krushchev and Brezhnev as Leaders*, p. 29.

4. John Prados, *The Soviet Estimate*, p. 41.

5. University Publications of America, Research Collections, *Documents of the National Security Council, 1947-77*, NSC 5602, February 1956, microfilm reel 4.

6. William Burrows, *Deep Black: Space Espionage and National Security*, p. 140.

7. Harry Schwartz, *Tsars, Mandarins and Commissars*, pp. 166-67.

8. David J. Dallin, *Soviet Foreign Policy After Stalin*, pp. 150-155.

9. *Beijing Review*, No. 48, Nov. 30, 1979, pp. 11-13.

10. *Beijing Review*, Vol. 29, no. 34, Aug. 25, 1956, p. 21.

11. See, for example, Adam Ulam, *Expansion and Coexistence*, p. 599.

12. Walter Clemens, *The Arms Race and Sino-Soviet Relations*, p. 25.

13. Ulam, *Expansion and Coexistence*, pp. 612-613.

14. Clemens, *The Arms Race and Sino-Soviet Relations*, Chapter 2.

15. Prados, *The Soviet Estimate*, p. 47.

16. The goal of dispersing U.S. nuclear targeting might also help explain an otherwise strange incident in 1958. In August of that year Warsaw officials told Western reporters that Poland was receiving nuclear weapons from the USSR. Had that statement been true, it would probably have provoked the NATO nuclear arming of West Germany, but Krushchev may well have hoped to send the United States off on a wild goose chase trying to find nonexistent missiles in Poland. See the *New York Times*, Aug. 7, 10 and 18, 1958, cited in Morton Halpern and Tang Tsou, "The 1958 Quemoy Crisis," in Morton Halpern, ed., *Sino-Soviet Relations and Arms Control*, p. 190.

17. Strobe Talbott, ed., *Krushchev Remembers: The Last Testament*, p. 269.

18. Prados, *The Soviet Estimate,* p. 77.

19. Prados, *The Soviet Estimate,* pp. 116-120.

20. University Research of America, Research Collections, *Top Secret Hearings of the Senate Committee on Foreign Relations,* microfilm reel 1.

21. Ulam, *Expansion and Coexistence,* pp. 611-612.

22. University Publications of America, Research Collections, *CIA Researc h Reports: Soviet Union,* microfilm reel 3.

23. Ulam, *Expansion and Coexistence,* pp. 623-624.

24. Horelick and Rush, *Strategic Power and Soviet Foreign Policy,* p. 78.

25. As Chapter 3 explains, Khruschev eventually came to fear Chinese-initiated confrontations with the United States, which could drag Moscow into a catastrophic and unwinnable war.

3

The View From Beijing: 1950–1960

Modern Chinese foreign policy has often been summarized as the search for wealth and power. The search was the more meaningful because imperial China had known both wealth and power for millennia. Beijing's defeats and humiliations at the hands of foreign powers in the nineteenth and twentieth centuries are too well known to require exposition here. The Nationalist government made headway against foreign leaseholds and treaties that had severely infringed upon China's sovereignty. Some of those gains were achieved even as Japan occupied most of the nation. However, it was the CCP that truly enabled China to regain its dignity by expelling unwanted foreign influences and presence. Though the anti-Western and anti-imperialist nature of the Chinese revolution drew it toward the USSR, the CCP's historical evolution did not foreordain the Sino-Soviet alliance.

Leaning to One Side

As the CCP rose to power during the 1946-1949 civil war, what made the leadership opt for the Soviet connection as opposed to the United States or a neutral international posture? The decision prompted considerable debate and maneuver within the CCP. Zhou Enlai favored a tilt to the West and was the most mistrustful of the USSR. Many of the communist military commanders, particularly Commander-in-chief Zhu De, favored an all-out pursuit of the civil war, eschewing US mediation. They therefore looked favorably on links with the USSR. A key party leader, Liu Shaoqi, also supported this view.[1]

It was Mao Zedong who ultimately decided the tilt toward Moscow. During World War II, Mao had sought to develop links between the CCP and the US war efforts in China. His 1944 request to visit Washington received no response. US arms would have been especially valuable to the CCP war effort since no arms were forthcoming from the USSR. All of Stalin's assistance from 1937 to 1941 had gone to Chiang Kai-shek. Mao's hopes for aid and recognition were dashed as Washington also committed itself totally to Chiang.[2] Mao felt prepared to recommence his long-simmering civil war with Chiang immediately after the Japanese surrender. Stalin pressured the CCP to cooperate with the US in seeking a political settlement with the Nationalists. In 1945, Stalin did not want China to upset his working relationships with the United States and Great Britain while he was consolidating his control of Eastern Europe. Neither Chiang nor Mao were eager for political compromise. Both felt that they could win a contest of arms. But the combination of Soviet desires and US power was sufficient to support two US mediation efforts between 1945 and 1946. Eventually, Mao perceived the negotiations as counterproductive. He believed that the United States favored Chiang, especially in terms of continued military support. From April through August 1946, Mao began to emphasize the need to struggle against Western imperialism, ultimately formulating his "paper tiger" thesis regarding the United States and its atomic arsenal.

Over the next three years, Mao sought to convert those CCP elements that had qualms about abandoning possible connections with the West. In a speech on June 30, 1949, Mao used the words of his critics to defend his own position:

> "You are leaning to one side." Exactly, . . . the 28 years' experience of the CCP have taught us to lean to one side, and we are firmly convinced that in order to win victory and consolidate it, we must lean to one side. . . . All Chinese without exception must lean either to the side of imperialism or to the side of socialism. Sitting on the fence will not do, nor is there a third road. . . .
>
> "Victory is possible even without international help." This is a mistaken idea. In the epoch in which imperialism exists, it is impossible for a genuine people's revolution to win victory in any country without various forms of help from the international revolutionary forces, and even if the victory were won, it could not be consolidated.
>
> "We need help from the British and US governments." This, too, is a naive idea in these times. Would the present rulers of Britain and the US who are imperialists, help a peoples' state? . . . Internationally we belong on the side of the anti-imperialist front headed by the Soviet Union, not to the side of the imperialist front.[3]

There were, however, eleventh-hour ploys to preserve a Western connection. A high-ranking official (Huang Hua) initiated a two-hour conversation with US Ambassador Leighton Stuart in May 1949, raising the issue of diplomatic recognition. At the end of that month, Zhou Enlai attempted a secret initiative with the United States. Through an intermediary, he reached the US consul in Beijing with a proposal whereby China would play a neutral role between the West and the Soviet bloc if the United States would agree to provide recognition and economic assistance. In going behind Mao's back, Zhou took a dangerous political risk. When the consul attempted to contact him directly, he broke off contact. On June 28, Huang Hua, in continued negotiations with Ambassador Stuart, said that Mao would welcome the opportunity to meet with Stuart if he would go to Beijing. The State Department refused permission lest it appear that the United States was softening its anticommunist position and weaken Washington's efforts to unite Western governments on a cautious policy regarding recognition of the CCP.[4] It is unlikely that a different US response to those initiatives would have changed the course of history. Given the rapid growth of the cold war in the late 1940s and the vulnerability of the Truman administration to demagogic charges that it had "lost China," an early accommodation with the CCP would have been difficult for the United States.

When Mao finally went to Moscow in December 1949, he had a range of objectives in mind. The Sino-Soviet treaty, at the very least, must commit Soviet nuclear and strategic power to the defense of the PRC. Second, the alliance must assist Chinese economic and military modernization. Mao might have expected the automatic support of the USSR in any Chinese conflict with Asian states.[5] More ambitiously, Mao hoped to reassert Chinese influence in Mongolia. Finally, he may also have sought assistance in developing Chinese nuclear weapons.[6]

In the prolonged negotiations with Stalin, Mao was barely able to win his minimal demands. Soviet assistance for economic development and modernization was niggardly during the first four years of the alliance. The majority of Soviet projects were concentrated in Manchuria, where the USSR still protected imperial interests and had signed a separate treaty with CCP regional leader Gao Gang. Since Stalin held most of the trump cards, and Mao had no US connection to use as leverage, it was not surprising that the treaty was heavily weighted in Moscow's favor.[7]

Revolutionary Foreign Policy

It would be unwise to focus only on the bilateral gamesmanship surrounding the 1950 treaty. Both nations had important commonalities in their foreign policies. On September 27, 1947, Politburo member Andrei Zhadanov made a landmark speech in which he said the world was divided between two "camps"—socialist and imperialist—locked in a struggle to the death. Communist parties worldwide were ordered to abandon their peaceful coalition and parliamentary road strategies and to turn to militancy and armed struggle.

In 1949, the PRC, like most newly founded revolutionary regimes,

favored a radical, confrontational foreign policy and was eager to see its revolutionary success replicated elsewhere. Beijing, of course, gave immediate
support to the Vietminh. But it also sought to develop an insurgency against
the neutral government of Burma and supported a major insurgency in
Malaysia. In the summer of 1950, China invaded Tibet and had prepared to
invade Taiwan.[8]

In his memoirs, Khrushchev claimed that Mao helped convince Stalin to
support the North Korean invasion of June 1950. The Chinese have not
denied that assertion. At the time of the Sino-Soviet Alliance, Mao Zedong,
even more than Stalin, was eager to probe for weaknesses in the West and to
expand communist influence among new nations emerging from colonialism.
Though Chapter 1 treated the onset of the Korean War in the general context
of Stalinist foreign policy, there are also distinctly Sino-American aspects to
be considered.

The Decision to Intervene

The "Chinese People's Volunteers"[9] entered Korea in October and November
1950 with little equipment. They fought not only the United States but the
international authority and prestige of the United Nations as well. Clearly
both the political and military costs were going to be very high. Stalin was
opposed to the idea as well.

Given the difficulties and dangers, why did the PRC go ahead with the
intervention? Most important was the threat perception. The United States
had entered the Korean War to repel an invasion. The decision to convert the
conflict into a war of conquest threatened the security of Manchuria, if not
China as a whole. Japan had used Korea as a stepping-stone for its occupation of Manchuria in the 1930s. The Truman administration assured Beijing
that no aggressive intentions were directed at Chinese territories, but similar
statements had earlier respected the sovereignty of North Korea. Second,
Truman's "neutralization" of the Taiwan Straits had forced the cancellation of
the PRC's invasion plan, making a confrontation with the United States seem
almost inevitable. Beijing still hoped that its intervention would not lead to a
wider war but rather to a negotiated settlement that would enable at least a
vestige of North Korea to remain as a buffer on China's Yalu River border.
Finally, Stalin's initial reluctance to support the PRC intervention was naturally kept secret from the West. Therefore, Beijing could count on the Sino-
Soviet alliance to protect it from massive retaliatory attacks from the United
States. Although the economic and human costs mounted to staggering figures as the war went on, Mao's basic premises supporting the intervention
were finally vindicated. North Korea was saved, and the high costs to the
United States made it more respectful of Chinese capabilities.

US Nuclear Threats and the End of the Korean War

A question intriguing US scholars is whether nuclear threats from Washington helped end the Korean conflict. No definitive answer can be provided until the archives in Beijing have been opened, but some observations are in order.[10] After first threatening to use the bomb against China, Truman admitted to British Prime Minister Clement Attlee in December 1950 that he was only bluffing. The Soviet spy, Donald Maclean, immediately obtained that information due to his "insider" connections in the British government and passed it to Moscow from whence it probably reached Beijing. The PRC showed no concern about Truman's threat, and the effective Soviet spy network may well have contributed to Beijing's confidence.

President Eisenhower threatened China with nuclear weapons immediately after assuming office in February 1953. He used the Panmunjom peace talks as the most direct of several channels to make his threat. Stalin died in early March. At the end of the month, the PRC showed the first signs of compromise regarding the US demands on prisoner repatriation. It cannot yet be finally determined whether the change in Beijing's negotiating position was due to the threat, the death of Stalin, or to a combination of both factors. Considerable time elapsed between Eisenhower's first nuclear threat in February and Beijing's final acceptance of US terms on June 4. However, nuclear threats had been renewed in May following a major Chinese offensive.

We now know that in Eisenhower's case, he was not bluffing. Indeed, only the objections of the US Army dissuaded him from employing tactical nuclear weapons on the battlefield without the benefit of delivering an advance warning to Beijing.[11] Unlike the earlier Maclean spy asset, Beijing was not privy to inside information regarding Eisenhower's true intentions. The president was personally convinced that his use of nuclear threat was a determining factor in achieving the Korean armistice. The threat may very well have effected the timing of the armistice, but the PRC had already achieved its basic purpose for intervention: guaranteeing the continuation of a communist government in North Korea.

Taiwan Under the US Nuclear Umbrella: 1954 to 1955

Eisenhower restated his nuclear threat against the PRC in the first case of the United States extending its "nuclear umbrella" to a third party. This occurred less than a year after the Korean Armistice during the so-called "first" Taiwan Straits crisis. The background of that crisis requires exposition.

In February 1953, President Eisenhower announced that the Seventh Fleet would no longer "shield" the PRC. Truman's 1950 "neutralization" of the Taiwan Straits had effectively separated the Nationalist and communist forces. Eisenhower effectively "unleashed" Chiang Kai-shek to recommence hostilities. The Nationalists used their control of offshore islands in a harassing blockade of China's central and southeast coasts. The Dachen Islands, two hundred miles south of Shanghai, interfered with trade to China's most important port. Mazu Island blocked the sea lanes to Fuzhou in Fujian Province, and Jinmen (Quemoy) blocked Fujian's second port of Xiamen. The PRC decided to counter this threat by shelling Jinmen and harassing long supply lines from Taiwan to the Dachen Islands by air and sea. The Nationalists were forced to abandon the latter. The withdrawal was assisted by ships of the US Seventh Fleet. At a press conference during the evacuation operations, Eisenhower was asked if he would consider the use of tactical nuclear weapons in a "general war" in Asia. He responded that he would use them under any circumstances in which they might be militarily useful.[12] In this instance, there was no indication that the PRC intended to attack US forces, but Eisenhower attempted to use the US nuclear arsenal as a coercive instrument to prevent an attack on the vulnerable islands of Jinmen and Mazu.

The 1954 Taiwan Straits crisis also resulted in a formal Taipei-Washington defense treaty by the end of the year. In January 1955, Congress passed a resolution expanding the president's defense authority to "related positions and territories" in the defense of Taiwan, effectively extending US defense responsibilities to the offshore islands. Also in 1954, the United States began forming the Southeast Asia Treaty Organization (SEATO), which was formalized the next year. Finally, Syngman Rhee of South Korea proposed a Northeast Asia equivalent of SEATO, which would include Taiwan, Japan, and the United States. While that proposal did not come to fruition, the combination of mounting US military presence and threats was not lost on Beijing. Clearly, it was time for the PRC to reassess its foreign policy. The US nuclear threat had continued even after the Korean War ended. There was an alarming anti-China drift developing among the Asian nations. A new, softer diplomatic line was needed from Beijing.

The Bandung Spirit

The PRC concentrated its 1954 to 1955 Asian diplomatic offensive on those countries that had not joined the US defense alliances. Zhou Enlai, then the PRC foreign minister, personally led the campaign beginning with a trip to Burma and India in 1954. His central message was peaceful coexistence as specifically defined by Zhou and Prime Minister Nehru of India. The five principles consisted of mutual respect for each other's territorial integrity and sovereignty, mutual nonaggression, mutual noninterference in each other's internal affairs, equality and mutual benefit (referring especially to commercial relations), and peaceful coexistence of differing political and social systems. Zhou pledged this basis of relations to Burma. The U Nu government, in return, promised to continue its course of neutrality. Zhou also privately assured the Burmese that the PRC would not assist the insurgency of the Burmese Communist Party. The Delhi portion of the trip was particularly warm and friendly. Nehru had already agreed to a commercial treaty with the PRC that implicitly recognized Chinese sovereignty over Tibet. India turned over to the PRC its trade outposts on Tibetan territory. Thus the single most difficult Indo-Chinese issue was temporarily resolved, though there was no boundary agreement.

Perhaps Zhou Enlai's greatest diplomatic tour de force came the following year at the Bandung conference of African and Asian States.[13] He mitigated the fears of the Southeast Asian states that their large Chinese populations might be used by Beijing as political instruments. (The insurgency in Malaysia, for example, had been ethnically Chinese.) Zhou called on all Chinese living abroad to adopt the citizenship of their resident nation. If they wished to keep Chinese citizenship, they should abide by the laws and customs of their resident nations. This was especially appreciated by Indonesia, and began a ten-year period of deepening friendship with Beijing. Zhou also pledged peaceful coexistence with Laos and Cambodia, and sought to establish better relations with Thailand and the Philippines. However, in the case of the latter two nations, he made no headway against their SEATO commitment. Finally, Zhou offered direct negotiations with the United States, which began at the ambassadorial level in August 1955.

There was a significant Sino-Soviet aspect to the Bandung period. It marked the emergence of a truly independent PRC foreign policy. As late as the 1954 Geneva Conference, most of China's diplomacy was done in conjunction with the USSR. The independent PRC policy formulation immediately diverged from Moscow. Zhou Enlai applied the peaceful coexistence principles differently. Malenkov and, later, Khrushchev sought an East-West great power détente, raising Chinese fears of superpower understandings at the expense of the PRC. Zhou offered peaceful coexistence only to those nations not in alliance against China. From Beijing's viewpoint, the principle of nonaggression was violated ipso facto by entering into a defense pact with the United States. This basic difference of interpretation surfaced following the 20th Congress of the CPSU and became an important factor as the Sino-Soviet rift widened in 1958 and 1959. By limiting the scope of peaceful coexistence to neutral and friendly nations, Zhou laid the foundations for Mao's "people's wars of national liberation" strategy at the end of the decade.

Despite Zhou's personal triumph, the so-called "Bandung Spirit" did not yield the results Beijing expected. Increased diplomatic recognition was insignificant. Only four nations established relations with the PRC between

1955 and 1957, the most important of which was Egypt. The UN embargo resulting from the Korean War remained intact.

In January 1956, Zhou suggested that it might be possible to liberate Taiwan by peaceful means and called for direct negotiations with the Nationalist government. However, the United States continued to supply Taiwan with the arms and equipment to shell the mainland, fly air strikes, and disrupt coastal shipping. In 1957, the US and Nationalist governments agreed to deploy Matador surface-to-surface missiles on Taiwan (under US operational control). These had a range of six hundred miles and could carry conventional or nuclear warheads.[14] Equally threatening, the United States assisted in the construction of an airfield suitable for stationing B-52 bombers in Taiwan. By the end of 1957, it was clear that China could not turn away the increasing US encirclement through solidarity with neutral nations and holding out an olive branch to Taiwan.

The Taiwan Straits Crisis of 1958

The growing military threat from Taiwan, fully backed by Washington, demanded a response. The islands of Mazu and Jinmen presented the PRC with its only point of leverage. Within artillery range from the mainland, both were vulnerable to siege. Moreover, the Nationalists had about 20 percent of their army on the islands (95,000 on Jinmen and 15,000 on Mazu). The surrender of such large garrisons would do much to undermine the morale and credibility of the Nationalist government. On August 23, intense shelling began with guns provided by the USSR earlier in the summer.

As Mao admitted in an inner-party speech two weeks later, he underestimated the US reaction. Six aircraft carriers headed for the Taiwan Straits laden with nuclear weapons, and US naval vessels resupplied the islands from outside the three-mile territorial limit with the help of armored landing craft. The PRC countered by announcing a twelve-mile territorial limit. The United States responded with a threat of retaliation against any interference with US ships three or more miles offshore. As part of the resupply, the Nationalist garrisons were provided with new eight-inch cannons which, the United States made clear, were capable of firing nuclear shells. The crisis began to ebb on September 5 when Zhou Enlai called for the resumption US-PRC bilateral talks and stated that China had no desire for war. The United States accepted Zhou's offer the next day.[15]

In subsequent years, the crisis gradually changed into parody. The PRC first announced that it would only shell Jinmen every other day. Later, the artillery barrages consisted of propaganda shells only. The Nationalist troops which spent much of their time picking up and destroying leaflets, launched propaganda balloons from the offshore islands. Finally, the PRC called a unilateral halt to this futile exercise when Deng Xiaoping mounted his political campaign for reunification with Taiwan in 1980 and 1981.

Beijing put the best possible face on the failure by inventing a post hoc explanation for beginning the shelling. The alleged intent had been to prevent the development of "two Chinas" by tying the Nationalists to the offshore islands. In forcing the defense of the islands with US support, the Nationalists were committed to maintain a presence there. Had they voluntarily abandoned the positions and retreated to Taiwan, one hundred miles of open water might have led to the evolution of a separate polity that was independent of the mainland and on which it had no claims.

The crisis did have one favorable result for the PRC. On October 23, 1958, Secretary of State John Foster Dulles and Chiang Kai-shek issued a joint statement in which the Nationalists pledged themselves not to use force as the primary means of recovering the mainland.[16] In subsequent months, harassment of shipping and aerial attacks tailed off. The 1958 crisis was the last large-scale clash in the Taiwan Straits. Thus the outcome was not a total defeat for the PRC.

The Sino-Soviet Aspect

The conventional wisdom interprets the importance of the Taiwan Straits crisis primarily in terms of Sino-Soviet relations.[17] It argues that the USSR failed to deter the United States from strong countermeasures and even stronger military threats against the PRC. This interpretation concludes that the lesson learned by Beijing was that the Sino-Soviet alliance could not be invoked on behalf of Chinese strategic interests. The alliance was one-way, benefitting of the USSR. Based on that perception, Beijing then decided to adopt military force building and defense policies that were increasingly independent from the USSR. From Moscow's viewpoint, Khrushchev learned that the Sino-Soviet alliance was dangerous; he could not control the initiatives of the Chinese leadership that might embroil the USSR in a Sino-American fight in which the Soviets had no direct national interest. The Taiwan Straits crisis was therefore seen as a major contributing factor in the emergence of the Sino-Soviet rift.

Two relatively recent studies, one by Jonathan Pollack and one by Gurtov & Hwang, have challenged the conventional wisdom, particularly in terms of the motives of Mao Zedong.[18] It does appear that Mao initiated the artillery siege without forewarning the Soviets. While Khrushchev personally approved the sale of the artillery to China, the Nationalists often engaged in artillery harassment of the mainland and shelled PRC merchant and fishing vessels that strayed within range of their batteries on the islands. Mao therefore could have wanted the Russian long-range artillery to use in counter-battery fire. The available evidence indicates that Mao failed to tell Khrushchev during his China visit in the summer of 1958 that the siege of the offshore islands was forthcoming.[19]

Mao Zedong took full responsibility for initiating the military action. Why did he run such a risk and what did he hope to achieve? The offshore islands were not specifically mentioned in the 1955 defense treaty linking Nationalist China with the United States. Taiwan and the Penghu Islands were specified as covered by the treaty provisions, but these fell outside the coastal territorial waters of the PRC, whereas Jinmen and Mazu were within sight of the mainland. Moreover, in 1955 Washington had encouraged Chiang Kai-shek to withdraw from the Dachen Islands, located offshore from Shanghai, and the Nationalists had done so without much military pressure from the PRC. It was thus possible that the United States would not intervene. Mao might have expected Washington to advise Chiang to pull his forces out of the exposed positions. The US leadership had not been at all happy about Chiang's military buildup there, and discussions had taken place in Washington regarding what obligations the United States had, if any, to defend the offshore islands.[20]

There were probably a range of objectives in initiating the attack. A minimum goal was the cessation of Nationalist harassment of intracoastal shipping in the waters of the Fujian Province. The best possible outcome would have been the surrender of the garrisons on the islands due to thirst and starvation. This would have delivered an immense military and political blow to the Nationalists, and the legitimacy and morale of the regime on Taiwan would have been weakened.

A major domestic propaganda campaign prepared the populace for military action against the Nationalists, and the offshore islands were a seemingly cheap means of providing a victory over both Chiang and his main source of support, the United States. Any US failure or inability to sustain the garrisons might weaken the credibility of the alliance, making the point to the people of the United States that supporting Chiang was a potentially dangerous undertaking. Finally, by undertaking the attack without previously clearing it with Moscow, Mao made a statement regarding the independence of China's defense policies. This was especially important at that time since Khrushchev was pressing Mao for command integration of the Red Army with the PLA and for Soviet military installations on Chinese soil.

What did the USSR do to support its ally in this crisis? After the shelling began, Moscow published two commentaries. The first was in Pravda on August 31. It warned the United States that a threat of attack on China was tantamount to a threat of attack on the USSR. The same article also defended fully the PRC right to attack the offshore islands.[21] The second commentary on September 5 did not repeat those warnings. Khrushchev sent a letter to Washington on September 7 in which he reiterated that an attack on China would be equivalent to an attack on the USSR. By that time, negotiations had been agreed to, but the crisis was not yet resolved.

The first US-escorted resupply ships arrived at Jinmen on the same day as Khrushchev's letter, and it was not at all clear that the Chinese would not fire on the US vessels.[22] Khrushchev penned a second letter on September 19 that contained even stronger language, specifically threatening a Soviet nuclear retaliation against the United States in response to a US nuclear attack on China, but this was too late in the game to be of tangible value to Beijing.

What other options did the USSR have? It was (and still is) very important to Beijing that the Taiwan issue be considered a Chinese domestic matter. A direct Soviet role in the offensive would have negated China's claim. When the United States did insert itself into the conflict and threaten the PRC, the Soviets countered with a threat of their own in *Pravda*.

In his inner-party speech of September 5, after the United States had reacted strongly in support of the island garrisons, Mao explained rather lamely that he had not anticipated the US actions. He made no mention of the Sino-Soviet alliance, nor of possible Soviet deterrence of potential US attacks on the PRC.[23] Gurtov and Hwang conclude that "Mao was not betrayed by the USSR."[24]

The 1988 memoirs of former Soviet Foreign Minister Andrei Gromyko tells a bizarre story regarding a proposal Mao made to him during the Straits crisis. Gromyko claims that Mao wanted to challenge the US forces, provoke them into attacking the mainland—even with nuclear weapons—and draw a US invasion force deep into China where it could be annihilated with Soviet nuclear weapons. Gromyko immediately rejected the idea without discussion.[25] The source is obviously biased, but Mao was sometimes capable of such wild theorizing. Left unexplained was how US troops were going to be drawn into invading China. US forces would have relied on sea and air power, along with nuclear weapons, to eliminate the threat to the offshore islands. No invasion would have occurred under the circumstances.

In October, Mao signed a Central Committee letter to the Soviet leadership thanking them for their support in the crisis.

> We are fully confident that should the events on Taiwan devolve into a war between China and the US, the USSR will unfailingly render assistance to us with all its strength. . . . We have already received powerful support from the USSR.[26]

Khrushchev claimed that the USSR gave full backing to the PRC and that it was Mao who lost courage and decided that an invasion of Jinmen and Mazu should not be attempted.[27] That assertion can probably be dismissed as self-serving. Secretary of State Dulles had indicated on September 4 that the

United States would help defend Jinmen and Mazu if the garrisons there proved unequal to the task.[28] The PRC was in no position to undertake an amphibious invasion facing the guns of the Seventh Fleet, even if it could find enough boats to launch such an attack. Khrushchev's claim also ignored the inability of the People's Liberation Army Air Force (PLAAF) to achieve air superiority over the Taiwan Straits, due in part to the newly supplied heat-seeking missiles provided the Nationalists by the United States. Without air superiority, an amphibious attack would have no chance of success. To Khrushchev's credit, he did offer to supply China with squadrons of interceptors from the Soviet Air Force and station them on the Taiwan Straits. This offer was seen by the Chinese as just one more effort to develop Soviet bases on Chinese soil.[29]

Perhaps the Soviets might have done more. Note that the first warning to the United States in *Pravda* came three days prior to the first US announcement that the seventh Fleet would participate in reinforcing and resupplying Jinmen. Thus, the USSR did not yet realize that it was facing a real, as opposed to a theoretical, confrontation with the United States. Significantly, the September 5 *Pravda* commentary did not include explicit references to the Sino-Soviet alliance, nor did it repeat the warning phrases from the article of August 31. It merely stated that the USSR was ready to provide "every kind of aid" to the PRC.[30] The dispatch of Foreign Minister Andrei Gromyko to Beijing on September 5 certainly did not indicate Soviet confidence in the situation. As all commentators have noted, Khrushchev's strong language in his letters to Eisenhower came after Zhou had already offered negotiations and made it quite clear that the PRC did not want to risk war with the United States.

In terms of Chinese motives, the crisis itself, and Soviet responses at the time, the balance of the evidence favors the new view rather than the conventional wisdom. The Soviet deterrent did not fail to protect China; rather, it was threatening to smother it. Khrushchev insistently demanded basing rights in the PRC, probably with the ultimate goal of command integration of the PLA and the Red Army. As Pollack concluded:

> Had Chinese leaders agreed to the conditions proposed by Soviet decision makers, it would have effectively stripped the PLA of its capacity to engage in autonomous military action. Moreover, it would have committed China's armed forces to long-term interdependence with Soviet military organizations, thereby assuring Soviet leaders a potent and ongoing means of leverage within the Chinese political process.[31]

The Taiwan Straits crisis did not begin a sequence of events ending PRC reliance on the Soviet nuclear umbrella. Instead, the attack on the offshore islands was Mao's announcement to Khrushchev that China would dictate its own defense policies without the expectation of active Soviet involvement. This interpretation leaves unchallenged the other half of the conventional wisdom, i.e., that Khrushchev was disillusioned and shocked by Mao's precipitous actions. Thus the crisis probably contributed to the 1959 decision to renege on the nuclear sharing agreement with the PRC.

The Great Leap Forward: Economics, Ideology, and Bloc Leadership

The years 1958 and 1959 also saw the PRC raise new and unexpected challenges to Moscow in areas other than national security policy. Mao sold the Great Leap Forward (GLF) to the CCP leadership in 1958 as a means of maximizing economic growth through labor-intensive methods. It was also intended to modernize the countryside through the institution of communes, combining agricultural, industrial, governmental, and social-service functions. Equally important, the GLF would lessen PRC economic dependence on the USSR and enable China to reduce its heavy debt burden.

The PRC had achieved rapid industrial growth during the First Five Year Plan (1953-1957) using the Stalinist model of a centrally controlled command economy, emphasizing heavy industry. However, the capital-intensive nature of the program and the forced dependence on Soviet technology and equipment proved very costly. The debt-service portion of Sino-Soviet economic exchange was not publicly revealed, but one estimate for the 1957-1959 period calculated that the Chinese returned at least 40 percent of their trade earnings from the USSR to pay the interest owed. Moreover, the nature of the bilateral trade exploited China's agriculture and raw materials base, two areas where the PRC most needed to husband its production capacity for the sake of its domestic economy.[32] The problem was partly due to the imperialist legacy of the Stalinist years and partly to the fact that China and the Soviet Union were not natural trading partners. The exports of both nations consisted primarily of raw materials and fossil fuels.

Nikita Khrushchev's economic priorities worsened the situation. In 1956, he suggested the gradual reduction or elimination of Soviet technical advisors in the PRC. Over the next two years, no additional credits were granted to Beijing. It was Moscow's goal to overtake the United States in economic output while refocusing foreign aid to the Third World nations where the struggle between socialism and capitalism was seen as vital for the future of the communist movement. The PRC viewed this as a slap occasioned by Khrushchev's strategy of peaceful coexistence with the West.[33] Thus the nature of Sino-Soviet economic relations and China's isolation from the West combined to help launch the daring and radical policy of the GLF.

National chauvinism and ideology also played significant roles. The

Maoist leadership expected rapid and dramatic results from the GLF. Two excerpts from Mao's speeches prior to launching the campaign reveal his confidence, as well as his growing disenchantment with the USSR as an economic model:

> In 40 years, the USSR has been able to produce only such a little bit of food and other stuff. If, in 18 years, we can equal what they have done in the last 40, it will naturally be all right, and we should do precisely that. For there are more of us, and the political conditions are different too; we are livelier, and there is more Leninism here. They, on the other hand, have let part of Leninism go by the boards; they are lifeless and without vitality.[34]
>
> Today the dogmatists advocate copying the USSR. Whom, I would like to know, did the USSR copy in the past? In the resolution of the 8th CCP Congress (1956), there is a passage dealing with the problem of technical reform. From the point of view of present conditions, this is inappropriate because it overemphasizes Soviet aid, but the most important thing is self-reliance. If we overemphasize Soviet aid, the question I would like to ask is, on whom did the USSR depend for aid in the past?[35]

Mao's viewpoint revealed in those inner-party statements came to be part of the public polemics of the 1960s.

In the first euphoric months of the GLF, greatly inflated production statistics caused the leadership to believe that the communes were totally successful. Beijing began to tout the new economic model as a significant advance on the historic road to true communism. The PRC claimed it would be the first nation to achieve the Marxist utopia.

Khrushchev had reason to be perturbed. First, the Chinese braggadocio constituted a violation of Mao's 1957 statement according sole bloc leadership to the USSR. The threat was not merely theoretical, Bulgaria and Albania quickly showed strong interest in the GLF, launching their own versions a year or two after the PRC. Second, Khrushchev's own domestic agricultural program was moving to the right, de-emphasizing some aspects of collectivization in the USSR and rendering him vulnerable to attack from the left.[36] Khrushchev responded by debunking the GLF as "pantsless communism," comparing it to the 1917-1921 "war communism" period of the USSR, thus denigrating it as primitive, scarcity-derived socialism. He later predicted that the USSR would achieve true communism by 1980, and other socialist nations would soon follow through Soviet-led mutual assistance.

When the GLF began to falter in 1959 and then collapsed disastrously in 1960 and 1961, Mao staunchly refused to make a public admission of error, though he did so in inner-party speeches. Domestically, he blamed the failure on three successive bad crop years (1959 to 1961). Politically, basic level cadres and poor reporting were culpable, but Mao placed the bulk of the responsibility on the USSR. The media propagandized the populace with a message designed to minimize the blame on Mao and the PRC leadership, claiming that their famine and hardships were due to Soviet perfidy.

The charges were based on two economic warfare measures implemented by Khrushchev in 1960. First, he pulled all 1,300 Soviet technicians out of China without warning in August 1960. They took their plans and blueprints with them, and critical supplies needed to continue construction were suddenly not available from the USSR. Khrushchev then compounded the injury by demanding every cent due on the PRC debt to the USSR. Much of the payment had to be in scarce foodstuffs.[37] Most Chinese still seem to believe that the USSR was a major cause of their post-GLF hardship. While the charges were true as far as they went, Beijing's propaganda line failed to provide the whole story. In February 1959, Khrushchev offered the PRC the most extensive aid package in the PRC's history: five billion rubles in goods and services over the next seven years.[38] Due to the strings that were attached and increasing mutual hostility, little was actually delivered. It was a vain but understandable effort to draw the PRC back into the Soviet economic orbit.

The fiasco of the GLF collapse, resultant famine, and stymied economic development over the next several years ended any remaining possibility that Mao Zedong could bid for leadership of the socialist bloc. Indeed, he lost much of his real power at home, though he continued to lead PRC foreign policy. Khrushchev applied all the economic pressure he could with the hope that Mao might be deposed completely by disaffected elements in the CCP who would then seek to repair the breach with Moscow. Sino-Soviet trade in 1962 was less than it had been in 1951.[39] However, the policy backfired, causing a common anti-Soviet policy among Maoists, non-Maoists, and anti-Maoists alike by 1961 and 1962.[40] The USSR had no chance of capitalizing on internal CCP rifts until early in the Brezhnev era some five years after the GLF had failed.

Conclusion

Having now looked at the Chinese side of the first decade of the Sino-Soviet alliance, how does this modify the judgments rendered at the end of the previous chapter? Strategic and national security issues still predominate, but Sino-Soviet amity would eventually have foundered due to worsening economic relations, ideology, and bloc leadership. However, without the Taiwan Straits crisis, the cancellation of the nuclear-sharing agreement, and crude "carrot and stick" economic pressures on Beijing, the deterioration would have been more gradual and potentially far more damaging to Mao's status within the CCP. The full extent of the GLF failure was not clear until 1960. Khrushchev's decision to apply economic pressure at that late date had no chance of success. The nuclear-sharing agreement was already dead, and China had announced its defense policy independence with the Taiwan Straits crisis two years earlier. Economic pressures are not sufficient to bring about political change; they must be used in conjunction with national security dependency (or interdependency). Theoretically, Khrushchev could have provided much more positive support to the Sino-Soviet alliance and thereby extended its effective life-span. However, as we saw in Chapter 2, that would have been at the cost of his détente with the United States. Given the strategic vulnerabilities of the Soviets at the time, Soviet-American détente naturally received first priority.

Notes

1. James Reardon-Anderson, *Yenan and the Great Powers: The Origins of Chinese Communist Foreign Policy, 1944-46*, pp. 141-147

2. Given the history of civil war between the CCP and the Nationalists and the breakdown of their alliance against the Japanese invaders in 1942, US military assistance to Mao Zedong could have been interpreted as a withdrawal of political support to the internationally recognized leader of China, Chiang Kai-shek.

3. Mao Zedong, *Selected Works of Mao Tse-tung*, Vol. IV, 1961, pp. 415-417.

4. William Stueck, *The Road to Confrontation*, pp.121-122.

5. Joseph Camilleri, *Chinese Foreign Policy*, pp. 50-51.

6. A Moscow television documentary on the history of nuclear weapons claimed that "the main goal" of Mao's visit to Moscow was to obtain the atomic bomb. *Foreign Broadcast Information Report, Soviet Union*, Aug. 3, 1988, p. 48.

7. The terms of the 1950 Sino-Soviet alliance are described in more detail in Chapter 1.

8. Ragtag invasion fleets gathered in China's ports as far north as Shandong beginning in the spring of 1950. Poor logistics and the absence of naval gunnery and air support of the communists was matched by the lack of readiness and abysmal morale of the Nationalist forces on Taiwan. The attack was scheduled for July. But for the intervening events of the Korean War (described in Chapter 1), the invasion might well have succeeded.

9. The euphemism, "volunteers," was intended to provide at least a veneer of deniability of national responsibility for the forces sent into Korea.

10. This discussion owes much to Richard Betts' analysis of US nuclear threats during the Korean War: *Nuclear Blackmail and Nuclear Balance*, pp. 33-47.

11. The US Army leadership felt that the mountainous terrain would degrade the effectiveness of battlefield nuclear weapons and that the nuclear option should be retained if it were necessary to expand the war into Manchuria. See Betts, *Nuclear Blackmail and Nuclear Balance*, pp. 39-41.

12. Betts, *Nuclear Blackmail and Nuclear Balance*, p. 59.

13. Zhou was fortunate to arrive alive in Indonesia. A probable Nationalist plot to blow up his airplane resulted instead in the destruction of an accompanying aircraft carrying journalists. The CIA has also been accused of planting the bomb aboard the aircraft, but another plot to poison Zhou while he was in Bandung was canceled by CIA Director Allen Dulles. It seems unlikely that the right hand would spare Zhou's

life while the left hand tried to kill him. William Corson, *The Armies of Ignorance*, pp. 360-366.

14. Camilleri, *Chinese Foreign Policy*, pp. 50-51.

15. Allen Whiting, "Quemoy in 1958: Mao's Miscalculations," *The China Quarterly*, #62, June, 1975, pp. 263-270.

16. Whiting, "Quemoy in 1958," p. 264.

17. This interpretation was well formulated in Harold Hinton, *China's Turbulent Quest*, pp. 90-93.

18. Jonathan Pollack, *Perception and Action in Chinese Foreign Policy*, an unpublished Ph.D. dissertation, University of Michigan, 1976, and Melvin Gurtov and Byong-Moo Hwang, *China Under Threat*, pp. 75-95.

19. Whiting, "Quemoy in 1958" and a note by Whiting in *China Quarterly* #63, p. 261.

20. Gurtov and Hwang, *China Under Threat*, p. 79.

21. J. Pollack, *Perception and Action of Chinese Foreign Policy*, pp. 149-150.

22. Morton Halperin and Tang Tsou, "The 1958 Quemoy Crisis," in M. Halperin, ed., *Sino-Soviet Relations and Arms Control*, p. 292.

23. Whiting, "Quemoy in 1958," CQ #62, p. 268.

24. Gurtov and Hwang, *China Under Threat*, p. 92.

25. *New York Times*, Feb. 22, 1988 p. 1.

26. Halperin and Tsou in M. Halperin, ed., *Sino-Soviet Relations and Arms Control*, p. 298-299.

27. S. Talbott, *Khrushchev Remembers, The Last Testament*, pp. 262-263.

28. Alice Langley Hsieh, *Communist China's Strategy in the Nuclear Era*, p. 123.

29. The date of Khreshchev's offer of air support is not clear--it may have been before or during the crisis itself. Gurtov and Hwang, *China Under Threat*, p. 89.

30. Pollack, *Perception and Action*, p. 183.

31. Pollack, *Perception and Action*, p. 350.

32. Camilleri, *Chinese Foreign Policy*, pp. 52-53.

33. Robert Freedman, Economic Warfare in the Communist Bloc, pp. 112-115.

34. Stuart Schram, *Chairman Mao Talks to the People*, p. 105.

35. Schram, *Chairman Mao Talks to the People*, p. 126.

36. Martin McCauley, *Khrushchev and the Development of Soviet Agriculture*, New York, Holmes & Meier, 1976, p. 112.

37. Through forced savings measures implemented by the central government, the PRC was able to repay all its debts to the USSR in 1965, including the military debt from the Korean War.

38. Adam Ulam, *Expansion and Coexistence*, p. 621.

39. Walter Clemens, *The Arms Race and Sino-Soviet Relations*, p. 29.

40. One leader who favored continued close military and economic relations with the USSR was Peng Dehuai, and he was removed from his defense ministry post after a failed confrontation with Mao in 1959. He had challenged the GLF policies a year or so too soon. Freedman, *Economic Warfare in the Communist Bloc*, p. 171.

PART 2
FROM RIVALRY
TO CONFRONTATION:
THE 1960s

4

Khrushchev's Swan Song: The Last Five Years

The last years of Nikita Khrushchev's rule were most vexing. The socialist bloc dissolved before his eyes, the Chinese leadership continuously attacked his foreign and domestic policies, and the Cuban missile crisis brought the USSR to the brink of war with the United States. The Soviet leader became increasingly concerned with neutralizing the Chinese ideological offensive and minimizing the growth of Beijing's power. Mao Zedong, for his part, came to categorize Soviet foreign policy as imperialist.

Bloc Disintegration

There were several efforts to save socialist bloc unity as the Sino-Soviet rift widened in the late 1950s and early 1960s. However, the "Moscow declaration" of October 1957 was the last compromise document of serious import. Revisionism and dogmatism were both excoriated, and Moscow's bloc leadership was reaffirmed. By the time of the Great Leap Forward and the Taiwan Straits crisis less than a year later, the document had lost cogency and relevance, although it was ritually invoked as late as 1962. As the rift became increasingly open and serious, some of the smaller and more vulnerable bloc members felt that new efforts should be made to maintain socialist solidarity. But international communist party conferences in Bucharest and Moscow in 1960 resulted in ambiguously worded declarations that did little to convey the impression of communist unity. Central to those conference failures was China's unwillingness to accept Soviet leadership of the bloc, or even to allow Soviet foreign policy principles to go unchallenged. The maintenance of bloc solidarity was less important to Beijing than the principles at issue.

The convoluted, abstruse ideological exchanges served as a stage for a struggle of another type. Moscow and Beijing were, for the first time, vying for the support of communist parties worldwide. Beijing made its first convert in the Albanian leadership. By late 1961, the USSR had virtually excommunicated Albania, forcing Tirana to rely heavily on China for economic and military assistance over the next sixteen years. As in the case of the Sino-Soviet rift, the growth of Albanian-Soviet differences was not due primarily to ideological differences, although rhetoric made it appear so. The root issue was one of national security for Albania. Tirana faced a real foreign threat from Yugoslavia. Stalin saved Albania from Tito's clutches just after World War II, and Khrushchev's efforts at rapprochement with Tito rekindled Albania's fears. Similarly, it was China's détente with Yugoslavia in the late 1970s that ended the close alliance between Tirana and Beijing.

The Moscow-Beijing competition for supporters divided virtually every communist party in the world, wrote finis to a coherent socialist bloc, and made "polycentrism" a permanent reality. With two poles in the socialist movement, the leverage of smaller nations and parties not in power was greatly enhanced. Nikita Khrushchev spent a great deal of time and energy during his last two years in office attempting to organize an international communist conference to expel the PRC from the movement. He failed because no combination of cajolery, bribes, and threats could deliver the near unanimity such a vote would require. Khrushchev had not merely lost control over the international communist movement, it had disintegrated "on his watch." That disintegration, along with his continuing failure to deal effectively with the China problem, contributed to his political demise in 1964.

The Absent US Response

Developments in the opening of the Sino-Soviet rift were followed closely by the US government.[1] By the time of the Kennedy administration, the dispute was believed to be profound and unlikely to be repaired in the foreseeable future. Secretary of State Dean Rusk, speaking for the administration in secret testimony before the Senate Foreign Relations Committee, described US policy as essentially passive. First, there were no plans to seek recognition of the PRC. The cost of sacrificing Taiwan would be too great and Beijing's anti-American hostility was too profound. Second, the United States would benefit from the Sino-Soviet dispute without taking any initiatives. As a result of its troubles with the PRC, Moscow would be more eager to seek détente with the West.[2]

The Sino-Indian Conflict

In the immediate post-Stalin years of 1954 and 1955, Soviet and Chinese policies toward India began to diverge gradually. Both communist countries favorably portrayed Prime Minister Jawaharlal Nehru's neutralist government as anti-imperialist and a model for peaceful coexistence. Divergence began when Nikita Khrushchev made his first trip to India in 1955 and publicly supported Indian claims to the Kashmir region. Since Pakistan had already aligned itself with the West, there seemed to be little cost in backing New Delhi in that territorial dispute. China did not follow the Soviet lead. Beijing simply called for a negotiated settlement. The PRC leaders probably realized that backing Indian claims would undermine their own position concerning the unresolved Tibetan-Indian border claims.

It was Tibet and its border that turned Sino-Indian relations from amity in the mid-1950s to open warfare in 1962. The Tibetan population grew increasingly restive under the Chinese occupation that began in 1950. By 1959, the situation had deteriorated into rebellion. The theocratic leader of the Tibetans, the Dalai Lama, fled to India, where he was given sanctuary. India quietly cooperated with the covert CIA support of the Tibetan insurgency.[3]

The border problem combined a colonial legacy with the unyielding terrain of the Himalayas. In 1912, Great Britain established the McMahon Line, demarcating the Indo-Tibetan border, a demarcation China never accepted. From Beijing's standpoint in the 1950s, the Aksaiqin region of the disputed territory was especially vital since it contained the only available pass through the Himalayas from Tibet north to Xinjiang. A road connecting the two regions was completed before the Indian government detected its existence. From New Delhi's viewpoint, China's preemptive road-building was highly provocative, especially since the Aksaiqin region bordered on Kashmir, the territory in dispute between India and Pakistan. The first serious border clash took place in September 1959 and was followed by a number of minor incidents that culminated in a major Chinese offensive along much of the border in September and October 1962. The Indian army was routed, and the PRC declared a unilateral cease-fire in November.

The focus here is not on the deterioration of Sino-Indian relations per se, but rather on Khrushchev's reactions to the emerging crisis. As early as the mid-1950s, the Soviet leader determined that Nehru and India constituted an important element in the Soviet Union's peaceful coexistence strategy. Nehru had advanced the concept and was also a founding father of the nonaligned movement. After Pakistan joined CENTO (the Central Treaty Organization), India became more important in geopolitical terms:

> A non-aligned India, friendly to the Soviet Union, would serve as an entry point for Soviet relationships with the neutral countries in general, would help keep Pakistan pre-occupied within the sub-continent and prevent the American sponsored alliances (CENTO and SEATO) from becoming geographically continuous and mutually reinforcing.[4]

By 1958, Khrushchev was pushing India forward in the international arena. When crises developed in Jordan and Lebanon, the USSR proposed a "Big Four plus one" summit meeting regarding the eastern Mediterranean issues. The additional state was to be India. While the conference proposal died on the table, it was surprising that India would be the nation considered to supplement France, the United States, Great Britain, and the USSR. The major powers all had economic and political interests in the Middle East, whereas India had none (not even the advantage of religious affinity).

Beijing had every reason to expect Moscow's support when the border clashes with India began and the bargaining positions on the McMahon Line became intransigent. The USSR always supported socialist-bloc allies in conflicts with bourgeois states; it was inherent in the basic concept of "proletarian internationalism." Khrushchev, however, broke precedent and adopted a neutral stance. The Soviet media treated the conflict as stemming from misunderstanding and described the territory as unworthy of armed struggle. Khrushchev cited the precedent of the post-World War II border dispute between Iran and the USSR which was eventually settled amicably by compromise. The Soviet leader later revealed his suspicion that China may have timed the border clash to undercut his visit to the United States.[5]

Immediately following his successful US trip, Khrushchev was in Beijing for the tenth anniversary of the founding of the PRC. In a private meeting with Chinese leaders, Foreign Minister Chen Yi began vilifying Nehru. By his own account, Khrushchev retorted that the Indian prime minister was the most progressive force in the nation apart from the Communist Party of India. He warned the Chinese not to alienate Nehru or weaken his position, since any successor government would be more reactionary. The Chinese responded by demanding that the USSR show ideological solidarity against a nonsocialist country. Khrushchev ended the exchange with two points: territorial disputes were not worth fighting over and the PRC must understand India's position. A weak, independent Tibet had constituted no threat, whereas a Tibet controlled by China had become a matter of national security concern.[6]

In December 1959, the USSR began to tilt its neutrality toward India by publishing New Delhi's notes to China without waiting for Beijing's replies. This was the first time that the USSR gave currency to noncommunist criticism of a communist power without simultaneous rebuttal.[7] The Soviets did not, however, accept the Indian territorial claims against China. Even in the late 1980s, Soviet maps still showed the Aksaiqin region as Chinese territory.[8]

In February 1960, Khrushchev again visited India, ignoring the mounting Chinese hostility toward Nehru. Soviet economic aid to New Delhi went up during the crisis period through the offer of a $375 million loan.[9] By 1961, Soviet nonmilitary loans to India amounted to more than twice the total amount provided to China from 1949 to 1961.[10] For the first time, military assistance was offered initially in 1959 in the form of transport aircraft and followed by various forms of weaponry. In 1962 this military aid culminated in an agreement to deliver a dozen MiG-21 interceptors and to provide co-production rights for the same aircraft. At the time, the MiG-21 was a very advanced fighter-plane. The Soviets had sold some to the PRC but were unwilling to give Beijing the production rights and associated technology. Moscow did show some sensitivity on this matter. The MiGs were not delivered to India until 1964, two years after the severe Sino-Indian border clashes.[11] However, by 1967 India had become the largest noncommunist recipient of Soviet foreign aid.[12]

Why did Khrushchev decide to tilt toward India and away from his erstwhile ally, the PRC? The decision to do so was precedent-breaking in terms of responsibilities within the socialist bloc. His actions certainly widened the breach between Beijing and Moscow. Why worsen relations with the Soviet Union's largest and most important ally in favor of the largest and most important neutral, nonaligned state? In retrospect, the policy may have been a mistake. However, there were mitigating factors that help explain the decision.

The USSR could not ignore Pakistan's position as a US ally. Soviet military assistance to India would help assure that Pakistan's armed forces would continue to be deployed to the south and west rather than toward intervention in the buffer state of Afghanistan. The security of Afghanistan was a significant factor in the equation. Primarily due to a festering border dispute, Pakistan closed the road from Kabul in 1955, thereby cutting off Afghanistan's sole means of exporting its products. This worked to the advantage of the USSR, which became Afghanistan's main trading partner.[13] However, the United States and Pakistani intention to pressure Afghanistan into a pro-Western alignment was obvious and continuing. Given the Soviet's basic national security strategy of a network of buffer states around its borders, this was indeed a serious matter.

New Delhi realized that its armed forces were underequipped and Nehru was determined to modernize and strengthen his forces. If Khrushchev had not agreed to the arms sales, India would certainly have bought the equivalent weaponry from Western powers. That, in turn, might well have weakened the friendly connection between New Delhi and Moscow, strengthening the leverage of the West in South Asia.

India made things easier for Khrushchev. Prime Minister Nehru encouraged Moscow's tilt toward India without undermining his own nonalignment principles.

(Nehru) regarded Soviet friendship as a counterweight to India's heavy dependency on the West and, increasingly from 1959 onwards, as a guarantee against China, whose intransigence he frequently contrasted with Soviet willingness to reach an accommodation with the West. In both senses, therefore, relations with the USSR were seen as a defense of non-alignment and an essential part of it.[14]

India and the USSR were also mutually supportive concerning nuclear diplomacy. Until the end of the 1950s, both nations called for the total abolition of nuclear weapons. Thus, there were sound reasons for a Soviet-Indian entente, but when the decisions were put in an "either/or" context, Khrushchev still seemed to slight an important ally in favor of a neutral nation.

Of course, Khrushchev could not foresee in 1959 how serious the Sino-Indian conflict would become. Initially he had simply tried to convince Beijing to seek a compromise. However, as other Sino-Soviet differences became apparent in 1959 and 1960, the alliance with Beijing diminished in importance while India became a de facto ally of Moscow in the Sino-Soviet dispute. New Delhi had primarily been of value to counterbalance the CENTO Alliance, but in the 1960s it also served to check the growth of Chinese power in Asia. During the Cuban missile crisis, the Sino-Indian border war was at its peak. There was a brief period during which Khrushchev repented of his tilt toward India. When faced with the prospect of an imminent war with the United States, the Soviet leadership realized that it needed its erstwhile Chinese ally more than friendly Indian neutralism. On October 25, 1962, *Pravda* published an article supporting China's position on the Sino-Indian border dispute. When the Cuban crisis was peacefully resolved some days later, though, the Soviets returned to condemning the Chinese attacks and calling for a peaceful resolution of the conflict.

The Cuban Missile Crisis

In the Sino-Indian border conflict, Khrushchev's actions were motivated primarily by his desire to strengthen Soviet influence in the Third World and among neutral nations. The Cuban missile crisis was a result of a more fundamental policy: attempting to assure national survival.

The events of October 1962 are too well known to require recounting here. The focus will instead be on Khrushchev's motives and objectives for putting the IRBMs in Cuba in the first place. It was clearly a dangerous and provocative course of action. There was a high risk that the missiles would be discovered before they were operational. A number of US reprisal actions were available to President Kennedy, regardless of whether the missiles were discovered before or after they were armed and operational. So why did Khrushchev do it?

The primary answer was the overwhelming US nuclear superiority at the time. Minuteman ICBM deployment had begun, and the Soviet ICBM force was still pitifully small, unreliable, and inaccurate.[15] Thus, Khrushchev sent IRBMs to Cuba to lessen the likelihood that the United States mount a first strike against the Soviet homeland, and to render the balance of power less unfavorable to the USSR.

A second possible answer derives from the exposed position of the IRBMs in Cuba. They would have been very vulnerable to low-level conventional air attack from fighter-bombers stationed in southern Florida. In a brinksmanship nuclear confrontation, the IRBMs would have to be fired first or they would almost certainly have been lost altogether. In today's argot, they were destabilizing "use or lose" weapons that might serve to increase the likelihood of a Soviet-American nuclear exchange rather than deter it. Therefore, Khrushchev might have intended to use the missiles as bargaining chips. He had scheduled a speech at the UN in November 1962, by which time the missile installations would have been completed. He might have used his speech to announce their presence and propose some trade-off with the United States.[16] The missile crisis caused Khrushchev to cancel his trip to New York. After the United States had discovered the missiles, he still successfully used them to bargain with President Kennedy. In return for withdrawing the IRBMs, he received a public pledge that the United States would not invade Cuba and a secret deal that guaranteed the removal of US IRBMs from Turkey some six months later.[17]

In the resolution of the crisis, Khrushchev later reported that China played an indirect role as an obstacle. Elements of the Soviet military leadership opposed the withdrawal of the Soviet missiles because of the Chinese (and Albanian) charges of appeasement and weakness that were sure to follow.[18] Khrushchev was able to overcome this resistance, but it indicated the increasing weight of the "China factor" in Soviet strategic thinking—as a rival rather than an ally.

The 1963 Atmospheric Nuclear Test Ban

By 1956, the USSR actively sought a test-ban treaty with the United States for the purpose of inhibiting US efforts to miniaturize warheads and develop mobile tactical nuclear weapons. In 1958, Moscow proposed a network of test-ban monitoring stations, including eight on Chinese territory.[19] Beijing publicly supported Moscow on this issue as late as August. However, the PRC leadership apparently said something quite different in private because in December, the USSR objected to the US demand that China also agree to test-ban terms. In January 1959, China further distanced itself from the USSR on nuclear diplomacy by voicing opposition to a nuclear-free zone in the Far East. By January 1960, Beijing declared its total independence in the nuclear field by proclaiming that China would not be bound by arms-control arrangements made by other nations.[20] A week after the US-Soviet atmospheric test-ban treaty was formalized on July 25, 1963, China proposed the total nuclear disarmament of all nations, a negotiating position it has continued to espouse.

On October 16, 1964 (ironically the very day the USSR announced Khrushchev's dismissal), the PRC tested its first atomic device. Beijing immediately declared "no first use" of nuclear weapons and called for an international conference of all nuclear powers to commit them to a no-first-use pledge.[21] This was to be the first step toward eventual nuclear disarmament. Beijing has maintained that policy position in subsequent years.

The test-ban topic is of interest here because of its impact on Mao Zedong's foreign policy. The test-ban negotiations did not cause Moscow to lose control of China's strategic and international security policies. That loss of control was long since a fait accompli. However, the effect of the negotiations was profound and far-reaching. Mao became convinced that China could no longer benefit from the bipolar system of international relations. His requirements for an independent foreign policy would inevitably arouse the hostility of both superpowers.[22]

In August 1963, following the signing of the limited test-ban treaty, Mao gave an interview to a visiting group of Japanese socialists. He described the USSR as an imperialist state and called for Moscow to return the "Northern Territories" (a group of islands north of Hokkaido) to Japanese control.[23] Chinese propaganda began attacking the Soviet Union directly rather than through indirect references, such as Yugoslavian revisionism. In 1964, Mao fully formulated his new foreign policy of a "united front against imperialism," and included France and Japan in the struggles against United States and Soviet imperialism, respectively. Once again, Soviet strategic policies provoked a hostile Chinese reaction. This time, the consequences went well beyond intra-bloc competition and fragmentation. China began looking abroad to create new international alignments that would challenge the underpinnings of Soviet (as well as US) national security policy.

Khrushchev's Demise

Careful students of Kremlin politics are in agreement that the removal of Nikita Khrushchev was not primarily due to his foreign policies. However, it must be noted that the Cuban missile crisis fundamentally damaged his effectiveness. It reduced his policy leverage over the Soviet military leadership, a consequence that was felt until the mid-1980s.[24] While domestic political and economic factors were central to Khrushchev's dismissal, the

Khrushchev era still provided a great deal of flamboyance in the international arena. He succeeded in developing the foundations for the later Soviet-American détente by breaking down cold-war barriers. But the cost was high. He could not avoid convincing the Maoist leadership that US-Soviet accommodation was at China's expense. What Khrushchev intended to be bipolar détente instead planted the seeds for the triangular relations that developed in the 1970s.

Notes

1. President Johnson appointed a new and unsophisticated CIA director in 1965, Admiral William Raborn. Raborn suggested that the agency should do a study on the Sino-Soviet dispute since it seemed potentially important to the United States. His veteran deputy director told him that the CIA had continuously studied the dispute since itas inception. Raborn asked to see the CIA materials. His deputy sarcastically asked him how he would like the existing reports delivered—in a wheelbarrow? Thomas Powers, *The Man Who Kept the Secrets*, p. 170.

2. University Publications of America, *Top Secret Hearings by the US Senate Committee on Foreign Relations, 1959-66,* Rusk testimonies of February 28, 1961, reel 2, and June 5, 1963, reel 5.

3. John Prados, *The Presidents' Secret Wars*, p. 162.

4. Geoffrey Jukes, *The Soviet Union in Asia*, p. 106.

5. Vernon Aspaturian, "The Domestic Sources of Soviet Policy Toward China," in Douglas T. Stuart and William T. Tow, *China, the Soviet Union and the West*, p. 40.

6. Strobe Talbott, ed., *Khrushchev Remembers, The Last Testament*, pp. 308-309.

7. Harry Gelman, "The Communist Party of India: Sino-Soviet Battleground," in A. Doak Barnett, ed., *Communist Strategies in Asia*, p. 116.

8. Information courtesy of Professor Rajan Menon, Lehigh University, Mar. 1988.

9. Robert O. Freedman, *Economic Warfare in the Communist Bloc*, p. 119.

10. Freedman, *Economic Warfare*, p. 139.

11. University Publications of America, Special Studies Series, *The Soviet Union, 1980-82 Supplement,* reel 3 frame 190, from *The Military and Security Dimensions of Soviet-Indian Relations*, Strategic Studies Research Memorandum, Strategic Studies Institute, US Army War College, June 1980.

12. Jukes, *The Soviet Union in Asia*, p. 260.

13. Jukes, *The Soviet Union in Asia*, pp. 261-262.

14. Jukes, *The Soviet Union in Asia*, p. 120.

15. The first-generation Soviet ICBM was scrapped as unworkable, though between six and nine ICBMs were deployed in 1960 and 1961. The Soviets had 190 heavy bombers at the time of the Cuban missile crisis and 1,000 medium bombers, of which a few hundred could have reached some portions of the United States on one-way ("suicide") missions. The United States had 133 ICBMs, 48 SLBMs, and 1,526 strategic bombers. Prados, *The Soviet Estimate*, pp. 118-121.

16. Adam Ulam, *Expansion and Coexistence,* pp. 661-672.

17. The IRBMs in Turkey troubled the Soviets more than similar installations in Western Europe since the latter were not capable of striking deep into the Soviet Union. They were intended instead to deter a European war or, failing that, to serve as "theater" weapons, striking targets in central and Eastern Europe. The missiles in Turkey amounted to an extension of US strategic striking power against the USSR itself, and would have provided only minutes of warning time if fired at Soviet cities.

18. Richard Betts, *Nuclear Blackmail and Nuclear Balance,* p. 177.

19. Walter Clemens, *The Arms Race and Sino-Soviet Relations,* p. 27.

20. Clemens, *The Arms Race,* pp. 28-29.

21. Clemens, *The Arms Race,* p. 86.

22. Joseph Camilleri, *Chinese Foreign Policy: The Maoist Era and Its Aftermath,* p. 77.

23. Ulam, *Expansion and Coexistence* p. 693.

24. The continued rapid buildup of the US ICBM force was probably the most important factor in the political power growth of the Red Army leadership. But in considering the end of Khrushchev's career, emphasis is on events that could be interpreted by domestic political rivals as "his mistakes."

5

Brezhnev and the Rise of the Soviet Military Threat

Failed alliances do not necessarily lead to military confrontation between the erstwhile partners. If 1960 is chosen as "the year" in which the Sino-Soviet alliance came to an end, based on Khrushchev's decision to recall all Soviet technicians and order the cessation of aid projects, then within nine years the two countries were on the brink of a major war. Why did this failed alliance have such a disastrous outcome? That is the topic of this chapter, which might be subtitled, "great powers hate to have other great powers on their borders."

With Khrushchev's ouster in 1964, there was a fleeting hope that relations might improve. The new leadership of Leonid Brezhnev and Aleksei Kosygin dropped Khrushchev's policy of economic warfare against the PRC and trade levels temporarily went up.[1] Exploratory political talks in Moscow between the USSR and China, however, were a fiasco. Drunken Soviet Marshal Rodion Malinovski scolded part of the Chinese delegation: "We have already ousted Khrushchev; you should follow our example and topple Mao."[2] The Chinese delegation, led by Zhou Enlai, discovered little or no substantive changes in Soviet policy positions and used the breach of etiquette as a pretext to break off the talks.

The stage was set for the devolution of the political dispute into a military confrontation. The Leonid Brezhnev leadership decided to strengthen the disposition of forces stationed in central Asia and the Soviet Far East. There had been a number of small-scale border incidents, and minority peoples in Xinjiang were restive. The Chinese had closed much of the northwest border with the USSR, but Beijing did not initiate any troop buildup on its side of the border. Brezhnev's decision to strengthen forces seems to have been primarily prompted by Mao's claims to vast areas of Soviet Central Asia and Siberia. Moscow also took a much stronger interest in the Vietnam War and tried to capitalize on that conflict to make gains against both China and the United States. The militarization of the dispute was heightened by Chinese foreign policy radicalism during the mass movement phase of the Great

Proletarian Cultural Revolution of 1966 through 1968 and the enunciation of the Brezhnev Doctrine justifying the invasion of Czechoslovakia in 1968. The process culminated in the border clashes of March 1969 and the subsequent mutual buildups and war preparations by both sides.

Territorial Issues

Contrary to popular belief, border issues were not significant when the Sino-Soviet rift began. The northeastern portions of the border are delineated by the Amur and Ussuri Rivers, and most of the rest of the 4,150-mile border (including the Sino-Mongolian segment) had been clearly demarcated by 1890. At a press conference in 1960, Zhou Enlai was questioned about Sino-Soviet border differences. He replied: "There are insignificant differences on the maps and they are very easy to resolve peacefully."[3]

The only competing claims of any size are in the Pamir Mountains of northwestern China, part of the Xinjiang Autonomous Region. As many as four thousand square miles are in dispute, though the territory is one of virtually uninhabitable high mountains having no vital interest to either nation. Thus, while unresolved problems remained, the issues were inherently worthy of little attention from two very large states. Rather, the border dispute became a barometer that registered the climate of the overall relationship. As summarized by one scholar on the topic, "The frequency and severity of Sino-Soviet border difficulties parallel the decline in friendly relations between the two parties."[4]

The first polemical exchange on the topic did not occur until the end of 1962. It was prompted by Khrushchev's crude attempt to undermine Mao's anti-imperialist credibility. He referred to British Hong Kong and Portugese Macao as "colonialist outhouses" in China's backyard.[5] He asked how it was that Beijing could advise other nations on standing up against imperialism. Beijing's rejoinder was pointed:

> In raising questions of this kind, do you intend to raise all the questions of unequal treaties and have a general settlement? Has it ever entered your heads what the consequences will be?[6]

Russia had taken more Chinese lands than any other country—over 600,000 square miles.[7] While other imperialist nations returned virtually all of their holdings to Chinese sovereignty, only the Soviet Union refused to return any of the lands it occupied.

Maps used in schools and sold in stores were used by the PRC to show that large areas of Siberia and Central Asia were "lost territories." A distinct element of Chinese revanchism entered the Sino-Soviet dispute. This in turn confirmed the Soviet's worst fears regarding Beijing's putative demographically driven expansionism into the underpopulated areas of Central Asia and Siberia. There was no real basis for such concern. The Chinese side of the Manchurian border is much less densely populated, much more underdeveloped economically, and without the transportation systems available on the Soviet side. The north and northwest border regions are comprised of deserts, grasslands, and mountains that account for over one-third of Chinese territory but less than 8 percent of its population. The Soviet leadership was well aware that China was in no position to expand across its northern borders.

Even if the PRC had been in a position to forcibly occupy Soviet territory, its demographic problems would be unchanged. Much of Central Asia is too dry for farming, and the permafrost in Siberia kills the roots of most food crops. Yet Soviet propaganda equated modern China under the Maoist leadership to the Mongol hordes of the thirteenth century that swept across Russia and Eastern Europe. There was an intentional effort to create a "yellow peril" psychology among the Soviet citizenry which seemed to be largely successful.[8]

Mongolia

In addition to the border question, there were other aspects of territorial relations that were troubling. As early as the 1949-1950 Sino-Soviet Treaty negotiations, Mao reportedly asked for a Mongolian/PRC merger.[9] Mongolia was the first Soviet satellite state, brought under Moscow's hegemony in 1921 and the prototype of "friendly" buffer states to protect the borders of the USSR. The Mongols accepted this status over the years because of the protection afforded by the USSR against China, which historically dominated the region. The Soviets carefully limited Chinese access to the Mongolian People's Republic (MPR) and refused most of Beijing's requests for more equity in economic and political influence there. The PRC made some headway between 1954 and 1964. As noted in Chapter 2, Khrushchev permitted limited Chinese emigration into Mongolia, and Beijing was allowed to provide a grant-in-aid to Ulan Batar.

In 1960, a formal Sino-Mongolian Treaty of Mutual Aid was signed, followed by a border treaty in 1962. The border was formally demarcated in 1964, but the scheduled meetings of boundary inspection teams were delayed until 1982.[10] The Maoist territorial claims that unduly alarmed the Kremlin probably had the same impact in Ulan Bator. As the Sino-Soviet dispute escalated, Moscow tightened its grip on Mongolia, and added it to the Council for Mutual Economic Assistance (COMECON, the Soviet-led economic bloc) in 1962.

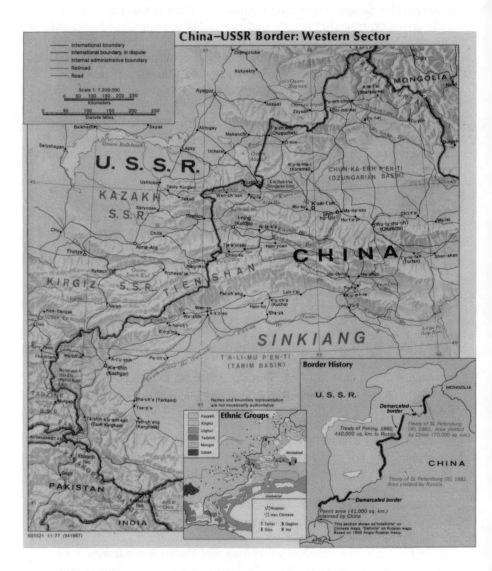

The Northwest Region

Restive Moslem minority peoples of the Xinjiang Autonomous Region further complicated the border issues. Rising radicalism associated with the Great Leap Forward (GLF) included more assimilationist policies toward the ethnic and religious minorities, making a mockery of the autonomous region concept. Those policies combined with the economic hardships that resulted from the failure of the GLF to cause an exodus of about 60,000 Uygurs and Kazakhs seeking political asylum on the Soviet side of the border between 1961 and 1963. Moscow allowed them to stay and then added insult to injury by publicly announcing that fact in 1963. The PRC response was to close the northwest portions of the border.

About this time, construction was halted on the last section of rail line linking Xinjiang with Soviet Central Asia. The line had been completed beyond the capital of Ulumuqi; on the Soviet side, it reached the Chinese border. Stopping construction on the the last remaining link clearly indicated that the PRC had reassessed its cost-benefit ratio. The rail line would boost commerce, but it would also provide a means for greater Soviet penetration and influence in Xinjiang. Moreover, it was a potential invasion corridor, although that possibility probably did not become a serious concern until the late 1960s.

Border Polemics

The Chinese pressed the border dispute in part because they felt they were the aggrieved party. This is an insufficient explanation, however. Tai-sung An, in his study of the Sino-Soviet border dispute, identified five reasons why Beijing took the offensive in the territorial polemics during the mid-1960s. The first, being to put Moscow on the defensive in the eyes of other communist nations, as well as some anticommunist countries, by portraying China as the victim of Soviet duplicity. Second, the PRC intended to inflame or provoke the irredentist passions of other nations, with potential or real claims against the USSR, (such as Japan, East Germany, Poland, Romania, and Finland). Third, Beijing wanted to demonstrate to the Afro-Asian world that the Soviets were the direct successors of Czarist Russia and fitted the mold of white colonialists in Asia. Fourth, the territorial dispute served internal political needs by serving as a unifying and rallying point for a population demoralized by the sufferings resulting from the failure of the Great Leap Forward. Finally, the PRC may have hoped to stop Soviet intrigues and the subversion of non-Han peoples in northwestern China by calling attention to Chinese claims in the region.[11]

Whatever benefits Beijing perceived in raising territorial issues, the long-term costs were high. Although Mao probably could not have foreseen the consequences, he put China at a distinct disadvantage. So long as the Sino-Soviet dispute was primarily ideological, China could compete with the USSR even as an economically underdeveloped, militarily weak, and internationally isolated nation. But the transformation of the dispute into geopolitical terms would lead to military confrontation in which the Soviets would hold the upper hand. While it was Brezhnev who initiated the militarization of the dispute, Mao must share the responsibility since he altered the nature of the Sino-Soviet rivalry.[12]

This escalation of polemics led Moscow to accede to formal border talks in February 1964, prior to Khrushchev's ouster from office. The two sides were unable to agree on a common approach. The PRC wanted to discuss broad principles and demanded a Soviet apology for the "unequal treaties" that Russia had imposed on China in the nineteenth century. Moscow rejected the demand, continuing to do so on the grounds that such an apology would call into question the legitimacy of all other Soviet territories acquired through Russian continental expansion in the eighteenth and nineteenth centuries.

According to Khrushchev's later account, Beijing initially made territorial demands in Siberia, including the cities of Khabarovsk and Vladivostok, though those were soon dropped in the negotiating process.[13] Khrushchev's claim is partially substantiated by Mao Zedong's June 1964 remark to visiting Japanese. Referring to Russia's territorial acquisitions under the czars, he warned that "China has not yet presented its bill." In the same month, Khrushchev attempted to put additional pressures on the Chinese side by threatening to exploit the minority nationalist feelings in Xinjiang.[14] In September, Khrushchev went much further, swearing that the USSR would take all necessary measures to ensure the inviolability of its frontiers, and that it would use all the means at its disposal to defend its borders, including the "up-to-date weapons of annihilation." This was the first Soviet nuclear threat against the PRC.[15]

Drawing the riverine borders also proved difficult, causing in turn problems regarding navigation rights. The usual international procedure is to accept the "thalweg" as the border, i.e., the middle of the main channel. This would cede Soviet-settled islands opposite Khabarovsk to China, so Moscow laid claim to six hundred of the seven hundred islands, thereby effectively drawing most of the border at the Chinese bank of the rivers. Beijing naturally refused to agree, and the talks ended acrimoniously in October (the same month in which Khrushchev was deposed).

Finally, the talks were further complicated by the issue of a nonaggression pact. At the end of 1963, Khrushchev had proposed a general international agreement on the renunciation of force for the settlement of territorial disputes. Some months later, after the border talks were underway, the PRC finally replied. Beijing accepted the borders as drawn in the "unequal treaties" but charged the USSR with recent violations of those borders, including the occupation of Chinese territory and provoking border incidents.[16] Until Soviet troops were withdrawn from the disputed areas, the PRC would not agree to negotiate a nonaggression pact. Beijing's unwillingness to pledge nonuse of force over the territorial problems may well have been a factor in the Soviet decision to strengthen its military posture on its eastern front.

Militarization of the Dispute

In July 1964, Mao Zedong made the first reference to the militarization of the Sino-Soviet dispute. He told a visiting Japanese delegation that the USSR had concentrated troops on China's northern border.[17] This may have been true, but not yet in terms of bringing additional forces to bear. There were only twelve to fifteen Soviet divisions in Central Asia and Siberia at that time, most of which were assigned either to internal security missions or to the defense of the Pacific Fleet headquarters in Vladivostok. Some units might have been reassigned to patrol the Chinese border, but Khrushchev did not deploy new forces to Central Asia and Siberia. That was a measure undertaken by the Brezhnev leadership.

The border issues and the failure of Khrushchev's use of economic levers to control Beijing seem to have been key factors in the decision to try military pressures. Since China had joined the nuclear club in 1964, Moscow could not rely merely on the single option of nuclear blackmail to protect its territory. The huge size of the Chinese People's Liberation Army (PLA) was quite enough to cause a reassessment of the Soviet posture in the region.

The Red Army troop buildup was initially quite modest, expanding the number of divisions to approximately seventeen by 1966. This enabled the Soviets to patrol the border more actively, but was far short of the forces needed to pose an invasion threat to the PRC. When the USSR occupied Manchuria at the end of World War II, it used seventy-five divisions against the diminished Japanese garrison remaining in Northeastern China. Eighteen divisions scattered along four thousand miles of Sino-Soviet border would have been incapable of sustained offensive actions against the much larger PLA forces. The number of additional border guard troops was estimated at only twenty thousand by 1966. However, the Red Army also changed its conscription system to increase its reserve forces to five million. This was done presumably because the Soviet leadership had to consider the possibility of a "two-front" war—fighting simultaneously in Europe and Asia.[18]

The initial buildup was followed in January 1966 by a new twenty-year friendship treaty between the Soviet Union and Mongolia that included secret clauses allowing Soviet troops to be sent to the MPR. There had been no Soviet military presence in the country since 1957. The 1966 agreement for the first time stipulated that Moscow would bear all costs of Soviet troops stationed in the country. The initial deployment consisted of two divisions and some aviation elements that were in place within a few months following the treaty signatures.[19] While the numbers of Soviet troops in Mongolia were not large, they were ominous since the natural geographic invasion corridor to Beijing runs from the MPR.

In 1966, the Sino-Soviet border became increasingly tense. In the spring, Beijing unilaterally announced new navigation regulations governing "foreign" (i.e., Soviet) vessels on border rivers. Among other things, the orders forbade the crews and passengers of Soviet boats from taking photographs, making maps, taking soundings, swimming, or fishing on the Chinese side of the rivers.[20] For their part, the Soviets harassed Chinese boats and fishermen on the Manchurian rivers. A number of small-scale skirmishes occurred at various places along the Soviet and Mongolian borders. The PRC claimed that there were a total of 4,189 border "incidents" between the time talks were broken off in October 1964 and the serious clashes of March 1969.[21] Those activities were probably best described as mutual intimidation tactics. However, the deployment of the first SS-4 and SS-5 MRBMs to the Soviet Far East in 1966 had to be perceived by Beijing as a national security threat, especially since they were soon accompanied by short-range rockets (SCUD and FROG models) that would only be usable against China, as opposed to other targets in Northeast Asia. However, unlike Khrushchev, the Brezhnev leadership did not indulge in verbal threats at that time.[22]

In 1967, Moscow began construction plans for the Baikal-Amur Mainline, a new rail link paralleling the Trans-Siberian Line but located further to the north. Thus it was less vulnerable to Chinese attack. Its nearest approach to the Chinese border is about two hundred kilometers.[23] While the main purpose of the line was to further the economic development of Siberia, its timing may well have been hastened by the increasingly hostile Sino-Soviet dispute.

As the Great Proletarian Cultural Revolution (GPCR) gathered momentum in 1967, so too did the Soviet troop buildup. Estimates differ, but by early 1969 the USSR had deployed approximately twenty-seven divisions on its territory and two or three in Mongolia.[24] The eastern littoral of Siberia contained more Soviet tanks and artillery pieces than did East Germany. There was a proportional increase in nuclear weapons and air-force deployments. True, those units also had the mission of defending the motherland against threats from Korea and Japan, but ground forces would be of greatest use against the contiguous neighbor of China. The Soviet forces were nearly all mechanized, thereby providing an immense tactical mobility advantage over the foot soldiers of the PLA. Equipment allocated to defend the eastern flank of the USSR was neither the best nor the latest in the Red Army inventory, and many of the units were not at full strength. However, the PRC did not initially respond with a concomitant buildup, and PLA equipment was both obsolescent and insufficient. Thus the Soviets soon established an overwhelming conventional force superiority in the border regions.

Moscow's Motives

What explained the increased rate of Soviet military commitment? Moscow was mute on the subject and did not even admit that a buildup was taking place. However the situation at the time would point to four factors, the first being China's increasingly confrontational posture during the GPCR. During the "Red Guard" phase of the GPCR, the Maoist leadership encouraged an outpouring of antiforeign chauvinism. Virtually all Chinese ambassadors were recalled home, the Foreign Ministry was taken over by "revolutionary rebels" in 1967, and the British Chancery in Beijing was burned a few weeks later by rampaging Red Guards. The USSR received plenty of "revolutionary" attention as well. The hostile riverine regulations of April 1966 were merely the first in a series of calculated provocations. The Soviet embassy in Beijing was under siege for weeks late in 1966. When nonessential embassy personnel and families left China (upon orders from Moscow), the Soviets were forced to run a gauntlet to the airport in which they were roughed up and humiliated. For several weeks, a Soviet merchant vessel and its crew were held hostage in the Manchurian port of Dalian because one of the crewmen had thrown a Mao button overboard after Red Guards had tried to forcibly pin it on his tunic. Soviet border guards in Siberia did discover one effective means for dealing with Red Guard groups who would troop to the river borders with giant portraits of Mao. The Soviets turned their backs, dropped their pants, and "mooned" the Great Helmsman. Chinese propaganda broadcasts calling for the overthrow of the Soviet leadership were jammed.

The Soviets began to consider the Maoist policies as "mad." That provided a second probable explanation for the Soviet troop buildup: opportunism. Since there was clearly no compromise to be found with the Maoists and since the GPCR caused immense disarray within China, a substantial Soviet force on the border might be in a position to intervene in support of an emerging anti-Maoist leader prepared to deal favorably with the USSR.[25] This, of course, did not happen, but it was not from lack of trying on the part of the Soviets. Chinese-language propaganda broadcasts were especially aimed at fomenting a military coup d'état.[26] Other broadcasts in minority languages fanned ethnic nationalism and separatism.

Growing PRC nuclear capabilities also played a role in the Soviet buildup. China's first test of a hydrogen bomb was in 1967, and the deployment of MRBMs was then underway. Those developments prompted Moscow to begin private signals to the United States regarding a possible preemptive attack on PRC nuclear facilities. As one anonymous Soviet official put it in July 1967: "If and when the time comes to do something about China, the USSR would expect the US to help."[27]

By 1969, Moscow had completed an anti-ballistic missile (ABM) system oriented against China.[28] Of course, any PRC nuclear attack on the USSR at that time would have been suicidal and could not even have reached metropolitan Russia, but the Soviets were prepared for the worst.

Racist paranoia was the final factor hastening Soviet buildup. When British Prime Minister Margaret Thatcher first met Brezhnev in the late 1970s, she raised the question as to why there was no progress in resolving Sino-Soviet tensions. Brezhnev replied emphatically: "Madam, there is only one important question facing us, and that is the question whether the white race will survive."[29]

The Zhen Bao/Damansky Island Incidents

After March 2, 1969, Moscow could throw charges of paranoia back into the faces of its accusers. On that date, Chinese forces sprung a carefully prepared ambush on Zhen Bao (Treasure Island in Chinese or Damansky in Russian) one of the larger islands along the Ussuri River. Soviet casualties numbered thirty-one dead and fourteen wounded in the two-hour battle, a death toll far higher from any previous skirmish. Moreover, this was no border-patrol accident. The ambush was clearly planned in advance, probably in response to orders from on high. Thus, the Soviets immediately went public with a detailed story of the action, whereas the Chinese were conspicuously silent in providing a factual account. Moscow took revenge on March 15 in a much larger clash at the same location. Red Army armor and artillery were extensively employed. The Soviets lost some sixty troops in a four-hour battle that saw several hundred Chinese casualties.[30] Here, attention is directed at the Soviet responses to the Zhen Bao incidents. (Possible motives for the Chinese ambush on March 2 will be considered in Chapter 6.)

The rate of reinforcement escalated drastically after the March clashes. By the early 1970s, there were about forty divisions confronting the PRC. By the mid-1970s, the figure was up to at least forty-eight divisions, numbering about 750,000 men, or 25 percent of the Soviet ground and air forces.[31] In the 1970s, the Pacific Fleet became the largest of the Soviet naval forces.

The Zhen Bao clashes also provoked a heated debate in the Soviet Politburo. Defense Minister Andrei Grechko advocated a strong nuclear attack on China's industrial centers to get rid of the "Chinese threat." Others proposed surgical strikes limited to conventional bombs, while some proposed avoidance of hostilities altogether. On different occasions, the Soviet leadership explored with President Nixon and Secretary of State Henry Kissinger the possibility of Soviet preemptive strikes against Chinese strategic weapons bases and manufacturing facilities. Both Nixon and Kissinger expressed strong objections to the latter plan. According to one "insider" Soviet account, US objections ultimately caused the USSR not to launch such an attack. Brezhnev instead opted for a major buildup of conventional forces, backed by ample theater and tactical nuclear weapons.[32]

The Soviets initially militarized the Sino-Soviet dispute in a calculated fashion, but the growing border troubles threatened to spiral out of control. Moscow's favorable position rapidly deteriorated. Brezhnev was unable to extract promises of help from Warsaw Pact allies. Immediately following the March clashes, a pact summit was held in Budapest, where the East European leaders politely pointed out to Brezhnev that the alliance was restricted to potential European conflicts.[33] The Soviets would have to face China alone. Still worse, the militarization of the dispute was proving to have long-term disadvantages:

> The Soviet policy makers were impaled on the horns of a dilemma. On the one hand, they had to defend their homeland and encourage the Chinese to negotiate a settlement. Together with the occasional use of minimal force, the border build-up did deter the Chinese from perpetrating another Zhen Bao Island incident and did keep them at the negotiating table. On the other hand, the Russians wanted to discourage the Chinese from modernizing their own military forces and from forming an anti-Soviet entente with the US. The build-up and the use of force against the Chinese, however, drove Beijing straight in that direction. . . . As the Kremlin solved its short-term security problem, therefore, it created a much greater long term threat. The cure turned out to be worse than the disease.[34]

The Brezhnev Doctrine

Chinese concern with the militarization of the border dispute was heightened by the reassertion of a Soviet policy governing relations among socialist nations. The latter was occasioned by the leadership of Alexander Dubcek in Czechoslovakia. In the "Prague Spring" of 1968, the nation moved toward freedom of the press and a multiparty system. The Soviets feared that those trends might well destroy communist control of the nation and remove it from their bloc. In August 1968, several Warsaw Pact nations, led by the USSR, invaded and occupied Prague in order to reverse Dubcek's policies.

The official Soviet rationale for the invasion became known as the "Brezhnev Doctrine."[35] It claimed that the importance of international proletarian solidarity among Soviet bloc nations outweighs the rights of national sovereignty. Therefore, if an ally adopts policies that constitute a "silent counter-revolution," it is incumbent on the USSR, as the bloc leader, to intervene and thus save the nation from itself while protecting the mutual security of all bloc nations. This was not a new policy; similar circumstances had surrounded the invasion of Hungary in 1956, an invasion that had been supported by all Warsaw Pact nations and China. The 1968 invasion of Czechoslovakia had sufficient justification to gain the support of all Warsaw Pact nations except Romania. It was also supported by North Korea, North Vietnam, and Cuba, nations that had faced military confrontations with the United States. For those nations bloc solidarity was vitally important to their sense of security.

A number of other communist parties and nations denounced the Soviet invasion. The Western European communist parties, Romania, Yugoslavia, and Albania, all attacked the Soviet action, but none were as vociferous as Beijing. Although the Brezhnev doctrine of "limited sovereignty" applied only to members of the Soviet bloc, Beijing claimed that it provided a rationale for a Soviet invasion of the PRC. None of the later published Soviet sources or memoirs indicate that Moscow was planning an invasion. The costs would have been far too high and the risks too great. However, the USSR did began to create a Chinese government in exile. For this purpose, they resurrected Wang Ming, whom Mao had ousted in 1938 and who had spent the intervening years living in total obscurity in the USSR. He became Moscow's primary spokesman denouncing the Maoist heresies.[36] Thus, if the GPCR happened to result in the complete collapse of the Chinese polity, the USSR might then intervene to restore "true" communism to the PRC.

The Soviets also convened a "schismatic" international communist conference intended to expel China from the socialist bloc, something Khrushchev had tried and failed to do in 1964. The conference was delayed by the Czech unpleasantness and a lack of enthusiasm on the part of some bloc members. When it finally convened in May 1969, the meeting was a disappointment to Moscow. The agenda had to be watered down in order to obtain the participation of a number of independent-minded parties, and the final document still included China in the list of socialist nations. The Soviet leadership stressed nationalism as a fundamental threat to the cohesion of communism, but that was not included in the final document. The document did say, however, that all communist parties and nations must eschew "striving for hegemony," which could be interpreted as a slap against the Soviet domination of its Eastern European neighbors, especially Czechoslovakia.[37] Finally, Moscow must have been disappointed at the refusals of both North Korea and North Vietnam to attend the conference. Needless to say, China did not attend, although Beijing received a pro forma invitation. Clearly, there were sharp limits to the levels of support Moscow might receive from its bloc partners in any showdown with the PRC.

The disappointing results of the meeting may have contributed to a temporary softening of Brezhnev's China policy. In a widely circulated article published shortly after the conference, he wrote that those allies who were "temporarily deluded" should be dealt with by "comradely, friendly polemics" and at times, "a certain restraint."[38] China was not specifically mentioned, but the implication was that the USSR was prepared to wait out Maoism in the expectation that it was only a temporary aberration. This could also have been a signal to Beijing that the USSR was not planning any imminent hostilities, but the Soviet reinforcements were still crowding the eastbound trains of the Trans-Siberian Railroad, and Wang Ming still posed the possibility of a Chinese communist party in exile. The Brezhnev "softline" message was lost on Beijing.

Brezhnev's Asian Collective Security Proposal

In Brezhnev's major speech to the Moscow Conference of June 1969, he first raised the idea of a multilateral Asian security agreement in conjunction with the long-standing proposal for a European security conference. It was not intended to be a military alliance. Rather, it was rooted in superpower détente and Third World nonalignment principles. Collective security was defined in terms of eight broad principles that included the themes of peaceful coexistence.[39]

The proposal was partly aimed at containing and perpetuating China's relative isolation in Asia. It was well timed since the domestic radicalism and violence of the GPCR had tarnished the image of the PRC, and Mao's support for Asian insurgencies (people's wars of national liberation) had contributed to China's isolation.[40] The Soviets, of course, were not about to admit that Brezhnev's plan had roots in the Sino-Soviet conflict. Within weeks of the Moscow Conference speech, Foreign Minister Andrei Gromyko sought to allay Asian suspicions that the initiative was aimed at China. He dismissed as groundless the claim that the proposal was directed "against some country or any group of countries." Three days later, Zhou Enlai denounced the plan as another step by "social imperialism" to create a "new anti-Chinese military alliance." Zhou claimed that the Soviets were "simply stepping into the shoes of U.S. imperialism" as the US alliance networks of SEATO and CENTO weakened.[41] The Asian nations responded negatively to Brezhnev's ideas. As one superpower was withdrawing from the region, there was little support for letting the other in through a back door. Specious claims that collective security was not aimed at China did not convince Asian leaders. They had no desire to become involved in the Sino-Soviet dispute as instruments of Soviet foreign policy. Even India, the Asian nation closest to

Moscow, refused to support the proposal. The Soviet leadership did not give up on the concept (as will be seen in Chapter 9, it was reformulated by Mikhail Gorbachev in 1986).

Later in the same month, President Nixon announced the so-called Nixon Doctrine. Its main thrust was that the United States would be reluctant to commit troops to the defense of Asian nations, apart from obligations already made. Instead the United States would serve as supplier and supporter of Asian states that would take a greater responsibility for their own defense. This was the starting point for Nixon's "Vietnamization" policy that saw the phased withdrawal of US combat troops from that embattled nation.

The Nixon Doctrine did not initially receive a warm welcome from Beijing. The New China News Agency dismissed it as an attempt to use "Asians to fight Asians." But Zhou's denunciation of the Brezhnev Asian collective security program "anticipated the differentiation between a receding US involvement in Asia and an expanding Soviet one that would underlie and justify the basic shift in the Sino-American relationship."[42] The increased Soviet presence in Asia was first manifested in India and was apparent in Vietnam by the late 1960s.

The Rise of Vietnam in Soviet Foreign Policy

Khrushchev showed little interest in Vietnam. He warned the Kennedy administration against growing US involvement in South Vietnam, lest the conflict be taken advantage of by Beijing and escalation ruin opportunities for Soviet-American détente.[43] He could see no victor in the conflict except for Beijing. Therefore, he tried to serve as a mediator in seeking a peaceful settlement, even to the point of pressuring Hanoi. In the last two years of Khrushchev's leadership, Soviet economic assistance to North Vietnam (the Socialist Republic of Vietnam, or the SRV) declined to a virtual halt even as the Kennedy administration increased US commitment to Saigon.[44] But the North Vietnamese could find nothing in the US position that was negotiable. Hanoi was committed to the reunification of the nation, and war was necessary to achieve that end.

The Brezhnev regime saw Vietnam as offering opportunities for the expansion of Soviet influence in East Asia. Soviet aid to the SRV (and North Korea) was restored in November 1964. A month later, Moscow warned the United States that it would not "stand with arms folded" while the SRV was subjected to aggression. This was the first time that the USSR threatened to take some counteraction to the rising levels of conflict in Vietnam.[45] Moscow stopped pressuring Hanoi to seek a negotiated settlement to the war. By March 1965, Soviet military aid to the SRV was rolling across Chinese rail lines toward Hanoi. By April, Moscow had already complained of

Chinese delays and interference with the Soviet materiel.[46]

Also in April, Moscow offered Beijing a "united action" proposal to provide extensive military assistance through China to Vietnam. Included in the offer were requests for overflight rights and the basing of Soviet air-force planes and personnel in Southwest China near the Vietnam border. The proposal strengthened the anti-imperialist credentials of the USSR that had become compromised under the Khrushchev leadership. It also put the Chinese in a bad spot. If they said no to the proposal, they would be letting down their socialist brothers in the face of mounting imperialist aggression. If they said yes, the USSR would finally get some of the basing rights in China that Khrushchev had vainly pursued with Mao. The PRC temporarily allowed overflight rights and worked out a formal agreement to continue the transhipment of Soviet materiel to Vietnam on Chinese rolling stock. Basing rights were denied as unnecessary for providing materiel support to the SRV.

Meantime, Soviet military and economic assistance to Hanoi went up sharply in 1965 and grew to $705 million in 1967, a figure that was more than three times the level contributed by Beijing.[47] As the war escalated between 1965 and 1967, it became clear that Vietnam would increasingly need sophisticated military equipment the PRC could not furnish. Through the remainder of the 1960s, Hanoi still managed to maintain its position of neutrality in the Sino-Soviet dispute, but Moscow had eclipsed Beijing in the quantity and quality of its aid to North Vietnam.[48]

Conclusion

The end of the 1960s saw unprecedented confidence in the USSR. In superpower relations, strategic parity was within reach. Relations among socialist nations were improved (i.e., the Czechoslovakian crisis had been resolved) and the 1969 Moscow meeting of international communist parties had finally been successfully convened, even though the conference did not formally expel China from the bloc. In the global arena, the USSR was clearly a power on the rise, with increasing influence in the Middle East, North Vietnam, and southern Asia. Stabilization of the superpower competition with the United States was on the agenda. The PRC remained the single most important and critical area of concern to the Soviets, but even that situation did not pose an imminent threat to Soviet security unless Moscow's own actions triggered a war with Beijing.

Undoubtedly, a root cause of the Sino-Soviet dispute in the 1950s and 1960s was Beijing's fear that the USSR and the United States might reach a superpower accommodation at the expense of China, which still had major national objectives requiring changes in the international correlation of forces. The discussion of the Khrushchev years in this book followed that general line of argument, though the emphasis is on the Soviet strategic weakness that forced Moscow to adopt policies conciliatory to the United States.

After the fear of a first strike by the United States was vitiated in the mid-1960s, the USSR developed new national security and foreign policies intended to make the Soviet Union a global power. The Kennedy-Khrushchev legacy of détente was undermined. On the US side, the bombing of North Vietnam was probably the most damaging action. On the Soviet side, its new activism in South Asia (where it brokered a peace between India and Pakistan), its role as arms supplier to the Arab nations (especially to Egypt after the 1967 Six Day War), and the invasion of Czechoslovakia led the United States to believe that Moscow was again launched on an aggressive foreign policy. The US leadership was increasingly concerned with the growth of Soviet global power. Under such circumstances, the PRC should not have feared a superpower accommodation at its expense. So why did the Sino-Soviet conflict become more heated and dangerous in this same time frame?

One answer was that Beijing in the mid-to-late 1960s gradually came to perceive Soviet ambitions in and of themselves as inimical to Chinese interests. Taken together, the Soviet-led militarization of the border dispute, the invasion of Czechoslovakia, and the concomitant Brezhnev Doctrine, along with increased competition for influence in North Vietnam and North Korea, were enough to cause both Mao and Zhou Enlai to begin listing the USSR ahead of the United States on China's "enemy list" in 1968.

Second, there were two areas of US-Soviet détente that survived the 1960s, and these were of particular concern to Beijing. First, the situation in Western Europe remained stable. A meeting of NATO ministers in December 1967 declared that "the threat from the Soviet Union to Western Europe is all but gone." Six months later, the Western powers proposed a "mutual and balanced force reduction" of conventional units in Eastern and Western Europe. Such lessening of European tensions would enable Moscow to transfer more of its troop units to the Asian theater, while the United States could commit more forces to Vietnam. Moscow and Washington continued to make progress regarding nuclear arms. The nonproliferation treaty was supported through the United Nations by both superpowers in early 1968. Beijing saw this not only as an attempt to perpetuate the superpower monopoly on nuclear coercion, but also to provide a nuclear umbrella over China's neighbors who signed the pact.[49] The first six years of the Brezhnev regime had seen profound changes in the posture of the USSR, almost all of which were threatening to China. Beijing was forced to respond.

Notes

1. Robert Freedman, *Economic Warfare in the Communist Bloc*, pp. 172-173.

2. *International Herald Tribune*, Feb. 6-7, 1988, citing a memoir by General Wu Xiuquan in *Dongfang Jishi*, Feb. 1, 1988. Wu was a participant in the talks.

3. *Pravda*, Apr. 1, 1978.

4. A fine summary treatment of modern Sino-Soviet border problems is Thomas Robinson's "The Sino-Soviet Border Dispute: Background, Development, and the March 1969 Clashes," *American Political Science Review*, Vol. LXVI, No. 4, Dec. 1972, pp. 1175-1202.

5. University Publications of America, *CIA Research Reports, China*, reel 3, frame 148.

6. Robinson, "The Sino-Soviet Border Dispute," p. 1178.

7. The 600,000 square-mile figure is by Chinese Nationalist accounting. For a detailed breakdown of the "lost territories," see Tai-sung An, *The Sino-Soviet Territorial Dispute*, p. 60.

8. A Soviet book that went too far with the "yellow peril" view was *Can the USSR Survive Until 1984?* by Andrei Amalric. He envisaged the breakup of the Warsaw Pact and the defeat of the USSR due to a war of attrition fought by Beijing. The book was published in English in 1970, but never sold in the USSR.

9. Robert Scalapino in Richard Solomon, *The China Factor*, p. 183.

10. US Department of State, Bureau of Intelligence and Research, International Boundary Study #173, Aug. 14, 1984, *China Mongolia Boundary*, pp. 5-6.

11. An, *The Sino-Soviet Territorial Dispute*, pp. 79-80.

12. Jonathan Pollack, *The Sino-Soviet Rivalry and the Chinese Security Debate*, pp. 4-8.

13. Strobe Talbott, ed., *Khrushchev Remembers: The Last Testament*, pp. 287-288.

14. Walter Clemens, *The Arms Race and Sino-Soviet Relations*, p. 71.

15. Harry Gelman, *The Soviet Far East Buildup and Soviet Risk Taking Against China*, p. 17

16. Richard Wich, *Sino-Soviet Crisis Politics*, pp. 31-32.

17. John Gittings, *Survey of the Sino-Soviet Dispute*, pp. 166-167.

18. Avigdor Haselkorn, *The Evolution of Soviet Security Strategy, 1965-75*, pp. 38-39.

19. Janos Radvanyi, *Delusion & Reality: Gambits, Hoaxes & Diplomatic One-Upmanship in Vietnam*, p. 185. Radvanyi was a Hungarian diplomat prior to his defection in 1967. His book contains a great deal of "insider" Soviet-bloc information in addition to its Vietnam War focus.

20. An, *The Sino-Soviet Territorial Dispute*, p. 84

21. Thomas Robinson, "The Sino-Soviet Border Conflict," in Steven Kaplan (ed.), *Diplomacy of Power: Soviet Armed Forces as a Political Instrument*, p. 268.

22. David Holloway, *The Soviet Union and the Arms Race*, p. 69.

23. Whiting, *Siberian Development and East Asia*, p. 101.

24. *Christian Science Monitor*, Mar. 27, 1969.

25. In one unofficial Chinese account of the later "Lin Biao affair," it is charged

that Defense Minister Lin himself was planning just such a use for a "provoked" Soviet invasion in 1971 which would have ended with the death of Mao Zedong. Yao Ming-le, *The Conspiracy and Death of Lin Biao,* Chapter 13.

26. Those broadcasts continued until stopped by Gorbachev in 1986.

27. University Publications of America, *CIA Research Reports-Soviet Union,* reel 4, frame 498.

28. Presumably this "anti-China" ABM system used the existing missiles deployed to defend Moscow and Leningrad against US ICBMs. The main addition that would have been required was a radar network covering the missile-approach paths from the PRC. C. G. Jacobsen, *Sino-Soviet Relations Since Mao: The Chairman's Legacy,* 1981, p. 112.

29. Freeman Dyson, *Weapons and Hope,* p. 183

30. Robinson, "The Sino-Soviet Border Dispute," p. 1189-1190.

31. Gelman, *Soviet Far East Buildup,* pp. 12-14.

32. Arkady Shevchenko, *Breaking With Moscow,* pp. 164-166.

33. Anatole Shub, *An Empire Loses Hope: The Return of Stalin's Ghost,* pp. 432-433.

34. Thomas Robinson, "The Sino-Soviet Border Conflict," in Steven S. Kaplan (ed.), Diplomacy of Power: Soviet Armed Forces as a Political Instrument, p. 288.

35. The Soviets officially deny the existence of the Brezhnev Doctrine, but it still serves as an accurate "short hand" for analyzing the circumstances under which the USSR has intervened against the sovereign interests of Soviet-bloc states.

36. Wich, *Sino-Soviet Crisis Politics,* p. 135.

37. Wich devotes Chapter 8 of *Crisis Politics* to the Moscow conference.

38. Wich, *Sino-Soviet Crisis Politics,* p. 161

39. Leszek Buszynski, *Soviet Foreign Policy and Southeast Asia,* 1986, pp. 41-63

40. Buszynski, *Soviet Foreign Policy,* p. 43

41. Wich, *Crisis Politics* pp. 181-182.

42. Wich, *Crisis Politics,* p. 181.

43. Roy Medvedev, *Khrushchev,* p. 196.

44. Donald Zagoria, *Vietnam Triangle: Moscow, Peking, Hanoi,* p. 43.

45. Daniel Papp, *Vietnam: The View from Moscow, Peking, Washington,* p. 45.

46. University Publications of America, *CIA Research Reports, USSR,* reel 4, frame 317.

47. Papp, *Vietnam,* p. 114.

48. Hanoi approved the Soviet invasion of Czechoslovakia in order to maintain bloc solidarity in the face of US military pressures, but the North Vietnamese leadership refused to support Brezhnev's Asian collective security proposal until after 1977. The SRV did not attend the "anti-China" Moscow Conference of 1969.

49. Melvin Gurtov, *China Under Threat,* p. 222.

6

China in Peril

As we have thus far seen, Beijing's fear of collusion between Moscow and Washington was a powerful factor in the development of the Sino-Soviet dispute. PRC propaganda continuously reiterated the theme that the two superpowers were attempting to divide up the world between them into informally recognized spheres of influence. Mao reportedly told Premier Kosygin in February 1965 that peaceful coexistence was "profitable only to the imperialists." He believed that the efforts by the two superpowers to establish a global condominium would eventually fail. World tensions would continue to grow and a war of unprecedented lethality would occur by about 1975 or 1980. Only such a world war involving both countries against the United States could restore Sino-Soviet relations and consolidate the socialist camp.[1]

Beijing's World View

Closely linked with the issue of Soviet-US collusion was the extent to which the communist bloc should support revolutionary and anti-imperialist wars by colonies and Third World nations against the Western powers. Mao was a strong advocate of such "people's wars of national liberation" (PWNL), whereas Khrushchev exercised caution lest local conflicts escalate into confrontations with the United States. Any such confrontation would have required a humiliating Soviet retreat due to the US doctrine of nuclear brinksmanship and Moscow's strategic weapons weaknesses.

After the Sino-Soviet dispute devolved into an open break in the early 1960s, Beijing's anti-imperialist position hardened and the moderating element of "peaceful coexistence" was largely absent from 1964 through 1968.[2] With the open and irreparable rupture between Beijing and Moscow, it was even more in China's interest to encourage PWNL since they decreased the chances of accommodation between the United States and the USSR.[3]

Mao's position was firmly rooted in Leninism, providing the appeal of orthodoxy in the PRC's worldwide struggles with Moscow for the loyalties of communist parties. Lenin explained the failure of the European proletariat to rise in revolution as due to the exploitation of Africa, Asia, and Latin America. The resources, labor, and markets of those continents had enabled the capitalists to create a "labor aristocracy" in Europe at the expense of the colonies and Third World nations. Thus, imperialism was the final and highest stage of capitalism. The collapse of the system would be brought about through the revolutionary and anti-imperialist struggles of the Third World. As those resources, markets, and labor supplies disappeared, the resulting economic crises in the West would finally result in the revolution that Karl Marx had predicted so long ago.

Khrushchev formulated his own version of this global view. He defined the Third World as a "protracted zone" of competition between the capitalist and Marxist systems. But for Khrushchev, economics constituted the core of the struggle. The superiority of socialism would be proven by its productivity, technical achievements, and social justice. In this formulation of peaceful competition between the two political-economic systems, neutralism would best serve the Third World nations in terms of foreign policy. For Mao, the emphasis was on revolutionary armed struggle against capitalist enemies within and imperialism from without. Peace would come after liberation.[4]

In 1964, Mao refined Lenin's argument by including an "intermediate zone." This was the group of nations that were capitalist and economically developed, but which also suffered from the exploitation of the most powerful imperialists, i.e., the United States. As the revolutionary struggle progressed, these nations would gradually realize that their best interests were with the new order. Beijing saw the process as beginning in concrete terms in 1964 with the establishment of diplomatic relations between Gaullist France and the PRC. The Western "intermediate zone" nations were also seen as good economic connections for the PRC, superior to the Soviet Union. In February 1964, Mao said: "We can do a little business, but we cannot do too much, for Soviet products are heavy, crude, high priced and they always keep something back [in the sense of technology transfer]. It is therefore better to do business with the French bourgeoisie who still have some notion of business ethics."[5]

World View and National Security Policy

Beijing pursued people's wars of national liberation throughout the 1960s with a single-minded dedication. Necessity played at least as important a role as did Leninist orthodoxy. With the Sino-Soviet alliance virtually defunct after 1960 and the UN embargo still in place from the Korean War period, China was isolated and vulnerable. If the number one enemy, the US, could be bogged down in a series of anti-imperialist struggles, it would be unable to apply its concentrated military power against the PRC. Indeed, Beijing had no other choice but to rely on this doctrine for its own defense. The leadership fully realized that they would have no help in defending China. Immense resources were committed toward developing a nuclear arsenal, but meanwhile the strategic weapons program itself increased the likelihood of a US attack. About a year before the PRC's 1964 initial nuclear test, President Kennedy considered mounting a preemptive attack to destroy the research, development, and production facilities associated with China's embryonic nuclear capability.[6] Apparently the risks were greater than the potential benefits, but Beijing had good reason to feel especially vulnerable during most of the 1960s.

Mao's protracted warfare strategy was touted as the ultimate defense for the PRC. No nation could successfully invade and occupy large areas of the PRC without paying a grievous price. Guerrilla warfare and small unit tactics would continuously harass lines of communication and pin down enemy forces deep within Chinese territory. Even the advent of tactical nuclear weapons did not change that reality. However, air and sea power could profoundly damage China's national capabilities and economy without an enemy even setting foot on Chinese soil. This would be true even without the use of nuclear weapons. Given the obsolescence of the PRC's air and naval forces and the absence of a nuclear deterrent until the latter half of the 1960s, China lacked a true "home defense" capability. Its best strategy was to keep the United States away from its shores and airspace by bogging Washington down in "brushfire wars" elsewhere.

The Soviet Variable. Mao's combination of world view and defense doctrine was challenged by the militarization of the Sino-Soviet dispute. As early as 1964, he began describing Soviet behavior in terms of imperialism (referring at that time to the Sino-Soviet border issue and Soviet control of Japan's Northern Territories). But Chinese propaganda made little headway against the socialist credentials of the USSR. So long as Moscow was perceived as fundamentally Marxian, it was difficult to place it in the same category as the United States. Meanwhile, the militarization of the dispute continued apace. On March 26, 1967, Foreign Minister Chen Yi expressed the belief that a border war between China and the USSR would begin sooner than a war between China and the United States.[7] Pressures mounted on Beijing to develop a national security policy against this new threat.

The 1968 Soviet invasion of Czechoslovakia and the enunciation of the Brezhnev Doctrine provided the PRC with additional ideological ammunition. Zhou Enlai coined the "social-imperialist" neologism to describe Soviet foreign policy, while the older slur of "revisionist" continued to be used against Moscow's domestic programs. In the autumn of 1968, Zhou and Mao both listed the USSR ahead of the United States in the litany of international threats.[8] China's denunciation of the invasion and warning to Romania that it might be the next victim of the Soviet Union was paralleled closely by the pronouncements from Washington, DC. This was the first time that the two countries arrived at a common position regarding the Soviet threat, but it was not to be the last.[9]

Even if Beijing succeeded in ascribing imperialism as the basis of Soviet foreign policy, the defense dilemma remained. Moscow's control over its Eastern European client states was ironclad, as evidenced by the invasion of Czechoslovakia, so there could be no wars of national liberation launched against the Kremlin. Third World brushfire wars provided no security for the PRC against the rising Soviet threat. The situation called for a fundamental foreign policy reformulation, but in the late 1960s, defense policy took precedence.

Coping with the Border Threat. The Soviet troop buildup between 1967 and 1969 and the Brezhnev Doctrine led Beijing to try direct counter-threats. The message was that Beijing would respond to any Soviet attack against its territory whether by air, sea, or land, regardless of whether the attack was conventional or nuclear. The response would be to create a major land war in Siberia. The best-known signal was the ambush of the Soviet patrol on Zhen Bao Island in March 1969, but a recent Soviet source puts that single attack into a larger context.

Vladimir Rybakov was a Soviet artilleryman attached to a unit stationed on the Ussuri River in 1968 and 1969. He personally witnessed one suicide attack by a sizable Chinese troop unit against Soviet positions. The unit was destroyed by a heavy artillery barrage that even included a FROG rocket (with a conventional warhead), and survivors were shot. In another instance, his battery targeted fire on Soviet territory during a night attack by a PLA unit. On more numerous occasions, PLA patrols would slip across the Ussuri under the cover of darkness to kill sentries and demolish Soviet ammunition dumps and warehouses.[10] To further impress the Kremlin with Beijing's willingness to undertake a hopeless war against the USSR, Lin Biao issued his so-called "General Order Number One" of 1969. That sweeping war preparations command included the physical removal of all persons from the area of the capital who could possibly be used by the Soviets as a puppet alternative leadership to the Mao-Lin group.[11] Moscow was thereby informed that even the occupation of Beijing would not end a Sino-Soviet war.

The scholar Allen Whiting coined a term for this Chinese form of deterrence. He called it "calculated irrationality," meaning that Beijing would threaten to undertake a military action in which it would certainly incur greater losses than would enemy forces. Yet the cost of the conflict would still be great enough to deter the aggressor.[12]

Strategic Weapons

By the time the Soviet military threat had become imminent in the late 1960s, the PRC possessed both nuclear and conventional military deterrence, having tested its first hydrogen bomb in 1967. More important, in 1965 and 1966, the PLA successfully completed dozens of troop-training MRBM launches—to a maximum range of about eight hundred miles. One launch used a live atomic warhead—the only such test ever undertaken by any nation to date. In 1966, Beijing began to deploy its new MRBM, with initial sites in Manchuria, targeted on cities and US military installations in Japan.[13] After the 1969 Sino-Soviet border clashes, targeting was reoriented against the USSR, though it was not until 1971 that the first missiles were placed in Qinghai in Northwest China.[14]

US reconnaissance satellites were unable to discover any of the locations until 1969. Concealment was vital since the rockets were liquid-fueled and required several hours to prepare for launching. Had their locations been known, it would have been a simple matter to destroy them in a preemptive strike. Since superior US spy satellites could not find the missiles, it may be assumed that the Soviets could not find them either.[15] The PRC also concentrated on medium-range bomber production. Production leveled off in the early 1970s when there were about one hundred TU-16 bombers in the inventory. To protect the aircraft, the bombers were frequently relocated among two hundred bases within striking range of Soviet targets.

It would have been suicidal for the PRC to have undertaken a nuclear exchange with the USSR, and its missiles could only have struck targets in Siberia and Central Asia. However, should the Soviets have initiated a first strike, Beijing could have destroyed the Trans-Siberian Rail Line, Vladivostok, Chita, Khabarovsk, and Tashkent in retaliation. No gain against China would have been worth that cost to the USSR.

The development of Beijing's small but sufficient nuclear deterrent in the late 1960s entailed military trade-offs. In 1965, the PRC began the development of an ICBM in order to have a nuclear deterrent against the continental United States. The technological challenges of an ICBM are much greater than those of a MRBM, and the test facility, which had been started in 1965, was torn down about 1970.[16] This change in nuclear-force building priorities must have been occasioned by the Soviet threat.[17] ICBM development did not resume until the mid-1970s, with the PRC's first successful long-range test finally occurring in May 1980. Meanwhile, the PRC rapidly developed an IRBM with a range of 1,200 to 1,500 miles and deployed the first of those missiles against the USSR in the early 1970s.

These initial missile deployments did not change the balance of power between the PRC and the USSR. Soviet military superiority along their common border was virtually unchallenged. Chinese forces remained as vulnerable as before to air and naval harassment or to ground-force incursions. The missiles provided one more variable for Soviet planners to consider should Moscow contemplate the use of force against the PRC.

Border Talks: Round Two

Chinese conventional and nuclear deterrence, together with US objections to a Soviet preemptive attack against the PRC, combined to prevent the outbreak of a Sino-Soviet war. However, tensions ran so high in the aftermath of the Zhen Bao clashes that it was in the best interest of both nations to defuse the military crisis lest some small border incident balloon into a larger conflict. Zhou Enlai was able to take advantage of Ho Chi Minh's funeral to meet with Premier Kosygin in October 1969.

In talks at the Beijing airport (on Kosygin's return trip to Moscow from Hanoi), Zhou agreed to drop a key Chinese precondition for negotiations, i.e., that the existing treaties be described as an "unequal" legacy of Russian imperialism. Zhou and Kosygin also agreed to cease armed provocations on the border and improve bilateral economic relations. Talks began a few months later, and both sides agreed to accept the status quo along the border until exact boundary locations could be mutually accepted.

Soon after that "second round" of border talks had begun, China raised a new demand for the withdrawal of all forces from the disputed territories. Since all lands at issue were under Soviet control, such a withdrawal would have amounted to a unilateral concession by Moscow. The unreasonable Chinese demand was probably a calculated decision to abort the negotiations.[18] The PRC was still too weak to obtain a favorable resolution, so no agreement was the preferred outcome. Meanwhile, the talks had served their purpose by reducing the likelihood of further border clashes.

Vietnam

As the threat to China's northern borders grew in the mid-1960s, so did the threat from the south. Beijing's national defense policy was known as a "dual adversary" approach. The PRC could not afford to neglect the US threat simply because of the militarization of the Sino-Soviet conflict. Beijing saw the Vietnam conflict as the best example of an ongoing people's war of national liberation. It had been the primary supplier to the Vietminh since the early 1950s and staunchly supported Hanoi in the face of the rising US threat. Following the retaliatory bombing raids associated with the Gulf of Tonkin incident in the summer of 1964, Beijing announced that aggression against the SRV would be considered the same as aggression against China. A dozen

MiG-15 and MiG-17 jet fighters were delivered to Vietnam, and large-scale troop exercises were carried out in South China.[19] When the sustained US bombing of North Vietnam began in 1965, China sent in PLA railway engineering and anti-aircraft artillery units to protect and maintain the lines from the Chinese border to Hanoi.[20] Eventually, some 120,000 Chinese troops were stationed there. As early as 1964, new airfields were constructed in China near the Vietnam border, with one being within twelve miles. These were as useful for the defense of SRV airspace as they were for defending China. Some additional infantry units were also redeployed into southern China.[21] Finally, Beijing issued a number of warnings between February and August 1965 that China would send "volunteer" forces to Vietnam if requested to do so by the SRV.[22] Such extensive PRC support was partly prompted by its "people's war" doctrine. In concrete terms, the Vietnam War seemed to offer an ideal opportunity to embarrass the Soviets, weaken the United States, and retard the progress of Soviet-American détente.[23]

While the relationship between Beijing and Hanoi was good in the mid-to-late 1960s, there were several troubling issues. First, the Vietminh refused to fight the war according to Chinese plans. Beijing wanted Hanoi to carry out a long-term guerrilla war in the south and avoid a dangerous escalation that might provoke the United States into strong and dangerous countermeasures. This strategy was enunciated in Lin Biao's famous September 1965 speech, "Long Live the Victory of People's War." Beijing and Washington had achieved a tacit mutual understanding in 1966. The PRC was not under imminent threat of US attack and, for its part, China would not directly intervene unless the war escalated to the point where the political survival of the SRV was at stake.[24] However, Hanoi insisted on countering US air power with its own main force infantry units that infiltrated into South Vietnam along the busy Ho Chi Minh Trail in 1966 and 1967. In addition to the threat of escalation, the SRV strategy also turned the Vietnamese armed forces into major "metal eaters." They badly needed large quantities of artillery, armor, and a sophisticated air defense system. Moscow was the only available source.

The Soviets made their "united action" proposal in April 1965. The PRC denounced the initiative, since it included provisions for stationing Soviet troops on Chinese soil. The proposal may have prompted the dispatch of PLA forces to Vietnam a few months later; if Beijing refused to cooperate with Moscow to ensure SRV security, then China needed to prove its unaided ability to protect Hanoi from US bombing and invasion threats. The Soviet proposal did generate a fractious policy debate in Beijing. Chief of the General Staff Department Luo Ruiqing favored accepting some form of the Soviet proposal since he was convinced that there was a serious danger of escalation. A renewed Sino-Soviet cooperative military effort could restore the credibility of the Soviet "nuclear umbrella" over China and deter the United States from direct action against the PRC. This argument was answered in Lin Biao's "people's war" manifesto, which called for a guerrilla war in Vietnam with strictly limited Chinese involvement and support. A war of that nature would not be apt to escalate into a direct Sino-US confrontation.[25] Luo lost the argument and his post in November 1965.

Even before Beijing received the Soviet "united action" proposal, it was under intense pressure to cooperate with Moscow in getting Soviet supplies to North Vietnam. A protocol for arms shipments across China was agreed upon in March 1965 (a month prior to the united action proposal).[26] The agreement allowed limited overflights of Soviet transport aircraft to Vietnam and the continuous use of Chinese railways for transshipping Soviet materiel to Vietnam. Troubles quickly developed with that arrangement. Beijing canceled the overflight rights in June 1967, and mob actions associated with the Great Proletarian Cultural Revolution (GPCR) caused a number of trains to be looted. On other occasions, Chinese equipment was substituted for more sophisticated Soviet weaponry. An arrangement was finally worked out whereby Vietnamese guards rode the trains from the Soviet border across China to Vietnam in order to safeguard the shipments.

Meanwhile, the PRC tried two different but equally unsuccessful arguments against the growing levels of Soviet support to Vietnam. The first was that the USSR need not send supplies to Vietnam at all. It could best help Hanoi's cause by putting pressure on West Berlin and creating a European crisis that would cause the United States to focus its military attention in that region.[27] Having found no audience for that ploy, Beijing tried more plausibly to persuade the USSR that it could most efficiently send military supplies to Vietnam by sea. The Soviets counterargued that such shipments would cause the United States to mine North Vietnam's harbors and make the situation worse; the only "sanctuary" from which North Vietnam could be safely resupplied was through the PRC. Chinese recalcitrance in facilitating the transshipment of Soviet materiel to Vietnam was only the first of a growing series of differences with Hanoi. China's own military and economic assistance to the SRV went down steadily between 1967 and 1970 (from $225 million to $180 million).[28] Following the Tet Offensive in 1968, the PRC opposed President Lyndon Johnson's offer of negotiations. Following the "people's war" scenario, Beijing wanted to keep the United States tied down in a long term struggle against guerrilla forces.

The Bankruptcy of People's Wars as Defense Strategy

Between 1965 and 1970, Vietnam received primary attention as the most important example of a people's war in action. However, Beijing made two attempts to expand the war in Southeast Asia. The first came in a secret meeting in 1967 at the Kunming Military Region Headquarters. This was an elaborately prepared session that brought together representatives of insurgent movements and disaffected minority peoples from throughout Southeast Asia. The purpose was to launch wide-scale guerrilla offensives wherever possible in Asia. Beijing apparently felt that the best way to deal with US escalation in Vietnam was to confront Washington with still more brushfire wars on the Asian mainland.

The first effort failed miserably. As a result of increased activities, with money and arms supplied from China, some of the insurgents fell to squabbling among themselves. In Burma, the most important Maoist leader was killed by his own followers in the White Flag party in 1968. Many of the hill tribes in Southeast Asia used their Chinese-supplied arms indiscriminately, even against each other in the case of the Shan and Kachin peoples. In Thailand, increased insurgent activities provoked more intensive government counterinsurgency efforts that may have caused a decline in the number of guerrillas active in northeast Thailand in 1968.[29]

In April 1970, a highly visible "summit conference of Indochinese peoples" convened in southern China. This conference was little more than a propaganda effort to mobilize national and international sentiment against US expansion of the war into neighboring Cambodia and Laos. China affirmed itself as a reliable rear guard for all three nations (SRV, Cambodia, and Laos), but it did not attempt to expand or generate additional guerrilla movements in the region.[30] People's wars of national liberation lingered on into the 1970s as part of China's revolutionary rhetoric. However, as a significant component of Beijing's national security strategy, the concept had reached a dead end by the end of the 1960s.[31]

Economic Costs

As the United States and Soviet threats escalated in the late 1960s, the PRC launched an unprecedented war preparations campaign. Mao called upon the populace to "dig tunnels deep and store grain everywhere." He initiated an extremely harmful program effort to make every province self-sufficient in grain production, regardless of soil and climatic conditions. However, the gravest long-term economic damage resulted from a campaign known as the "Third Front." This was a thirteen-year program to develop new defense and heavy industial production in the interior provinces, especially in Southwest China. The purpose was to enable China to fight on against invaders even after its major cities had been destroyed or invaded.

Little infrastructure existed in the southwestern provinces, but the area was attractive due to its near continuous cloud cover and remoteness from other industrial targets. Establishing rail lines and roads, electrical power, supply networks, and building the factories and machinery collectively entailed enormous costs. At its peak, in the period from 1966 to 1970, the Third Front absorbed just over one-half of the entire national capital investment. Equally troubling were the long-term consequences. The factories proved inefficient and costly to operate. Over the past ten years, many have closed their doors. Meanwhile, pressing needs went begging in China's industrial heartlands for upgraded transportation systems, power grids and new factory equipment. Those effects are still being felt as China enters the 1990s. It is estimated that the gross value of industrial output in China today would be some 10 to 15 percent higher than the current levels if the Third Front had never been undertaken.[32]

The Third Front was an extreme manifestation of the Chinese sense of national threat as it entered the decade of the seventies. The new Nixon administration expanded the Vietnam War into Cambodia and Laos, so the danger from the United States was undiminished. The Soviet threat from the north combined the Brezhnev Doctrine, nuclear intimidation, border clashes, troop buildup, and increased Soviet influence around China's periphery, including India, Pakistan, and the SRV. US-Soviet détente made it appear that the two superpowers were about to collude against China.

There have been systematic studies of threat and threat perception in international relations. One of the principles developed reads: "The more benefit a nation can derive from harming our interests, the more threatened we are likely to feel."[33] In the transition from the 1960s to the 1970s, powerful political forces in both Moscow and Washington felt that the world would be a better place without Mao and Maoism. Beijing needed more effective foreign and defense policies to meet the situation.

Notes

1. William E. Griffith, *Sino-Soviet Relations, 1964-65*, p. 75. See also University Publications of America, *CIA Research Reports, USSR*, reel 4, frame 313.

2. Richard Lowenthal, "The Degeneration of an Ideological Dispute," in Stuart and Tow, China, *The Soviet Union and the West*, p. 68.

3. Adam Ulam, *Expansion and Coexistence*, p. 698.

4. Mao's unremitting emphasis on PWNL led to a rare diplomatic misstep by Premier Zhou Enlai. During an African tour in 1965, he declared that "Africa is ripe for revolution." Most of the governments had recently achieved their independence and only a handful of colonies remained. Zhou's sweeping statement threatened the new order in Africa more than it did the old. He spent much of his trip explaining away his statement.

5. Stuart Schram, *Chairman Mao Talks to the People*, p. 39.

6. Banning Garrett, "China Policy and the Constraints of Triangular Logic," in K. A. Oye, R. J. Leiber, and D. Rothchild, eds., *Eagle Defiant*, p. 240.

7. Melvin Gurtov and Byong-Moo Hwang, *China Under Threat*, p. 213.

8. Richard Wich, *Sino-Soviet Crisis Politics*, p. 65.

9. Wich, *Crisis Politics*, p. 58.

10. Vladimir Rybakov, *The Burden*, pp. 104-105, 154-157.

11. Kenneth Lieberthal, "The Background in Chinese Politics," in Herbert Ellison, ed., *The Sino-Soviet Conflict: A Global Perspective*, p. 8.

12. Allen S. Whiting, *The Chinese Calculus of Deterrence*, 1975, pp. 204-208.

13. John Wilson Lewis and Xue Litai, "Strategic Weapons and Chinese Power: The Formative Years," *CQ*, #112, Dec. 1987, p. 550.

14. Lewis and Xue, "Strategic Weapons and Chinese Power," p. 551.

15. H. Nelsen, *The Chinese Military System*, pp. 70-73.

16. The initial ICBM test site was at Shuangchengzi, Inner Mongolia. It was developed during the period of nuclear sharing with the USSR. The location was close to the Mongolian border and extremely vulnerable to attack from Soviet forces stationed there. When the ICBM test facility was eventually restarted, it was placed in southern Manchuria, much further away from the northern border.

17. Thomas Robinson, "The Sino-Soviet Border Conflict," in Steven S. Kaplan, (ed.), *The Diplomacy of Power: Soviet Armed Forces as a Political Instrument*, pp. 288-289.

18. Robinson, "The Sino-Soviet Border Conflict," p. 282.

19. Daniel Papp, *Vietnam: The View From Moscow, Peking, Washington*, p. 39.

20. AAA troops were promised as early as January 1965, and the engineering units were positively identified in North Vietnam by US intelligence immediately upon their dispatch in June 1965. Elements of a coastal defense division were also sent to Vietnam in June. Andrew Wedeman, *The East Wind Subsides*, p.80. See also New York Times, Jan. 17, 1965, p. 1, and Aug. 12, 1966, p. 4.

21. Papp, *Vietnam*, p. 37.

22. Papp, *Vietnam*, p. 75.

23. Joseph Camilleri, *Chinese Foreign Policy*, p. 74.

24. Papp, *Vietnam*, pp. 79-80

25. For a more detailed discussion of the Luo Ruiqing case, see Uri Ra'anan, "Peking's Foreign Policy Debate, 1965-66," in Tang Tsou, ed., *China in Crisis*, Vol. II. See also Gurtov and Hwang, *China Under Threat*, pp. 167-181; Donald Zagoria, *Vietnam Triangle*, Chapter 3, and Jay Taylor, *China and Southeast Asia*, pp. 37-48.

26. Janos Radvanyi, *Delusion and Reality: Gambits, Hoaxes and Diplomatic One-upmanship in Vietnam*, p. 152.

27. Radvanyi, *Delusion and Reality*, p. 167.

28. Papp, *Vietnam*, p. 114.

29. Nelsen, *Chinese Military System*, pp. 202-203.

30. Papp, *Vietnam*, pp. 147-148, 161.

31. Chalmers Johnson, *Autopsy on People's War*, Chapters 6 and 8.

32. The discussion of the Third Front is derived from Barry Naughton, "The Third Front: Defense Industrialization in the Chinese Interior," *China Quarterly*, Number 115, September 1988, pp. 351-386.

33. The quotation is from D.G. Pruit, "Definition of the Situation as a Determinant of International Action," in H. G. Kelman, ed., *International Behavior*. However, for a better treatment of this topic, see Raymond Cohen, *Threat Perception in International Crisis*, 1979.

PART 3

ENTER, DEUS EX MACHINA, UNCLE SAM: 1970–1988

7

Sino-American Détente and Beijing's New World View

Previous chapters have shown that the United States played a major role in global events from 1950 to 1970, though it did so from the Olympian heights of the world's greatest military and economic power. Moscow could do little to change the direction of US policies, and Beijing could do far less. The 1960s saw the first important Soviet influence in US foreign policy. Beginning with the Cuban missile crisis in 1962, Washington avoided confrontation with Moscow. From the time of the atmospheric test-ban treaty the following year, US presidents sought to find areas of mutual benefit between the two superpowers. China remained a negligible factor in US decision-making, with the notable exception being the Vietnam War.

In the 1970s, the situation changed markedly. Washington embarked on a policy of détente with Moscow, followed shortly by the opening to Beijing. The era of triangular relations began. It was an era in which diplomacy, linkages, and economic carrots eclipsed strategic weapons sticks. Both Moscow and Beijing interacted with Washington rather than reacting to US initiatives, which had previously been the norm. Between 1973 and 1976, the United States enjoyed the so-called "pivot position" in the triangle. Since Beijing and Moscow remained at daggers' point, both feared the other might reach strategic accommodations with the United States. Each wooed Washington, thereby effectively maximizing the influence of the United States within the triangle. In this process, Moscow was the primary loser. It first lost its long-term advantage of being the only power with normal diplomatic communications with the other two nations. Second, Moscow had to prevent the emergence of a Beijing-Washington axis, which was a much stronger possibility than an alignment between the two superpowers against the PRC. Moscow had limited options, and it made the worst of them.

US Policies: Nixon Through Carter

Because of the emergence of the triangle in the 1970s, this chapter departs from the previous Sino-Soviet format by including a separate section on US foreign policy, focusing on national security objectives. On the most basic level, Nixon's trip to the PRC represented a belated US recognition of the Sino-Soviet dispute. In 1950, Secretary of State Dean Acheson explained the US failure to establish diplomatic relations with the PRC by claiming that Beijing was simply an extension of Moscow and that the government did not truly represent the aspirations of Chinese nationalism. By the end of the decade, that specious argument was totally defunct.

Nonrecognition in the 1960s was based on the international threat posed by the PRC through its "people's wars" strategy. Pentagon intelligence documents of the mid-1960s placed the long-term Chinese threat above that of the Soviet Union. The combination of the Vietnam conflict and Mao Zedong's revolutionary foreign and domestic policies were used to support such threat assessments. Presidents Kennedy and Johnson made little effort to take advantage of the Sino-Soviet dispute by demarches toward Beijing. Instead, they hoped to gain from the rift by finding Moscow more amenable to compromise with the United States. There was no attempt to practice triangular diplomacy. Secretary of State Rusk emphasized Chinese hostility to the West and the need for continued staunch support of the Nationalists on Taiwan.

Richard Nixon realized the importance of an opening toward China, as first shown in a Foreign Affairs article published a year before his election in 1968.[1] His vision was especially commendable given the radicalism of the Great Proletarian Cultural Revolution (GPCR) and the intensity of the Vietnam conflict at the time. As Nixon's chief foreign policy advisor, Henry Kissinger strongly favored an approach to Beijing, incorporating it as an essential component in his grand strategy of détente with the USSR. Kissinger clearly understood the advantages of triangular diplomacy, and he also hoped that the PRC might help the United States disentangle itself from Vietnam.

> By accepting the emergence of China as a great power whose interests had to be given due consideration, American diplomacy was perhaps hoping that a tacit agreement might be reached between the two nations about their respective spheres of influence. Such an understanding might permit the US to pursue its policy of military disengagement in IndoChina in the knowledge that its political and economic dominance in other parts of Asia would not, as a consequence, be subject to serious challenge.[2]

A number of signals were sent by Washington between 1968 and 1970 to indicate its interest in establishing a new relationship. They ranged from simply using the name, "People's Republic of China," for the first time in US governmental argot, to suspending the Seventh Fleet patrols in the Taiwan Straits, to loosening the tight trade and tourism restrictions imposed against the PRC. Showing an awareness of US/PRC mutual interest in confronting Soviet expansionism, President Nixon announced in February 1971 that he would not become a participant in the Sino-Soviet dispute and the United States would therefore have nothing to do with "any condominium or hostile coalition of great powers against either of the large communist countries."[3] Translated into plain English, the United States would not negotiate with Brezhnev regarding his Asian collective security proposal.

It took four years for Nixon to reach China. A number of delays and stumbling blocks were US-related. The first mistake came immediately after Nixon was sworn into office. China had decided to test the waters with the new president and offered the "five principles of peaceful coexistence" as the basis on which Sino-US relations could be improved and stabilized. (Briefly, these are mutual recognition of the sovereignty and territorial integrity of competing nations, nonaggression, noninterference, equality, and mutually beneficial economic relations.)

Nixon failed to make an appropriate response. At his first news conference on January 27, 1969, he did not acknowledge the coexistence offer from Beijing, but he enthusiastically welcomed talks with the USSR that would enable both nations to build anti-ballistic missile systems. In his second news conference some six weeks later, Nixon made explicit the anti-China rationale of the ABM talks: "I would imagine that the Soviet Union would be just as reluctant as we would be to leave their country naked against a potential Chinese Communist threat."[4] The new administration had competing defense and foreign policy priorities. In order to sell the ABM to Congress and the public, the Chinese nuclear threat was invoked. The proposed ABM system could not defend against MIRVed ICBMs, which the Soviets were then beginning to develop.

Probably as a result of Nixon's rebuff, the foreign policy coalition led by Zhou Enlai that had offered the olive branch to Washington temporarily lost influence in Beijing, so what might have been the Sino-US détente of 1969 was delayed until 1972.[5] In the intervening years, the widening of the Vietnam War into Cambodia and Laos again slowed the development of the embryonic communications. Beijing could hardly negotiate with the United States when it was expanding the war along China's southern borders.

The US/Japan partnership also caused unusual difficulties for Beijing. In 1969, President Nixon and Prime Minister Eisaku Sato issued a joint communiqué that stipulated that the "security of the Republic of Korea is essential to Japan's own security." It went on to make a similar assertion regarding Taiwan's importance to Japan.[6] The PRC began a steady drumbeat warning of Japanese remilitarization. Beijing criticized the 15 and 17 percent increases in the Japanese defense budgets of 1970 and 1971, as well as the rapidly developing arms industry. Zhou Enlai asserted that the Nixon Doctrine had turned Japan into a US military "vanguard in the Far East."[7] However, it is unclear whether Beijing's concern with Japan's military and regional power potential delayed the opening to Washington. Japan granted diplomatic recognition to the PRC immediately after the Nixon trip, taking the international lead in developing trade and economic ties with the PRC. Sino-US détente was probably a prerequisite for transforming Japan from a threatening enemy to China's economic partner.

An international trend toward recognition of the PRC was underway between 1969 and 1971. Twenty countries established diplomatic relations with Beijing, and it was seated in the United Nations through a resolution favorable to the PRC; its terms required the expulsion of the Chinese Nationalist representatives from the organization. This new international legitimacy was due to a number of factors, including the end of GPCR radicalism and an effort by the Chinese to reestablish normal diplomatic ties. China's ambassadors, who had been recalled between 1966 and 1968, were returned to their posts in 1969.

The Nixon administration also claimed some credit for the trend toward ending China's isolation. In the summer of 1969, the President ordered Henry Kissinger to privately encourage other countries to grant recognition to Beijing.[8] The USSR at the same time was quietly discouraging additional recognition for Beijing due to its border confrontation.

In the preliminary negotiations carried out between Henry Kissinger and Zhou Enlai in July 1971, the United States made a key concession that enabled the Nixon visit to proceed. Washington agreed that "Taiwan is Chinese" (as stated in the Shanghai Communiqué issued at the end of Nixon's 1972 trip). From Beijing's standpoint, this greatly reduced the Taiwan problem. The Nationalists were seen as a fading force, losing legitimacy and international backing. Over time, the biggest problem would be that the Taiwanese population might declare the island a nation separate and distinct from China. With the US renunciation of that possibility in 1972, Beijing could afford to wait since Taipei had no place else to go.

The success of Nixon's opening did not immediately lead to other breakthroughs in bilateral relations, but two benefits to the United States soon followed. First, China played a supporting role in the US extrication from Vietnam. Beijing agreed not to oppose peace talks. It did continue to stand behind Hanoi's most important negotiating demands, namely that the bombing of the SRV cease and that all "foreign" forces leave South Vietnam. However, Mao privately suggested to the SRV foreign minister that Hanoi give up its demand that President Thieu be removed prior to a negotiated political arrangement for the future of South Vietnam.[9] Beijing also continued to restrict the levels of military assistance provided to the SRV (although that trend predated Sino-US détente). The second major benefit came in additional bargaining leverage in Moscow, especially reflected in the Strategic Arms Limitation Talks (SALT I).

There were a number of factors limiting direct US/PRC cooperation in the early and mid-1970s. China's continued insularity and the US policy of "equidistance" between Beijing and Moscow restricted both economic and political ties. Washington made no attempt to develop joint plans with Beijing for containing the Soviets, lest the delicately constructed détente with the USSR become unglued. Preparations for the Helsinki Accords began the year following Nixon's visit to the PRC. Beijing was opposed to the meeting from the outset.[10] If major issues in East-West relations were resolved in the European theater, then the USSR could concentrate its forces against the Chinese. The Helsinki Conference met as scheduled in 1975 and was probably the high watermark of US-Soviet détente. European boundaries were "guaranteed" by all participants, but, fortunately for Beijing, the conference did not lead to an East-West rapprochement in Europe.[11] Finally, 1973 and 1974 saw the Watergate crisis overwhelm and eventually destroy the Nixon presidency. During this period, what little energy and attention remained for foreign affairs was devoted to the Middle East and the consequences of the 1973 Yom Kippur War between Israel and Egypt.

The caretaker Presidency of Gerald Ford was also preoccupied with domestic matters, especially runaway inflation and the scandals associated with the congressional hearings regarding wrongdoing within the US intelligence community. Ford did visit China, but the trip was not successful. He felt disinclined to further US/Chinese cooperation because normalized relations would require terminating US presence in Taiwan. The collapse of both Cambodia and South Vietnam in 1975 made it important that the United States not "abandon" another ally in East Asia.[12] It was imperative that President Ford adopt this position due to the political threat being mounted on his right by Ronald Reagan.

In economic relations, the PRC was initially treated the same as the Soviet Union in accordance with the equidistance policy. High technology and military items were denied to both nations, though that policy changed perceptibly in 1974 and 1975 when Washington let its European allies know that it was not averse to "defensive weapons" sales to Beijing. The first major contract was with Rolls Royce for production rights and associated technology for the Spey jet engine, negotiated in 1975 and 1976. The thinking in Washington was that the military imbalance between Moscow and Beijing should not be allowed to grow worse lest the Soviets be tempted to take advantage of their immense superiority in weapons and mobility. By using European powers to assist China's defenses, Washington could still claim equidistance, and the likelihood of a Sino-Soviet war would be reduced. The 1974 Jackson-Vanik amendment also served to tilt US economic policy in favor of Beijing. That law prevented the extension of credits to the USSR and made it impossible for Moscow to achieve "most favored nation" (normal) trade status with the United States until the Soviets allowed free Jewish emigration to Israel.

The first year of the Carter administration saw a continuation of nominal equidistance. However, beginning in 1978, Soviet expansionism, particularly its activities in the horn of Africa, provided ammunition for the Zbigniew Brzezinski view that the United States should play its "China card" against the USSR. As national security advisor, Brzezinski was the primary architect of normalizing relations with the PRC in 1978 and 1979. The establishment of full diplomatic relations required that the United States abrogate its defense treaty and break relations with Taipei. This was done on January 1, 1979. Deng Xiaoping visited the United States at the end of 1978 and spoke of a "strategic alignment" between the United States and China against Soviet hegemonism in East Asia. In 1980, a special new category was added to the US Export Administration Act enabling Washington to sell high technology equipment to Beijing. Until that date, the PRC had shared the same export restraining category as the USSR and Warsaw Pact nations. In the same year, the PRC was granted "most favored nation" trade status.

Trouble was waiting down the road, however, since no agreement had been reached concerning the thorny problem of US military sales to Taiwan. The normalization documents stipulated that Beijing and Washington agreed to disagree. The end of the 1970s also left a bitter domestic legacy. Congress, alarmed at the president's hasty abandonment of Taipei, passed the Taiwan Relations Act, which restated US interest in the security of the island.

Four important political groups were alienated by the content and method of Sino-American normalization.[13] The first group emphasized the need to preserve US honor and reliability in world affairs by maintaining commitments to proven allies. Second were those who felt that we were jeopardizing much more important long-term agreements with the USSR by aligning ourselves too closely with the PRC. Another element was suspicious of Beijing and Chinese communist intentions. Finally, some congressional leaders felt that too much secrecy and too little open debate had characterized the normalization process. Collectively, these groups would provide valuable support for the new China policy formulated by presidential nominee Ronald Reagan in the 1980 election.

Through Chinese Eyes: Confronting the Polar Bear in the 1970s

By the time Richard Nixon was elected president, the PRC had concluded that the Soviet Union represented the primary threat to Beijing, though one faction within the Politburo continued to advocate a "dual adversary" approach: a pox on both your houses. The latter position, favored by Defense Minister Lin Biao, was difficult to sustain in the face of Vietnamization and the Nixon Doctrine on the one hand and continued Soviet military confrontation on the other. During 1970-1971, Lin was sliding down a slippery slope, having first lost Mao's confidence on a series of domestic policies. The 2nd Plenum of the 9th Party Congress in September 1970 agreed to seek gradual improvement of relations with the United States. In December, through the visiting US journalist Edgar Snow, Mao proffered an open invitation to Nixon to visit China. Two months after Henry Kissinger's exploratory talks with Zhou Enlai in July 1971, Lin Biao was dead, and the last domestic obstacle was thus removed.[14]

The Chinese leadership realized from the outset that it was entering a strategic triangle and was prepared to play that game. The "three worlds" theory that Mao had formulated as the framework for the PWNL strategy in the 1960s adapted well to triangular relations since it implicitly rejected the concept of bipolarism. Mao told Kissinger in their first meeting that he did not want the United States "standing on China's shoulders to reach Moscow."[15] In other words, the Chinese wanted to be treated as equals, not as a mere lever that Washington might use to extract more favorable agreements from the Soviets.

Beijing also soon showed that it was not trying to use Sino-American détente as a method to reach accords with Moscow. While avoiding provocative military actions along its northern borders, the PRC stiffened its negotiating positions. In addition to demanding Soviet troop withdrawal from all disputed territories, Beijing added the pullout of forces stationed in Mongolia as yet another precondition to Sino-Soviet talks. In reality, the PRC had no intention of reaching an accommodation with Moscow at this time. The military balance was overwhelmingly against the Chinese, so rather than negotiate from weakness, they preferred to wait. The only successful Sino-Soviet negotiations in the 1970s dealt with narrow technical issues of mutual interest, most notably, navigation rights on the Ussuri and Amur Rivers.

Regarding Taiwan, the Chinese got most of what they wanted in the Shanghai Communiqué. In that document they refused to pledge nonuse of military force against the island (and have continued to hold the same position to the present day). Beijing readily agreed to try peaceful means first, but it kept its options open. As noted above, both governments were determined not to let the arms sale issue prevent normalization of relations in 1978 and 1979. Although the 1979 Taiwan Relations Act was a setback, its terms were general, and no legislative statements of intent could offset the fact that all US forces were gone from the island and the US embassy in Taipei was shut down. In the 1970s, the Taiwan issue was eclipsed by the enormity of the Soviet threat. Beijing was careful not to abandon its fundamental principles on the matter: that the island was a province of China, that Taipei/Beijing relations were thus domestic Chinese affairs, and that no foreign power had any right to interfere. While protecting those principles, Beijing willingly put the Taiwan issue on the back burner in order to stabilize its relationship with Washington.

After the initial flush of success accompanying the Nixon visit, the PRC was disappointed with the limited results of the opening to Washington. The continuation of US-Soviet détente, the US policy of "equidistance," and the denial of advanced technology transfer to the PRC contributed to the disappointment. In the latter half of the 1970s, however, the situation began to change. Three factors emerged that led Beijing to seek its "strategic alignment" with the United States. First, US-Soviet détente foundered, and the new power alignment in Indochina led to parallel US/China interests in Southeast Asia. Finally, Japan began to "tilt" in favor of Beijing and to the detriment of the USSR. The first of these factors will be discussed in the next chapter when Moscow's viewpoints are considered, but both the Indochina and Japan aspects are best treated here.

Beijing, Hanoi, and Indochina

Quite apart from the long historical legacy of Sino-Vietnamese hostility, Hanoi had a number of reasons to be disappointed in Beijing. It was Zhou Enlai above all others who had been responsible for the "half-a-loaf" victory at Geneva in 1954.[16] The Vietminh had soundly defeated the French but received only a divided nation as its reward. Later, the PRC tried to tell the SRV how to run its war. When it came to grand strategy, General Vo Nguyen Giap owed no intellectual debt to Mao Zedong. Beijing's blatant opposition to the initial peace talks in 1968 was a case of interference with Hanoi's national sovereignty. Relations were further strained by Beijing's obstructionism on the vital problem of Soviet military supplies. During the height of GPCR radicalism and violence, transport delays sometimes lasted for months.

While troubling, those Sino-Vietnamese issues were not allowed to interfere with the basic objective of defeating the common enemy, the United States. It was only after the Treaty of Paris in 1973 that divisive issues began to erode the Sino-Vietnamese alliance, an alliance that no longer had a mutual security objective. The first issue to arise was a territorial dispute. Beijing had long claimed the islands of the South China Sea extending all the way down to the waters north of Indonesia and west of the Philippines. But it was only in 1974 that Beijing took direct action in support of such claims. In January, a small amphibious force invaded and overwhelmed the South Vietnamese garrison in the Paracel Islands, which lay in the Gulf of Tonkin and east of North Vietnam. While held by Saigon, Hanoi also had claims on this territory. The only warning provided was a diplomatic note to the SRV in December 1973 that China would begin oil exploration in the Gulf of Tonkin within a month.[17] Oil was found, though it is not a major deposit, and wells are currently producing to China's benefit.. North Vietnam protested but could do little about it. The Paracels are within MiG range of Hainan Island and thus can be easily protected from Vietnamese counterattack.

Chronologically, the next issues for Beijing dealt with Vietnamese reunification and Hanoi's objective of an Indochina confederacy. Beijing argued in favor of the National Liberation Front (NLF) establishing itself as the government of South Vietnam, with the merger of North and South a deferred goal.[18] Hanoi instead dissolved the NLF immediately after the fall of Saigon. The PRC also feared that the collapse of Cambodia and the Vietnamese domination of Laos might lead those nations to consider supporting the Brezhnev Asian collective security concept. Beijing entered into negotiations with the United States to obtain coalition governments in both of those nations, which would keep some US presence and interest as a counterweight to that of the USSR.[19] Hanoi was having none of this. It secured its hold on Laos through its domination of the communist armed forces, the Pathet Lao. The rapid victory of the Khmer Rouge in Cambodia prevented the possibility of a negotiated transfer of power there. The victory initially worked to Beijing's advantage since the Khmer Rouge leadership feared the Vietnamese plans for confederation even more than did the PRC.

The grotesque radicalism of the new Khmer Rouge regime was accompanied by a justifiable fear of Vietnam's intentions. That combination soon led Cambodia to flex its muscles against Vietnam. The first gesture was symbolic; Cambodia became Kampuchea, a name derived from the Champa empire that had dominated all of mainland Southeast Asia in the twelfth and thirteenth centuries. More concretely, Kampuchean military forces immediately occupied small islands to the south of the Vietnam/Kampuchean border that were claimed by both nations. Vietnam also undertook an aggressive initiative. A salient of Kampuchean territory aptly dubbed "the parrot's beak" juts into Vietnam toward Saigon (Ho Chi Minh City after 1975). Vietnam began to redraw that portion of the border by evicting many Kampuchean villagers. Widespread border skirmishing soon followed and grew into serious firefights in 1977.

Beijing's response to this emerging confrontation between Phnom Penh and Hanoi was to firmly support the former. This was not a new Chinese policy. The PRC had been a staunch friend of the Sihanouk neutralist government during his sixteen-year reign (ending in 1971). The PRC favored a Balkanized Indochina. Zhou Enlai had made that quite obvious during the 1954 Geneva Conference. The Chinese opted to overlook the genocidal nature of Pol Pot's Khmer Rouge. Kampuchea played too important a role as a check against Vietnamese hegemony in Indochina. Therefore, during 1977,

Beijing provided large amounts of military aid and hundreds of PLA advisors. The Khmer Rouge armed forces rapidly expanded their army and developed for the first time a small air force and navy.[20] Naturally, Hanoi was well aware of Beijing's strong military support of Phnom Pen and this contributed to an atmosphere of overt hostility in Sino-Vietnamese relations.

Also during 1977 and 1978, Hanoi began a domestic socioeconomic program of eliminating small-scale capitalism. Most of the petite bourgeoisie in both northern and southern Vietnam were overseas Chinese, known as the Hoa in Vietnamese. The government's tactics were harsh. Families were offered the choice of moving to the starvation conditions of the "new economic zones" (land reclamation projects) or of "escaping" from Vietnam with governmental collusion, leaving their property behind. Most chose to leave with 160,000 Hoa fleeing across the border to China while even more boarded small boats for extremely hazardous voyages to Malaysia, Hong Kong, and Indonesia. The SRV leadership had a secondary reason for the expulsion of the Hoa. As Sino-Vietnamese relations worsened, there was a fear that the overseas Chinese might become a fifth column for Beijing. Beginning in late 1978, rather than simply allowing the Hoa to escape, SRV authorities began to march large groups of them up to the Chinese border and force them across at gunpoint. According to PRC sources, by mid-1979 the Hoa refugees in China totaled 250,000.[21]

Beijing initially demanded a halt to the persecution and the repatriation of all Hoa, along with the restoration of their lost property. When this had no effect and the rate of emigration kept rising, the PRC sent merchant ships to Haiphong in order to provide a humanitarian means of emigration to those being forced out. However, no agreement could be reached, and the ships returned empty to China. Clearly, the Hoa issue was a major factor in the devolution of Sino-Vietnamese relations.

There was an economic dimension as well. Following the fall of Saigon, the PRC stopped all military aid to Hanoi, despite Vietnam's need of the latter to consolidate its military victory. In the spring of 1978, the last of the civilian economic assistance programs was ended, and hundreds of Chinese technicians and advisors were recalled. The SRV responded by joining the Soviet-led COMECON economic bloc.

The ultimate break came in November 1978 when the SRV signed a military alliance with the USSR. With the Soviets available to protect them from Chinese military power, the SRV invaded Kampuchea in December; within a matter of weeks it drove the Pol Pot regime into a remote mountainous salient of the Northwest.

Deng Xiaoping was visiting the United States as the Vietnamese consolidated their occupation of Kampuchea and installed a puppet government in Phnom Penh. He raised the prospect of administering a lesson to Vietnam and received the tacit approval of the Carter administration by virtue of its public silence.[22] The Chinese invasion began the third week of February 1979, and a unilateral withdrawal followed some three weeks later. Beijing made it clear from the outset that this was a limited application of force. No air power was used, geographic penetration was only about twenty-five miles along most of the front, and Vietnam was informed that the Chinese would withdraw as soon as they had administered their "lesson." By sharply restricting its military objectives, Beijing reduced the likelihood that the Soviet Union would retaliate by attacking Chinese territory. Indeed, the Soviets showed remarkable restraint, limiting their reactions to propaganda, a major military resupply of Vietnam, and a strong naval presence in the Gulf of Tonkin.

The outcome for China was not a happy one. The PLA succeeded in the sense that it got in, did a lot of physical damage, and then got out. However, the invasion force did not acquit itself well militarily. Its casualties numbered some 20,000, and Chinese units had not even fought main force Vietnamese divisions. Still worse, the invasion had no effect on Hanoi's military stranglehold over Kampuchea. Vietnamese units were not redeployed to defend the motherland. The attack cemented, rather than fractured, the Vietnam-Soviet military alliance. Finally, China found itself in the same uncomfortable situation as the Soviets of having to face the prospect of a two-front war.

The regional and bilateral issues that separated Vietnam from China between 1974 and 1978 should not be ignored in terms of their contribution to the onset of hostilities. However, Eugene Lawson, in his in-depth study of the origins of the conflict concludes:

> The Sino-Vietnamese relationship was determined primarily by global strategic considerations. It was shaped less by bilateral or even regional issues between the two than by the relations each had with Moscow and Washington. . . . The current Sino-Vietnamese animosity is not a product of age-old rivalries, but of the strategic choices each made as to how to maximize its security and where—Moscow or Washington—each could obtain greater strategic benefit in an uncertain world.[23]

By 1978, Thailand and the entire Association of Southeast Asian Nations were no longer viewed by Beijing as a US-manipulated, anti-China alliance. Rather, Thailand became a "front line" state, cooperating with the PRC in the containment of Vietnam. The United States supported China's position in the UN, where both nations fought to keep the Pol Pot government as the "legitimate" internationally recognized polity. Washington also saw to it that Japan did not proceed with its plans to provide economic assistance to Hanoi. US power and that of its allies was fully aligned with Chinese objectives in Southeast Asia.

Japan's China Tilt

In modern history, Japan was to East Asia what Germany was to Europe—the key to the regional balance of power. Prior to World War II, Japan was unquestionably the most powerful country in the region. Following its defeat, its threat potential had to be controlled. To that end, Japan was demilitarized "permanently" through its postwar constitution. This was insufficient from the PRC viewpoint since Japan was allowed to develop its heavy industry and high technology, which would enable it to become a military power on very short notice. Japan was also the ally of the United States, and it allowed the presence of US forces aimed in part at containing China. This was especially true of the US bases on Okinawa.

From 1950 to 1964, China's Japan policy was to undercut the government and the US alliance by staunchly supporting the Japanese Communist Party. That approach was unsuccessful. The Communists were far too weak and the Liberal Democratic Party far too strong. In 1964, when Mao began to develop his "three worlds theory," Japan was categorized as one of the nations in the "second intermediate zone" which, over time, would come to realize that it was also being exploited by the major imperialist nations. It could thus be brought into a united front with the socialist and Third World nations. The Liao/Takasaki trade agreements of the 1960s weakened the UN embargo against China and held out to Japanese corporations the lure of the potential China market. But it was the Nixon trip of 1972 that opened the door. Full diplomatic relations between Japan and China were established that same year. The "Japan formula" was devised, allowing Tokyo to keep its commercial interests in Taiwan even after severing diplomatic relations with the Republic of China. Most of the industrialized states that recognized Beijing in the 1970s did so on the basis of that model.

Japan and China are natural trading partners, with the PRC providing raw materials, fossil fuels, and agricultural products while Japan exports machinery and electronics and provides technology transfer through the sale of licensing rights. The mid-1970s saw multibillion-dollar deals worked out between Beijing and Tokyo in which Japan would first supply machinery and technology and China would later repay through energy supplies, enhanced production in extractive industries, and agricultural commodities. Although China was still only a small percentage of Japan's export market (under 5 percent) the future looked bright since China's needs were so great. Disillusionment and financial difficulties would plague Sino-Japanese relations in the 1980s; in 1978 and 1979, however, such problems were only distant clouds on an otherwise clear horizon.

Tokyo was simultaneously being wooed by Moscow. Siberian development was a priority item, and the minerals, oil, and gas of that region could be sold to Japan on a cost-effective basis. Indeed, due to the distances involved, Japan was the natural market rather than European Russia. The Soviets made offers which would have traded concessionary prices and guaranteed supplies in return for Japanese investment capital. Tokyo was strongly tempted to accept such deals, but when Beijing privately raised its voice in protest, the Japanese backed away from large-scale joint efforts with the USSR.[24]

There was also a major bone of contention between Tokyo and Moscow that contributed to Japan's "tilt." A group of islands known as the Northern Territories lie just northeast of Hokkaido. These were occupied by the USSR at the end of World War II. Moscow claimed that they were part of the Kurile Islands, granted to the Soviets in the instruments of surrender signed aboard the battleship Missouri. The Japanese claim that the islands are an extension of the northeast coast of Hokkaido. The Soviets adopted an unyielding negotiating stance on this question in 1960, and began harassing Japanese fishermen in the area. The tough stance was occasioned by the renewal of the US-Japanese alliance. As the United States moved toward full normalization of relations with the PRC in 1978, both nations saw the possibility of including Japan in the "strategic alignment." A Sino-Japanese friendship treaty was concluded in August 1978 that included language calling for cooperation against any effort to establish "hegemony" in East Asia. Hegemony was well established as the Chinese code word for Soviet expansionism. Despite additional language insisted on by the Japanese, which said that the treaty was not directed against any nation, Japan was universally perceived as moving toward an anti-Soviet triple entente with the United States and the PRC. About the time of the signing of the Sino-Japanese treaty, Deng Xiaoping said: "Strengthening Japan's defense capability and the US-Japan security treaty is a natural course."[25] A few years before 1978, such a statement from a Chinese leader would have been inconceivable.

Afghanistan

The Soviet invasion of Afghanistan in December 1979 brought US/PRC strategic cooperation to its peak in 1980. Defense Secretary Harold Brown visited Beijing in January and offered, for the first time, to sell US arms to China. The two governments cooperated in the multinational covert operation to supply and arm the mujahedeen. Arms came primarily from Egyptian arsenals, paid for by Saudi Arabian oil money, and were replaced by new US military equipment.[26] China also supplied small arms and mines, but much of its assistance was in food and other civilian necessities. Pakistan provided the access to the guerrilla fighters.

Perhaps as a result of Defense Secretary Brown's visit, the PRC also agreed to an unprecedented joint venture in intelligence collection. As a result of the Iranian revolution, the United States had lost its most important listening post for monitoring Soviet missile tests. Probably as a direct result of the Soviet invasion of Afghanistan, the PRC agreed to allow the United States to establish an electronic intelligence site high in the Pamir Mountains. This was a nearly ideal site for monitoring the Soviet missile test range. The arrangement naturally required that the intelligence gathered be shared with the PRC, and Chinese technicians were trained in the use and maintenance of the equipment.[27]

As the 1970s came to a close, Soviet expansionism and militarism seemed to provide a limitless source for strategic cooperation between China and the United States. Virtually all noncommunist states in Asia, with the exception of India and Burma, were to one degree or another helping forward this new international power alignment. A reversal of positions had occurred. The decade had opened with the PRC under threat and ended with the "international correlation of forces" (to borrow a Soviet phrase) shifting against Moscow. Soviet policies contributed to that reversal. It is to the perspectives of the USSR that we now turn.

Notes

1. Richard Nixon, "Asia After Vietnam," *Foreign Affairs,* Oct. 1967, pp. 111-125.

2. Joseph Camilleri, *Chinese Foreign Policy,* p. 131.

3. Camilleri, *Chinese Foreign Policy,* p. 129.

4. Raymond Garthoff, *Détente and Confrontation,* p. 217.

5. Thomas Gottlieb, *Chinese Foreign Policy Factionalism and the Origins of the Strategic Triangle,* pp. 97-114.

6. Greg O'Leary, *The Shaping of Chinese Foreign Policy,* p. 200.

7. O'Leary, *The Shaping of Chinese Foreign Policy,* pp. 202-203.

8. Henry Kissinger, *The White House Years,* p. 179.

9. Garthoff, *Détente and Confrontation,* p. 255, citing Seymour Hersh, *The Price of Power,* p. 442.

10. A new theme emerged in Chinese propaganda: the so-called "feint to the East." The term was first used in 1973. Beijing described the Soviet buildup on China's borders as an elaborate ploy to encourage Western Europe to let down its guard. But Europe, according to the Chinese, was always Moscow's goal. Only Western Europe could provide the industrial capacity and expertise to save the Soviets from their own failures. China had nothing of value to the USSR that it did not already possess in abundance. See Robert Sutter, *Chinese Foreign Policy After the Cultural Revolution, 1966-77,* p. 39, and C. G. Jacobsen, *Chinese Foreign Policy After Mao,* p. 84.

11. The "mutual, balanced, force reduction" (MBFR) talks, which followed logically from the Helsinki accords, soon stalled, leaving NATO and Warsaw Pact forces undiminished.

12. Robert Sutter, *The China Quandry,* p. 3.

13. Sutter, *China Quandry,* p. 5.

14. Lin died as a direct result of his challenges to Mao's leadership, but exactly how he died remains a matter of contention. Beijing's official story claimed that Lin was killed in a plane crash in the Mongolian People's Republic while fleeing to the USSR.

15. Kissinger, *The White House Years,* p. 763.

16. See Chapter 3.

17. Eugene Lawson, *The Sino-Vietnamese Conflict,* p. 277.

18. The NLF was recognized by all communist nations and some neutral countries as the legitimate government of South Vietnam. The SRV had little use for the NLF except as a lever against the US-supported government led by President Thieu. After the conquest of Saigon, the SRV saw the NLF as little more than a nuisance.

19. Lawson, *The Sino-Vietnamese Conflict,* Chapter 8.

20. Vietnamese sources, which are hardly unbiased, claimed that the Khmer Rouge went from six divisions in 1975 to nineteen divisions at the end of 1978. While those figures are probably inflated, there was a major expansion, and it was funded by the PRC. *Asiaweek,* Mar. 16, 1979, p. 13.

21. Lewis Stern, "The Vietnamese Expulsion of the Overseas Chinese," *Issues and Studies,* Vol. 23, No. 7, July 1987, p. 114.

22. In private conversations with Deng, President Carter voiced his opposition to the planned Chinese attack on the SRV. King C. Chen, *China's War With Vietnam,* 1979, pp. 91-92.

23. Lawson, *Sino-Vietnam Conflict,* p.7.

24. Allen Whiting, *Siberian Development and East Asia,* p.139.

25. Ed Olsen, *US Japan Strategic Reciprocity,* p. 144.

26. President Anwar Sadat revealed the operation to US television journalists shortly before his assassination.

27. John Prados, *The Soviet Estimate,* p. 275.

8

The Devolution of Soviet Foreign Policy: 1970–1980

Moscow entered the 1970s full of confidence and ready to play the role of a global power. It dealt with the United States as an equal, and sought to stabilize superpower relations. Brezhnev also supported a European concord that would insure continued Soviet dominance in Eastern Europe. Finally, Moscow felt prepared to take new initiatives in the Third World. Those auspicious beginnings turned to dust; by the end of the decade, the USSR found itself in an increasingly untenable position.

Brezhnev Puts on a Mao Jacket

Détente, warding off the threat of nuclear war for mankind and responsive to the most profound aspirations of all peoples, is also creating favorable conditions for the struggle for national liberation and social progress.

Politburo member Andrei Kirilenko (1977)

One of the ironies of the Sino-Soviet dispute was the reversal of the Soviet and Chinese positions regarding people's wars of national liberation (PWNL). The Cultural Revolution period of the late 1960s saw the concept at its zenith in China. By the mid-1970s, however, the PRC diligently pursued normalized state-to-state relations with the governments it had previously sought to overthrow, while the USSR supported liberation struggles and Marxian movements in Africa and the Middle East. This development did nothing to repair or lessen the Sino-Soviet split because the schism was based on differing national security perceptions rather than ideological positions. After the opening to the United States in 1972, PWNL became less relevant to China's security and economic objectives. The USSR, had achieved true strategic parity with Washington, built a large blue-water navy, and fielded an impressive airlift capability. It could well afford the risks associated with extending its influence into new regions, especially since the United

States was struggling with the traumas of Watergate and its failure in Vietnam.

During the preliminary negotiations of the SALT I Treaty, begun in 1970, it was clear that "parity" to Brezhnev meant not just strategic weapons, but a global rather than Eurasian regional role for the USSR. His force-building programs pointed in that direction as early as 1965. He merely awaited his opportunities. The first came with Vietnam where, by 1967, the USSR eclipsed China as the primary supplier of military equipment. The Asian Collective Security Proposal of 1969 did not meet with a positive response, but it did reveal the readiness of the USSR to play a major role in shaping the future of the existing nation-state system extending from Northeast to South Asia.

The 1971 Soviet-Indian Treaty

One of Brezhnev's best opportunities to support a liberation struggle came in South Asia in 1971. It was an ideal situation. Pakistan was a geographically and ethnically divided nation. East Pakistan had grown restive and sought independence. India was already quite friendly with the USSR, and Pakistan was the only noncommunist ally of China. Despite those factors, Moscow was initially unwilling to make a firm commitment to New Delhi against Pakistan. Brezhnev had mediated the end to the 1965 Indo-Pakistani war, and he was trying to develop additional leverage in Pakistan. In the late 1960s, the Soviets even sold weapons to the Pakistani armed forces. Thus, when East Pakistan grew restive and unstable, Brezhnev at first favored a political solution rather than the dismembering of the nation. It was India that pressed for more active measures. Assurances from Moscow were needed before the Indian army could take the offensive. Though the Soviets had negotiated a friendship treaty with India in 1969, they had not initialed the document, probably for fear of losing influence in Pakistan.

It may have been the US opening to China in 1971 that caused the Soviets to finalize the treaty, although the timing is somewhat problematic.[1] Henry Kissinger stopped in India on his way to Pakistan and his secret mission to China. According to Indian sources, he told the leadership that in any future Indo-Pakistani war, if China intervened on the side of Pakistan, India could not expect automatic US assistance such as it had received in the Sino-Indian border clashes of 1962.[2] Such a statement would certainly have added incentives for New Delhi to sign a pact with Moscow, but the Indians were probably already committed to that course. Zhou Enlai correctly stated that Moscow resurrected the treaty after "it had lain for two years in a drawer in the Ministry of Foreign Affairs."[3] Zhou claimed that it was the US opening to China combined with Brezhnev's Asian Collective Security program that caused the Soviets to put the treaty back on the table.

In any case, the agreement came into effect on August 18, 1971. India then intervened in support of separatist East Pakistan, renamed as the nation of Bangladesh. The Indian forces triumphed in the field, Pakistan was weakened, and China looked like a feckless ally since it did not intercede. The outcome of the war also served Brezhnev's efforts to "contain" the PRC. The partition of Pakistan replaced a pro-Chinese buffer state (East Pakistan) with one that was pro-India (Bangladesh).[4]

In March 1972, a few months after the conclusion of the war, Pakistan's President Zulfikar Bhutto paid a state visit to Moscow, presumably for the purpose of persuading the Soviets to return to their more evenhanded South Asian policies of the late 1960s. He came away with very little. India, and perhaps the United States, had led Moscow into supporting a successful people's war of national liberation. In terms of Soviet objectives, the outcome could not have been better if Brezhnev had planned it all from the beginning.

Africa and the Middle East

The Soviets also deepened their involvement in the Arab world, undertaking a massive refitting of the Egyptian armed forces after the 1967 Arab-Israeli War, and becoming the major suppliers to Syria and Iraq. In another striking similarity to Mao's foreign policies of the 1960s, Brezhnev was quite willing to support an anticommunist regime as long as it was anti-US. In 1975, Moscow concluded the largest arms sale in its history to a noncommunist country. The buyer was Colonel Khaddafi's Libya. As a fundamentalist Moslem, he was staunchly anticommunist, but he had evicted the US Air Force from its bases outside Tripoli. Also, he could and did pay cash for his arms, thanks to an immense income generated by oil exports. Foreign exchange has always been scarce in the USSR. The relationships Moscow developed with Iraq and Syria were similar to its relationship with Libya. The Iraqi government was busy executing communists both before and after its arms deal with the USSR.[5] In the case of Syria, oil money was not readily available, but since it is a frontline state opposing Israel, the political benefits to the USSR outweighed current account costs.

In the mid-1970s, the collapse of Portugal's African empire provided new opportunities in Angola and Mozambique. Marxian liberation governments were brought into power with Soviet assistance in both instances. African liberation movements needed more than just arms, especially once they had succeeded in taking power. Cuba offered troops and advisors in the tens of thousands. The Soviets provided transportation and logistics. Direct risks to the USSR were thereby minimized and no domestic problem of Soviet casualties resulted. The troops dispatched to Africa were mostly black

Cubans which prevented the charge of white neocolonial domination under the guise of socialist solidarity.

In 1977 and 1978, the Soviets were able to capitalize on hostilities between Ethiopia and Somalia to gain a presence in the horn of Africa. While initially supporting Somalia, the opportunity presented itself in 1978 to switch sides and back the larger, more important nation of Ethiopia. The monarchy had been overthrown and a radical-left military junta was in control. The switch of support from Somalia to Ethiopia was intriguing since the former was strategically located. In 1976, the US chief of naval operations told the House Armed Services Committee that Soviet bases in Somalia enabled the USSR to control the northwest corner of the Indian Ocean and the southern access to the Suez Canal. The chief of naval operations went on to say that in wartime, the United States would not contest the area. Somalian bases would also enhance Soviet ability to disrupt the flow of oil from the Persian Gulf. Ethiopia did not offer comparable strategic advantages. It had greater political influence than did Somalia and was formerly aligned with the West under Emperor Haile Selassie.[6] At least in the case of Africa, Brezhnev seemed more interested in political influence than in enhancing Soviet global military capabilities and weakening those of the United States. It is now the US Navy that has port-of-call privileges in Somalia and controls the access to the Suez Canal and (to a lesser degree) the Persian Gulf.

Détente in Europe

One of the preconditions allowing Moscow to undertake a more active global role was stability on its western front. The Soviets were offered an unprecedented opportunity to stabilize their relations with Western Europe through the good offices of Chancellor Willy Brandt of West Germany. His "Ostpolitik" initially frightened Moscow since it carried the potential of Western economic and political leverage in Eastern Europe. Soviet concerns were laid to rest by three factors: Bonn's acceptance of the German borders as redrawn by the USSR after World War II, a German-Soviet non-aggression pact completed in 1970 and, finally, the establishment of diplomatic relations between East and West Germany.

US forces remained stationed in West Germany, but there were some indications that Brezhnev favored their continued presence. A withdrawal of US forces might well have weakened the Warsaw Pact and encouraged political and economic relaxation in Eastern Europe. In the early 1970s, Senator Mike Mansfield led a concerted effort to reduce US troop commitment to Germany. There was a realistic chance of success, but it was short-circuited by Brezhnev's acceptance of an earlier offer for "mutual, balanced force reduction" (MBFR) negotiations. President Nixon was able to defeat the Mansfield effort since any unilateral reduction would weaken US bargaining leverage in the pending negotiations.[7]

The breakthrough on the "German problem" enabled Brezhnev to move forward toward a general European understanding: the Helsinki accord of 1975. That apogee of East-West détente was attended by all European nations (except Albania), as well as the United States and Canada. It sanctified the post-World War II borders as redrawn by the Soviets in Eastern Europe and amounted to de facto recognition of Eastern Europe as a zone of Soviet hegemony. The trade-off was Moscow's acceptance of two relatively low-cost pledges: to respect human rights and not to intervene in the sovereign affairs of other nations. The signatory states pledged that they:

> would refrain from any intervention, direct or indirect, individual or collective, in the internal or external affairs falling within the domestic jurisdiction of another participating state, regardless of their mutual relations.[8]

At the time of its signing, it looked as though the Helsinki accord had put East-West relations on a new and favorable footing. The means of achieving peaceful coexistence finally seemed to have been found. Between the Czechoslovakian crisis of 1968 and the Polish crisis of the early 1980s, the USSR enjoyed a decade of relatively untroubled European relations. Western trade, investments, and technology transfer to Eastern Europe and the USSR improved markedly during that period.

However, the Helsinki spirit did not long prevail in the area of strategic relations. Serious issues arose in the late 1970s. The Western European nations of France and Great Britain were the first to sell arms to the PRC (with tacit US support, as noted in the previous chapter). In 1978, Brezhnev sent threatening letters to the heads of state of both nations, as well as a warning letter to Italy. He described the arms sales as hostile acts and threatened nonspecific damages to the bilateral relations between Moscow and the nations involved in arms sales.[9] The late 1970s also saw the deployment of the Soviet SS-20 IRBMs. The sites were located so that all of Europe (apart from the tip of the Iberian Peninsula) was within range of Moscow's MIRVed warheads. NATO responded in 1979 with the so-called "two-track decision" in which European-theater nuclear-arms reduction talks would be attempted. If those failed, the United States would deploy its new Pershing II IRBMs in Western Europe to offset the SS-20s. Thus, the net gains in Europe for the Soviets were restricted largely to improved economic relations and an absence of crises. Moscow's European defense burden remained as heavy as before.

Strategic Arms Limitations with the United States

Earlier chapters described the rapid Soviet strategic arms buildup after more than a decade of being held nuclear hostage by the United States. As the 1970s began, the Soviets had caught up, although their MIRVs were still in the development phase. The leadership of both nations realized that this was an opportune time to stabilize and better define the "rules of the game" in US-Soviet nuclear competition. There were three successful precedents from the 1960s: the atmospheric test-ban treaty, the nuclear nonproliferation treaty, and the cap on anti-ballistic missile (ABM) deployments. Limiting strategic arsenals was more difficult than any of those previous agreements, both in terms of the complexity of determining what constituted a fair balance and in the problem of verifying compliance. Nonetheless, in the atmosphere of détente, excellent progress was made during the negotiations in Moscow in 1972.

The Soviets attempted to add a clause dealing with third-party nuclear threats to either superpower. It proposed "joint retaliation against a country that launched a provocative nuclear attack."[10] The intent was clearly to involve the United States with the USSR in an anti-China nuclear axis. The proposal also implied the potential of global nuclear policemen roles for the "big two." While the latter might have been appealing to the Nixon/Kissinger leadership, the cost would have been too high. The embryonic détente with Beijing would have been imperiled and Kissinger's "equidistant" triangular approach to the two major communist powers would have been lost. This failed Soviet bargaining ploy did not prevent the successful conclusion of the SALT I treaty, but it did indicate Moscow's strong desire to counterbalance rising Chinese power.

Moscow's China Policy After Zhen Bao

The Soviets tried to control Beijing with both carrots and sticks, but the emphasis was on the latter. Political threats based on separatist potential within China were tried. A "Free Turkestan" movement was created on Soviet soil, with a military force based on the Uygur political refugees of 1962 and led by a famous figure among the Uygurs, General Zunun Taipov. Thus, if Beijing escalated the Sino-Soviet conflict, it might lose the vast northwest territory of Xinjiang.[11] The Soviets also informally indicated that diplomatic relations might be established if Taiwan were to become an independent nation. The same offer was proffered to the Tibetan independence movement in exile in India.[12]

On the military front, the USSR continued the buildup along the Chinese border through 1974, peaking at some fifty divisions consisting of about

750,000 men. Troop levels remained stabilized until 1980, when more nuclear forces were deployed to the Soviet Far East, led by the new triple-warhead MIRVed SS-20 and followed by the supersonic Backfire bomber. As the theater nuclear capability grew, the manpower commitment shrank. By 1981, many of the divisions were reduced to "category 3" status, denoting a skeletal force less than half the full manpower complement. Estimates of total troop strength ranged from 450,000 to 530,000 throughout the 1980s.[13] The one exception to this unilateral troop reduction was in the Mongolian People's Republic, where the number of Soviet divisions increased from two to three in 1978, and went up again to six in 1980.[14] The increased strength in Mongolia kept a certain amount of pressure on Beijing. Geographically, the ideal corridor of attack against the national capital would be from the MPR. Perhaps the increased forces in Mongolia were intended to partially compensate for the troop reductions elsewhere along the PRC's northern border.

Soviet weaponry, equipment, and war-fighting potential continued to be upgraded in Central Asia and Siberia. By the early 1980s, for example, the six armored divisions flanking Manchuria received the powerful T-72 main battle tank, and late-model interceptor aircraft were deployed on an enlarged network of airfields. In 1978, a Far East theater command was established at Ulan Ude, the first such command established on a permanent basis in peacetime.[15]

By contrast, Soviet carrots held out to China were few. In 1971, the USSR suggested a "non-use of force" agreement and expanded the concept in 1973 by proposing a formal nonaggression pact.[16] Also in 1973, Moscow offered to "apply international law" to its riverine border dispute with Beijing.[17] This would have conceded many of the islands to the PRC and probably indicated a genuine desire for a Manchurian border settlement. As previously noted, the PRC was not then seriously interested in negotiations. It accepted the nonaggression principle and proposed stabilizing relations based on the five principles of peaceful coexistence. China also demanded Soviet troop withdrawal from all disputed territories. In 1978, Beijing further stiffened its negotiating posture by demanding a drawdown of Soviet forces in the Far East and Mongolia to levels of the early 1960s.[18] By accepting in principle the nonaggression concept, the PRC signaled to Moscow that it had no belligerent intentions on Soviet territory. The associated demands guaranteed that Beijing would not be forced into negotiations until it was in a better position vis-à-vis the USSR.

Emergence of an Anti-Soviet Entente:
Japan, China, and the United States

Excluded from military and economic presence in Japan by the US occupation at the end of World War II, the USSR has yet to sign a peace treaty formally ending hostilities. Moscow conditioned such a treaty on the with-drawal of the 47,000 US forces stationed in Japan and the abrogation of the Tokyo-Washington defense treaty. The Soviets also continuously occupied the Northern Territories—four islands just northeast of Hokkaido. As long as Japan was just another ravaged victim of the war, this hard-line position was viable. However, as Japan grew into a major economic power in the 1960s and 1970s, the policy became outworn.

Unfortunately for Soviet national interests, the Brezhnev leadership lacked vision and statesmanship, especially in the latter half of the 1970s. Premier Alexei Kosygin, for example, insulted Japan in 1977 by suggesting that Finland should serve as a model for Japan's relationship with the USSR.[19] Moscow was unavoidably engaged in a competition with Beijing for political power and influence in Japan.[20] Had the USSR been sensitive to issues of Japanese sovereignty and national pride, it might very well have won the contest.

Prior to the Helsinki Accords, the USSR felt that any unilateral conces-sion regarding postwar borders with Japan would open a Pandora's box in Europe. After 1975, there were precious few reasons not to remove this affront to Japanese nationalism. There are no historical linkages between the Japan-Soviet and Sino-Soviet border disputes. A Soviet willingness to com-promise with Japan would not weaken its bargaining position with Beijing, especially since a compromise on the riverine boundaries was already offered as early as 1973. The Soviets have justified their continued control of the Northern Territories as vital to the submarines of their Pacific Fleet. Japanese ownership of the islands would marginally improve its anti-submarine war-fare (ASW) capability against the USSR. However, ASW considerations are poor justification for the continued alienation of the most powerful economy in Asia and a natural economic partner in the development of Siberia.

The 1978 Sino-Japanese treaty was the result of several factors. Soviet intransigence and the economic opportunities for the China trade were proba-bly the most important influences. Also, the United States encouraged Tokyo to make a pact with the PRC. Following the treaty, the Soviets made the worst of it by building a highly visible military presence in the Northern Territories. Three airfields were constructed, and MiGs were deployed. About 2,300 ground forces were permanently stationed on the islands.[21] Amphibious invasion exercises may have been intended to frighten Japan but angered the nation instead.

In subsequent years, the defense budget grew and Japan agreed to under-take the responsibility for its own naval defenses out to 1,200 miles. This required an immense expansion in its anti-submarine warfare capability. In time of war, such enhanced Japanese naval and air capacity would more than offset the marginal utility of the Northern Territories to the USSR. Moreover, the Soviet forces on the islands would be hostage to those same Japanese air

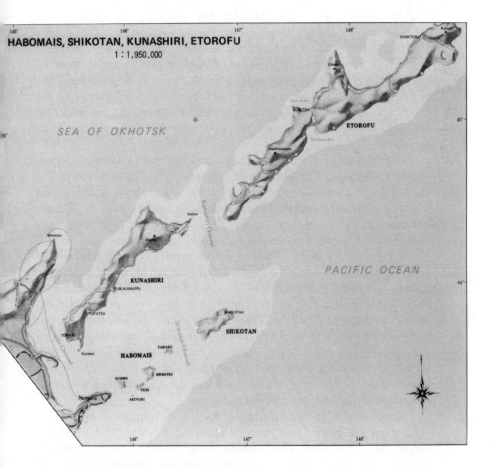

Northern Territories

and naval capabilities. Japan's basic foreign policy has long been friendship with everybody in order to maximize economic opportunities and minimize threats. The Soviets made that impossible in their bilateral relationship.

Afghanistan

This landlocked country was for centuries a weak monarchy. It borders three of the five Soviet socialist republics, which are predominantly Moslem. Political power was dispersed among tribal chieftains in the mountains. The populace is tough and martial, and virtually every adult male owns a rifle and knows how to use it. Because of its weak central government and intertribal conflicts, Afghanistan has never posed an offensive military threat to its neighbors.

A territorial dispute between Pakistan and Afghanistan developed immediately after Pakistan gained its independence. Kabul did not accept The Durand line, the boundary drawn by the British. Pathan tribal lands were cut by that line, and Afghanistan claimed sovereignty over the tribe. In 1955, the Pakistan leadership closed the Kabul/Peshawar road to exports from Afghanistan. The road was better suited to pack animals than trucks, and the Afghans were too underdeveloped to rely on exports. Still, the Khyber Pass provided virtually the only access to the outside world. In the same year, Kabul requested military aid from the United States, which was rejected because Afghanistan had earlier refused to join the US-sponsored Central Treaty Organization. The Eisenhower administration viewed neutral nations as unworthy of US security assistance. Afghanistan's increased isolation from the West provided Moscow with an opportunity. Khrushchev visited Kabul later in 1955 and offered both arms and trade assistance. The Soviets improved the road north from Kabul, allowing the Afghans to trade with the outside world via the Trans-Siberian Railway.

Moscow also provided other economic development assistance. Natural-gas and cement reserves were exploited for export to the USSR at bargain-basement prices. The favorable terms obtained from those extractive industries, combined with extensive credits, soon rendered Afghanistan an economic dependency of the USSR. Major efforts by Moscow ensured that it stayed that way until the mid-1970s. Afghanistan ranked third behind India and Egypt as a noncommunist recipient of Soviet loans, credits, and grants between 1955 and 1975, and first in terms of per-capita receipt of Soviet largess.[22] Afghanistan still remained neutral in the sense that it belonged to no alliance system, but it was clearly in the Soviet economic orbit.

The monarchy was overthrown in 1973 and replaced by a republic. The Afghan Communist Party then became active. The president, Mohammed

Daoud, was far from a Soviet puppet; he sought to reduce Afghanistan's dependence on the USSR. In 1974, negotiations began between Kabul and Tehran. The Shah of Iran, with the support of the United States, tried to draw Kabul into a Western-tilted, Tehran-centered regional economic and security sphere. Iran signed a two-billion-dollar, ten-year economic assistance agreement.

> Iran would have supplanted the Soviet Union as Kabul's largest donor had subsequent events not intervened. Planning was initiated for a rail network linking Afghanistan to Persian Gulf ports, which would also have ended Afghanistan's land-locked status and its dependence on Soviet trade and transport outlets. Over the next year, Daoud was encouraged to break with the domestic communist groups which had been instrumental in bringing him to power. In September, Daoud dismissed 40 Soviet trained officers and concluded officer training agreements with India and Egypt. Most important, Daoud also announced that he would establish his own National Revolutionary Party and ban all others including, of course, the communists.[23]

In March 1978, Daoud signed a friendship agreement with Pakistan and seemed to be prepared to accept the Durand Line as the boundary between the two nations. An official state visit to the United States was scheduled for September.

Moscow could not abide the idea of losing a buffer state on its border, especially after major political and economic commitments had been made. The tools were at hand to deal with the problem. Both the Khalq and Parcham factions of the communist party had strengthened their political bases and had considerable influence within the officer corps of the armed forces. The communist coup took place in 1978, resulting in the death of Daoud, his cabinet, and his entire clan. While Moscow may not have directly ordered the coup d'état, it had prepared the groundwork for just that development.

Unfortunately for the Soviets, Afghan communists were split into two irreconcilable factions. In the internecine struggles that immediately followed the coup, the leader of one wing, Babrak Karmal, lost out and went into de facto exile in Moscow. The government fared badly from the outset. As a profoundly Moslem and traditional society, the tribesmen refused to accept communist leadership and the social revolution being pressed upon them. The traditionally weak central government soon had trouble controlling the provinces. Hundreds of experienced bureaucrats were purged from the small central government. Army morale dropped; mutinies and desertions became serious problems. A greater Soviet civilian and military presence was required to keep the regime afloat. In April 1978, just prior to the communist coup, there were approximately 350 Soviet advisors in Afghanistan. In

December 1979, just prior to the military intervention, Soviet advisors numbered about 7,200.[24]

Afghanistan was becoming a morass in which the Soviets were stuck. In December 1978, Moscow and Kabul signed a friendship treaty that further committed the Soviets. That action might have been partly prompted by the Sino-Japanese treaty some months earlier and the normalization of US-Sino relations that took place at the end of the year. The game of encirclement and counterencirclement in Asia was particularly intense at that time. The Moscow-Kabul treaty did nothing to improve political stability; the government itself was deeply divided between the two top leaders in Kabul: Hafizullah Amin and Nur Mohammed Taraki. The Soviets, who felt that Amin was the source of much of the problem as the more radical of the two leaders, attempted to engineer his removal in September 1979. The plan backfired; in a shoot-out, it was Taraki who lost his life. Amin declared the Soviet ambassador persona non grata and began desperate efforts to make personal contact with the president of Pakistan. The Soviets feared that Amin was about to replicate the 1973 performance of Anwar Sadat when he threw out the Soviet advisors and realigned Egypt with the West.

Meanwhile, between August and October 1979, a Soviet military fact-finding mission led by a dozen generals finally concluded that the only hope for continued communist control of Afghanistan lay in rebuilding the armed forces. It further concluded that only the USSR would be able to accomplish this task, which would require about six months to complete. About the second week of December, the Soviet leadership decided in favor of military intervention. Three motorized rifle divisions, brought up to strength by the addition of local reserves, were positioned to intervene. An airborne division was already largely committed to Afghan territory. The direct assault on Amin's headquarters began on Christmas day. Amin was killed in the fighting. Babrak Karmal returned to Kabul from Moscow and immediately issued the request for Soviet military intervention.[25]

Moscow's concerns about the political and diplomatic directions of the Afghan republic were probably the primary motives for supporting the weak leadership of the coup d'état and for the later military intervention. Secondarily, a socialist Kabul fitted Brezhnev's desire to expand Soviet power and his ideology of advancing communist revolutions in Third World nations. Once committed to supporting a Marxian government, it would have been very dangerous to let it fall a year later. Such a collapse would have been a severe ideological setback for the Soviet Union. The military intervention can be seen as a reassertion of the Brezhnev Doctrine. History is supposed to move forward toward socialism, not backward into counterrevolution. Almost as important would be the message sent to Moscow's European allies that counterrevolution might succeed. Brezhnev had no choice but to intervene in 1979. He may even have believed his generals when they told him that the direct involvement of Soviet forces would be short-term.

Less likely were the motives assigned by the Carter administration. First, Afghanistan would serve as a stepping-stone to direct access to the Indian Ocean, thus providing the USSR with an ice-free port. This putative motive has been used for numerous worst-case scenarios of future Soviet expansionism all around the southern littoral of the USSR. The logistics of rail construction linking such a port to existing Soviet trackage are daunting. Even more difficult would be keeping such a line open through hostile territory. The political costs would be very high, especially in the Moslem and Arab world. Finally, security problems in coping with Pakistani retaliation would be open-ended.

A second motive assigned by some Kremlinologists was to outflank Iran in preparation for an invasion after the death of the Ayatollah Khomeini. The purpose of such an invasion would be to control the Persian Gulf and thus hold hostage the major energy supply for Western Europe and Japan. However, control of Afghanistan does not help in invading Iran. Beyond the Afghan-Iran border lies a large desert without rail lines and with few roads. The invasion route is from the north, not the east. The military occupation of Aghanistan, by tying down troops and military resources, made a Soviet invasion of Iran more difficult and less likely.

A number of negative reasons help explain Brezhnev's decision to send in troops. US-Soviet détente was already in serious trouble. The SALT II treaty looked like it was going to fail in the US Senate. Washington had established diplomatic relations with the PRC and was moving to grant Beijing "most favored nation" trade status without proffering the same offer to Moscow. The NATO arms budgets were on the upswing.[26] Thus, the political costs of intervention seemed minimal. The United States could not do much more against the USSR than intensify current policy trends. Brezhnev also had reason to believe that the United States would do little beyond protesting the Soviet occupation. Washington had accepted the 1978 coup d'état, recognized the government, and even maintained its economic assistance to Kabul. It also failed to protest the December friendship treaty with the USSR. The military intervention would confirm the political realities in Afghanistan rather than change them.[27]

Whatever the motives, the international consequences of the Soviet occupation were soon apparent. US Defense Secretary Harold Brown was in Beijing about a month after the invasion and offered US military arms sales to the PRC. The multilateral covert operation began to supply the mujahedeen resistance forces in Afghanistan. The reaction to the Afghanistan invasion marked the apogee of the Sino-American strategic alignment.

But for Afghanistan, there was a possibility that Sino-Soviet détente might have begun in 1979 rather than the latter half of the 1980s. Early in 1979, the PRC formally notified Moscow that it would not renew the Thirty

Year Treaty of Friendship and Cooperation, due to expire in 1980. Accompanying this pro forma notification was an offer to undertake broad negotiations with the USSR to establish a new general understanding for bilateral relations. This was the first time since 1964 that Beijing had shown a willingness to negotiate anything more than immediate and specific problems with Moscow. The talks were in their preparatory stages at the time of the invasion of Afghanistan. Naturally, Beijing broke off the negotiations. Those talks might have been fruitful since Beijing finally had the confidence to deal with the USSR. Normalization of relations with the United States had been accomplished, the Sino-Soviet border had seen no serious incidents for years, and the PRC was involved in a stalemate with Vietnam in Indochina. Those conditions still applied when the talks finally began in the mid-1980s, and bilateral relations did improve.

Conclusion

The decade had started well for Moscow. Gains were made in South Asia and the Middle East, shortly followed by unprecedented opportunities in Africa. But Brezhnev had overreached Soviet capabilities and made more enemies than friends. The loss of Egypt as an ally in 1973 was the first major setback. Brezhnev must bear the blame for the failure to capitalize on opportunities to improve relations with Japan. One study of the Brezhnev years described the 1976-1978 period as "drift" followed by "crisis" in 1979 and 1980.[28] Although he was to live until late 1982, Brezhnev's foreign policy ossified in the late 1970s. Initiatives and vision were lacking. In retrospect, it is easy to understand how Moscow was drawn into Afghanistan, but the intervention was very costly in terms of relations with China, the West and the Arab world. Afghanistan also resulted in more Soviet war dead than at any time since World War II: 13,310 as of May 1988, plus 35,478 wounded and 311 missing.[29]

The costs of empire in Eastern Europe continued to grow. The USSR could no longer afford massive subsidies to the economies of those states, all of which had a higher standard of living than did the Soviet citizenry. This was driven home to Moscow through the "Solidarity" labor union crisis in Poland. Fortunately for Brezhnev, the Polish military leadership made it unnecessary for the USSR to undertake a costly occupation of that country.

New commitments via the Cubans in Angola and the Horn of Africa were becoming bottomless money sinks, although nowhere near as costly as the support required for the Cuban economy itself. The 1978 Vietnam alliance required not only weapons, but substantial quantities of food that the USSR could ill afford to provide. The opportunities for a stable relationship with the West and a concomitant reduction in defense expenditures had disappeared by the end of the 1970s. The United States soon followed the Western Europeans in assisting the military modernization of the PRC. The major powers of the Western and Asian regions were lining up against the USSR. Brezhnev had sailed the Soviet ship of state into waters laden with shoals and reefs.

Notes

1. The Soviet-Indian treaty came into effect on Aug. 18, 1971, a month after Henry Kissinger's trip to Beijing, but final negotiations seem to have been completed in April. Of course, there were a number of indications that a US-Sino opening was in the offing prior to Kissinger's dramatic secret flight to Beijing.

2. Archer Blood, "Through the Looking Glass: The Indo-Soviet Treaty," University Publications of America, Special Studies Series, *The Soviet Union, 1980-82, Supplement,* Research Memorandum, Strategic Studies Institute, US Army War College, microfilm reel 3.

3. Archer Blood, "Through the Looking Glass."

4. Richard Thornton, *Soviet Asian Strategy in the Brezhnev Era and Beyond,* p. 33.

5. Adam Ulam, *Dangerous Relations,* p. 132.

6. Patrick Rollins, "The USSR and Black Africa" *The Soviet Armed Forces Annual,* 1978, pp. 260-61.

7. C. G. Jacobsen, *Sino-Soviet Relations Since Mao,* p. 18.

8. The nonintervention pledge directly contradicted the Brezhnev Doctrine. Robin Edmonds, *Soviet Foreign Policy,* p. 148.

9. Alan J. Day, ed., *China and the Soviet Union, 1949-1984,* p. 172.

10. Adam Ulam, *Dangerous Relations,* p. 15, citing Gerard Smith, *Doubletalk: The Story of the First Strategic Arms Limitation Talks.*

11. Thomas Robinson, "The Sino-Soviet Border Conflict," in S. Kaplan, *Diplomacy of Power,* p. 286.

12. R. Scalapino, "China and Northeast Asia," in R. Solomon, *The China Factor,* p. 208.

13. In 1981, the author was given the 450,000 figure by a senior US official specializing in Far Eastern affairs. The 530,000 figure comes from a 1983 monograph by Gerald Segal, *The Soviet Threat At China's Gates,* p. 9.

14. Thomas Hart, *Sino-Soviet Relations,* p. 49.

15. Richard Solomon and Masataka Kosaka, "Nuclear Dilemmas and Asian Security," in their own volume, *The Soviet Far East Buildup,* p.5.

16. Harold Hinton, "Sino-Soviet Relations: Background and Overview," in Douglas Stuart and William T. Tow, *China, the Soviet Union and the West,* p. 16.

17. C.G. Jacobsen, *Sino-Soviet Relations Since Mao,* p. 89.

18. H. Hinton, "Sino-Soviet Relations," in Stuart and Tow, *China, the Soviet Union and the West,* p. 19.

19. Hiroshi Kimura, "Soviet and Japanese Negotiating Behavior," *Orbis,* Vol. 24, No. 1, Spring 1980, pp. 56-57.

20. The United States, of course, has been the dominant foreign influence on

Japan since World War II, but that bond did not prevent Moscow from establishing mutually beneficial relations with Tokyo.

21. *Far Eastern Economic Review,* Dec. 15, 1983, p. 33.

22. Siddieq Noorzoy, "Soviet Economic Interests in Afghanistan," *Problems of Communism,* May-June 1978, p. 46. The outlay totaled $1.265 billion.

23. Richard Thornton, *Soviet Asian Strategy in the Brezhnev Era and Beyond,* pp. 53-54.

24. Raymond Garthoff, *Détente and Confrontation,* p. 899, citing estimates from the US embassy, Kabul.

25. Garthoff, *Détente and Confrontation,* Chapter 26, supplemented by a 1981 presentation made by Marshall Shulman to the Southern Center of International Studies, Atlanta. Shulman was a Soviet affairs advisor in the Carter administration.

26. Jacobsen, *Sino-Soviet Relations Since Mao,* pp. 114-115.

27. Garthoff, *Détente and Confrontation,* p. 924.

28. Edmonds, *Soviet Foreign Policy,* Chapters 16 and 20-23.

29. *New York Times,* May 26, 1988, p. 1, citing figures provided by the Soviet Defense Ministry. At the time of final Soviet withdrawal in February 1989, Western estimates calculated Soviet fatalities at over 14,000.

9

Ronald Reagan and the End of the Sino-American Strategic Alignment

Although the two superpowers have professed a desire to defend peace and wish not to be valued on a par with one another, their actions regrettably can lead to only one conclusion: that they are now locked in a bitter confrontation for world hegemony by force of arms.

Beijing Review, May 20, 1985

During the Nixon and Carter administrations, Beijing feared that US-Soviet détente would work to the strategic disadvantage of China. This could have occurred in the area of nuclear weapons; the Soviets pushed for explicit anti-China language in both SALT I and SALT II. It was in the common interest of the United States and the USSR to slow nuclear proliferation and prevent the rise of significant new nuclear powers. More generally, an atmosphere of détente between Moscow and Washington would weaken the threat perceptions on both sides, enabling the USSR to concentrate more of its power against the PRC and reducing the incentives for the United States to engage in such Chinese ventures as the "Four Modernizations" (agriculture, industry, science and technology, and the military). Those realistic concerns on the part of the PRC gave the United States an advantage in the strategic triangle.

After 1980, Beijing no longer had to concern itself on this account. Virtually all communications between Moscow and Washington were at a standstill. In terms of the strategic triangle, the PRC replaced the United States in the swing or "pivot" position. That desirable status is achieved when (1) the pivot stands to gain from a certain amount of normal contact with the other two wings of the triad, (2) the pivot's leverage depends on both wing players' concerns lest a coalition develop between the pivot and one of them, and (3) the pivot's leverage depends on the competition of the other two players for its friendship.[1] Beijing took advantage of its position to put its relations with the Soviet Union on a more stable and less-threatening basis.

President Reagan and the "Evil Empire"

During the presidential election campaign of 1980, Ronald Reagan made it
clear that things were going to be different under his presidency. Like Jimmy
Carter, he ran against Washington. But Carter's "outsider" appeal in 1976
was based on a revived morality and return to basic American values.
Reagan's outsider appeal was to American chauvinism. He blamed his presidential predecessors (especially Carter) for allowing the decline of US power.
He presented the electorate with an external threat, the so-called "window of
vulnerability." Reagan's visceral anticommunism carried the conviction that
the Soviet Union was embarked on a long-term effort to achieve global domination. In pursuit of that goal, Moscow was preparing, if necessary, to fight
and win a nuclear war with the United States.

In the first term of his presidency, Reagan engaged in an overt arms race,
especially in nuclear weapons. Therefore, strategic arms limitation talks were
canceled, and negotiations on theater nuclear forces were conducted under
circumstances that caused the Soviets to break them off.[2] The US also can-
celled advanced negotiations on a comprehensive test ban. There would be
no US-Soviet agreements made at Beijing's expense in the field of strategic
weapons.

Another important Reagan strategy for dealing with the Soviet threat
consisted of "raising the costs" for Moscow. The Soviet economy was in bad
shape in the early 1980s. Factoral productivity had been declining.
Maintaining a firm grip on Eastern Europe was increasingly expensive. The
Solidarity crisis in 1980 and 1981 showed the Soviet inability to keep the
Polish economy afloat. If the United States maximized the economic burdens
for the USSR wherever possible while simultaneously engaging in a rapid
military buildup, then Moscow would be in a difficult situation. It would
either have to retrench its empire, or cut into its force development programs
while imposing still more austerity on Soviet consumers.[3]

Abroad, Washington ceased normalizing economic relations with
Castro's Cuba, and sought to intensify the anti-Vietnamese armed resistance
in Kampuchea. The so-called Reagan Doctrine confronted Marxist Third
World nations with CIA-supported paramilitary covert actions. Arms aid to
the Afghanistan resistance grew by geometric proportions over the level initially provided by the Carter administration. In 1987, the budget for the support to the mujahedeen was $660 million.[4] In Western Europe, the United
States lobbied hard, though unsuccessfully, to prevent the construction of a
natural-gas pipeline from western Siberia. Admittedly, the NATO partners
were too dependent upon Middle East energy supplies, but the pipeline
would provide new infusions of convertible currency and lessen the Soviet
economic crisis.

In brief, the Reagan administration confronted the Soviets on virtually every front.[5] Collectively, the competitive and hostile policies toward the USSR had three important effects. First, Beijing no longer had to seek leverage and bargaining points to win US support for anti-Soviet positions. The process was almost reversed. For example, Washington first offered to sell arms to the PRC in 1981 without any lobbying on the part of Beijing. Second, the renewed superpower rivalry made Brezhnev understandably eager to seek détente with his other major enemy, the PRC. Finally, Beijing did not have to concern itself with US-Soviet relations. Reagan was in no mood to seek mutual accommodation with the nation he claimed was behind most of the strife in the world. China thus gained the pivot position in the strategic triangle because both superpowers sought its cooperation while confronting one another.

Asian Allies and Enemies

Taiwan

There were other elements involved in dealing with the Soviet threat that harmed Sino-US relations. First, Ronald Reagan felt that the United States was getting a well-deserved reputation as a feckless ally. He set out to strengthen bilateral and multilateral alliances and to prove that the United States could "stand by its man." In candidate Reagan's mind, one of the best and most faithful of US allies had been the Republic of China (ROC) on Taiwan. He felt that Carter betrayed the Nationalists when he unilaterally abrogated the mutual defense treaty in order to get full diplomatic relations with Beijing. That was a poor trade in Reagan's eyes, and one that should be corrected by re-recognizing the ROC. Naturally, this made for bad relations with Beijing from the outset of his administration. Cooler heads prevailed, and the president was dissuaded from restoring diplomatic relations with Taipei. To make up for it, Reagan approved unprecedented arms sales to the ROC. Due to heavy congressional opposition, the package did not include the "F-X" export version of the F-16 interceptor, but it did provide qualitative, as well as quantitative, upgrading of the Nationalist military, especially in air defense and anti-submarine warfare.

Unfortunately, the arms deal was being debated in 1981 at the same time that the PRC proffered its most attractive reunification offer to Taipei. The offer allowed the Nationalist government to remain in control of Taiwan, keep its armed forces, and have no communist officials on Taiwan, while providing Nationalist leaders with concurrent appointments in Beijing. The capitalist economic system would be preserved, and free-trade access to the mainland would be provided. The ROC would give up its sovereignty and independent foreign policy, although it could continue to make commercial agreements with foreign nations. Beijing charged that the Reagan administration, by making a large arms deal with Taiwan at that point in time, deliberately sought to undermine the reunification offer.

In reality, the PRC offer to the ROC would have been rejected in any case. Taipei has fared very well domestically and in the international economy despite losing diplomatic recognition from most nations. From a Taiwan perspective, there would have been little to gain and a great deal of risk involved in accepting the PRC offer. Beijing has since abandoned the "packaged" reunification approach and now emphasizes the gradual building of economic and social ties between the two polities, with political cooperation eventually following. That approach has received a much warmer reception in Taiwan. However, the fact remains that Beijing tended to blame the Reagan administration for the failure of its reunification proposal.

Korea

Reagan's efforts to strengthen US ties with another Asian ally, South Korea, also proved to have adverse consequences for both Beijing and Washington. Chun Doo Hwan (then the chief of Seoul's military government) was one of the first foreign heads of state received in the Reagan White House. The US/South Korean alliance had been strained by President Carter's efforts to remove US forces from South Korea, even though he was eventually persuaded not to do so. Partly to reassure Seoul and reaffirm the alliance, Reagan offered to provide F-16 aircraft to the South Korean Air Force. This caused a serious problem for Kim Il-sung in North Korea since his most modern fighter was the MiG-21, which dated from the early 1960s.

For years, Kim had carefully balanced his position in the Sino-Soviet dispute. In the 1970s, however, he had tilted more toward Beijing. He was forced by the Reagan arms sale to go hat-in-hand to Moscow to seek more advanced aircraft that only the Soviets could provide.[6] The USSR agreed to supply MiG-23s, but the price was high. First, the Soviet Pacific Fleet received port-of-call privileges in an ice-free North Korean deep-water port.[7] Second, the Soviets received overflight rights, which enabled them to more easily reach Vietnam from Vladivostok. The Reagan administration initiated a qualitative arms race in Korea that the three previous US administrations had avoided. Still worse, North Korea came into closer alignment with the mutual adversary of both Beijing and Washington.

North Korean economic and strategic dependency grew sharply in this decade. In 1980, the USSR accounted for 22 percent of North Korea's imports and 26 percent of its exports. In 1985, those figures jumped to 47 and 37 percent, respectively.[8] During Kim's 1984 trip to Moscow, an agreement was reached for a direct rail line between Pyongyang and the Trans-

Siberian, thereby bypassing Chinese territory. Eastern port expansion was begun to handle Soviet transit cargoes to and from Japan and Indochina. The rapid development of economic dependence upon Moscow was not solely the result of decisions made in Washington, D.C. North Korea could not pay its debts to European and Japanese creditors and had to seek new infusions of capital that did not require convertible currency repayments. Moscow obliged.

China must also bear some of the responsibility for North Korea's drift toward Moscow. In the 1980s, the PRC increasingly pursued a "two Korea" policy. Trade with South Korea grew sharply in the early 1980s. By 1987, it exceeded the levels of trade with North Korea.[9] According to a spokesman from the PRC embassy in Washington, the decision to increase trade with Seoul originated as part of a larger plan to re-establish links with Taiwan. South Korea and Taiwan are international competitors on a wide variety of manufactured products. South Korea now receives low-cost raw materials and energy supplies from nearby China. Taiwan must import higher-priced industrial inputs from Australia, the United States, and the Middle East. Over a period of time, such a competitive edge for Seoul may cause Taipei to also seek direct trade with the PRC. At least, that is Beijing's strategy.[10]

The PRC negotiated directly with the Seoul government on hijacking crises involving Chinese naval craft and air force planes. Limited travel and sports competitions were allowed between the two countries, and China did not follow North Korea's lead in boycotting the 1988 Summer Olympics that were held in Seoul. North Korea also toyed with, and then rejected, the Deng Xiaoping model of economic liberalization. These factors probably contributed to Kim's concessions to the Soviets as well as to his decision to restore ambassadorial relations with China's other enemy, Vietnam.[11]

The Beginnings of Sino-Soviet Détente

Washington had set the stage for improved Sino-Soviet relations. It merely required the presence of a script. Border talks were reconvened in 1982 after a three-year hiatus due to the invasion of Afghanistan. The discussions initially made little progress, but were continued as an indication of normalizing state-to-state relations. The negotiations enjoyed a more positive atmosphere than any bilateral talks since the early 1960s.

Bilateral trade went up sharply, doubling for three consecutive years (1982-1985).[12] However, Beijing insisted that a true rapprochement with the USSR could not take place until the "three big obstacles" were removed. They were: the Soviet military presence on China's border and in Mongolia, the Soviet occupation of Afghanistan, and Soviet support for the Vietnamese occupation of Kampuchea.

On the one hand, the PRC simply had less need of the United States as a strategic partner against the Soviet threat. On the other hand, Beijing could count on the Reagan administration to support its goals in Afghanistan and Indochina. Therefore, the PRC could and did distance itself from Washington. In 1982, Deng Xiaoping moved the territorial integrity of China (reunification with Taiwan and sovereignty over Hong Kong) up to number two national priority in the 1980s. This divisive issue with Washington ranked behind the economic modernization of China, but for the first time was listed ahead of "anti-hegemonism."[13]

Beijing's Gains in Washington

The Reagan administration was slow to understand the seriousness of China's reorientation. In 1981, Secretary of State Alexander Haig made his first official visit to Beijing and offered to sell weapons to the PRC at the same time as arms were provided to the ROC. He was rudely rebuffed. Some of Beijing's strongest anti-US rhetoric was issued at the conclusion of the Haig visit:

> US government is bent on giving Taiwan international status as an independent political entity. Anyone who thinks that China will have to swallow that bitter pill because it needs American support in combatting Soviet hegemonism should remember the Sino-Soviet split. . . . In the late 1950s, China waged a resolute struggle against . . . bullying . . . in order to defend the principles of independence, sovereignty, and equality, not hesitating to bear the consequences of a break.[14]

Once the PRC threatened to sever relations with Washington while simultaneously pursuing new initiatives with the Soviet leadership, the Reagan administration reconsidered its policies. The result, dubbed "Shanghai II," was signed in August 1982. Beijing won a commitment from Washington to gradually reduce the quantitative levels of arms sold to Taiwan and to freeze the level of sophistication at current standards. Beijing yielded little in return. It still refused to renounce the use of force, but did state that the "fundamental policy" was to strive for the peaceful reunification of the motherland.

In 1983, the United States upgraded China's access to dual-use technology. The PRC was reclassified as a "friendly, non-aligned country." This facilitated Beijing's purchases of advanced equipment and electronics that could have military applications. After two years of tough negotiations regarding export quotas, the PRC also won most of its demands in that field. The tailspin in Sino-US relations was halted, but yet another serious problem arose.

In 1984, President Reagan made his first state visit to the PRC and signed a treaty to sell nuclear-power equipment and technology to the Chinese. When the treaty was submitted for ratification, some senators objected on the grounds that Beijing was guilty of nuclear proliferation and thus was not eligible for US nuclear technological assistance. The charge was probably true in terms of China's military cooperation with Pakistan. Former President Z. A. Bhutto, in his death cell memoir, referred to a 1976 international agreement that he felt would be his "greatest contribution to the survival of our people."[15] He may well have been referring to a secret nuclear-sharing arrangement with the PRC. In the early 1980s, US intelligence and congressional sources claimed that China helped Pakistan design its first nuclear weapon, which was eventually completed (though not yet tested) in November 1987.[16]

The treaty ratification deadlock was finally broken by two Chinese initiatives. First, Prime Minister Zhao Ziyang issued the following statement in January 1984: "China does not engage in nuclear proliferation ourselves, nor do we help other countries develop nuclear weapons."[17] (Note the careful use of the present tense.) In the same month, the PRC agreed to join the International Atomic Energy Agency and abide by its monitoring and safeguard procedures on fissionable materials. Those measures mitigated Beijing's continued refusal to sign the UN Nuclear Non-Proliferation Treaty.

While the nuclear proliferation issue did not create the polemical outbursts seen from Beijing during the first term of the Reagan administration, it did reveal that China's relations with a neighboring ally might take precedence over those with the superpowers. It almost seemed that the relationship with Pakistan outweighed rational national-security policy-making. A nuclear-armed Pakistan may possess a more effective deterrent against future wars with India, but a Pakistani bomb was sure to prompt a response. While India had tested an atomic device in 1974, it had refrained from the production of nuclear weapons. Once it was clear that Islamabad was launched on a nuclear-arms program, New Delhi responded by starting production of nuclear bombs and warheads in late 1986. By 1988, it was producing them at the rate of about twenty per year.[18] India also has missiles capable of reaching any target in Pakistan. Their range would probably cover much of the PRC as well.

The 1968 Non-Proliferation Treaty epitomized the superpower nuclear condominium. Both Washington and Moscow believe that the spread of nuclear weapons makes nuclear wars more likely. While the Chinese have not developed a public policy position on this sensitive topic (apart from the Zhao Ziyang statement cited above), such medium-sized powers as China, France, and Great Britain do not share all of the concerns of the superpowers.

An argument can be made that nuclear proliferation reduces the likelihood of both conventional and nuclear war.[19] As Beijing rhetorically asked in a propaganda document of 1963, "Did the danger of nuclear war become greater or less when the number of nuclear powers increased from one to two?"[20] A condition of mutual deterrence between the two major powers in South Asia might end the string of disastrous defeats suffered by Pakistan at the hands of India. A Pakistani bomb would also relieve Beijing of the extended deterrence responsibility of protecting Islamabad from potential Soviet military threats. Since the essential nuclear technology had already been provided to Pakistan, Beijing could then afford its later pledge of proliferation abstinence.

Japan

In the emerging entente among Beijing, Washington, and Tokyo in the late 1970s, it was the Japanese who were the most reluctant partner. Japan drew back first from the arrangement. This was made easy because the leadership never admitted that they were part of an entente in the first place. If Japan were seen to be in any sort of alliance arrangement with China, it would not lessen Soviet pressures on Japan, but would increase the danger of involvement in the Sino-Soviet confrontation.[21] When China invaded Vietnam, Tokyo refused to support the "pedagogical war" and demanded the withdrawal of Chinese forces. Like Vietnam, Japan has its own territorial dispute with Beijing over the Senkaku Islands, which lay between Taiwan and Okinawa. The islands shelter a sizeable off-shore oil deposit, so more than uninhabitable rocks and fishing rights are at stake, especially to the energy-deficient Japanese nation.

Foreign economic policy plays an unusually important role in Japan's international relations. This is quite understandable in a nation that lacks resources and must depend upon imports for most of the basic necessities of life. In February 1978, Japan signed a $20 billion, eight-year trade package with the PRC, one of the largest bilateral economic deals in history. The agreement provided for Japanese sales of machinery and technology transfers to be paid for by Chinese raw materials, foodstuffs, and oil. The deal did not work well. The PRC found itself unable to meet the export requirements of the agreement. Therefore, in February 1981, Beijing canceled contracts on seventeen steel-making and petrochemical plants.[22] Partly as a result of the defaults, Japanese exports to the PRC dropped 40 percent in 1981 compared to the previous year.[23]

The most famous canceled project was the Bao Shan steel complex under construction near Shanghai with Japanese money and technology. The site was poorly planned in terms of geology, local transportation, and access to electric power. The advanced alloy steels to be produced required high-grade iron ore that was not available in China. Australia was the nearest source. Cost overruns and delays became so onerous that the PRC canceled the contracts and defaulted on over $1.2 billion owed to Japanese suppliers. The firms involved were overextended, and some required governmental assistance to avoid bankruptcy. The project eventually restarted under a much longer-term arrangement and with the help of the Japanese government, but all parties concerned were disillusioned by the experience. Adding further injury, China's oil exports did not reach expected levels.

Understandably, the cautious Japanese businessmen were reluctant to throw good money after bad.[24] The PRC counted on Japan as its number one investor in the "open door" economic policy, but that role was soon taken over by tiny Hong Kong. Japan did not even remain China's major trading partner. In 1986, Hong Kong again overtook Tokyo. Between 1982 and 1987, there were no more long-term bilateral economic pacts between the two countries.

In 1985, university students in Beijing spontaneously demonstrated in the streets against what they perceived as unfair Japanese economic policies. (China had a $6 billion deficit in the $19 billion two-way trade in 1985.) The demonstrations were subsequently echoed in several other major urban centers. By 1987, the PRC criticized basic Japanese foreign economic policy rather than the specific issues within their bilateral relations.

> Japan seems to be solely interested in earning foreign exchange from the South and penetrating the home markets of the North. . . . It lacks the foresight of making a greater contribution to the countries of the South by channeling its surplus capital into the area instead of dumping it in the US and West Europe in pursuit of short-term economic goals.[25]

The devolution in Sino-Japanese economic relations was finally slowed—if not halted—in 1988. A new pact that had been negotiated over the previous two years accorded "national treatment" to Japanese firms operating in the PRC.[26] The same negotiations led to a concessional loan package totaling some $6.37 billion over a five-year period, beginning in 1991. It will enable the PRC to expand trade beyond its own capacity to earn foreign exchange. In 1988, Beijing achieved a favorable two-way trade balance for the first time in years.[27]

Finally, the two nations had difficulty in dealing with each other from a sociocultural standpoint. In rewrites of Japanese school textbooks undertaken in 1982 and again in 1986, the government softened the language regarding Japanese aggression in World War II, glossing over such heinous events as the "rape of Nanjing." The PRC demanded that the books be withdrawn and rewritten. Tokyo acceded to most Chinese demands for revising the texts. In 1985, Prime Minister Nakasone visited a shrine honoring Japan's military dead from World War II. Also buried there were some individuals who had been executed as war criminals after the 1945 surrender. Beijing protested this visit, but to no avail. In 1986, a Chinese student dormitory in Kyoto was the subject of an ownership claim filed by Taipei. The Japanese courts found that the historical ownership rights did fall to the ROC on Taiwan. The PRC mounted a major propaganda campaign that confused private ownership rights with issues of national sovereignty.

In 1987, Beijing revived the old charges that Japanese militarism was a danger to Asia. This was occasioned by Japan's exceeding its previous self-imposed limit of one percent of its gross national product devoted to the defense budget. The People's Daily predicted that the level would continue to rise until "the state of affairs will get out of control."[28] Japan does have the world's eighth largest military force, but it is small when compared with its immediate neighbors.[29]

One well-respected Western scholar visited both Japan and China during 1987 in order to draw out the attitudes of officials regarding each other. He concluded that "one cannot describe Sino-Japanese ties in terms of a love/hate relationship because there is no love there."[30] Most important to the focus of this study, rising tensions between Tokyo and Beijing would be a powerful force furthering Sino-Soviet détente. The closest cooperation between China and the Soviet Union occurred between 1937 and 1941 when both nations faced a direct Japanese threat. Moscow has already tried to raise the specter of renewed Japanese militarism to justify to Beijing its strengthened presence in the Pacific.[31] Perhaps the 1988 improvements made in bilateral economic relations will improve the outlook for the 1990s. If not, the only beneficiary will be the USSR.

China's Reorientation

In addition to the negative factors provided by Washington and Tokyo, the PRC had its own reasons for finding a new foreign-policy equilibrium in the 1980s. There were positive opportunities inherent in the strategic deadlock between the superpowers. For example, the following analysis was offered in a 1981 unclassified report prepared for the Chinese Foreign Ministry:

> The West European countries have tended to emphasize the need to maintain détente with the USSR. . . . They have considerable economic and military strength, and have their own calculations for supporting détente which are not a result of their weakness nor the lure and pressure of the USSR. . . . It is possible, if détente is implemented, for West Europe to impose certain restraints on the USSR and strengthen its position vis-à-vis the US. Some Europeans believe that in the stalemate between the two superpowers, this policy will provide Western Europe with the key to a greater opportunity for diplomatic maneuvering.[32]

A mere six years earlier, Zhou Enlai had denounced détente in Europe as a Soviet ruse to lull NATO into a false sense of security.[33] If, in the 1980s, West Europeans can now benefit from détente with the Soviets, why would not the same factors apply to Beijing?

In addition to the above analogy with Western Europe, a number of unique factors helped Beijing capture the "pivot position" in the Moscow-Beijing-Washington triangle. First, Secretary of State Alexander Haig and Deputy Assistant Secretary for East Asia John Holdridge were both convinced that good relations with China were important in the global efforts to contain the USSR. This perceived need for China provided considerable leverage for Beijing as it pressed the United States for concessions on Taiwan, technology transfer, and trade advantages. Beginning new negotiations with the USSR would serve to strengthen that leverage.[34]

Second, Soviet inability to consolidate its position in Afghanistan, Beijing's ability to keep the guerrilla war alive in Kampuchea, the crisis in Poland, and the internal economic problems in the USSR all served to convince the PRC that Soviet expansionism had bogged down. Moscow's threat potential seemed increasingly long-term rather than immediate.[35] Although there were as many as fifty-three Soviet divisions deployed east of the Ural Mountains by the mid-1980s, only forty were east of Lake Baikal and those collectively numbered only 370,000 men.[36] About thirty-two of those divisions were in the vicinity of the Chinese border. Nearly half of the Red Army divisions in the Soviet Asia were at one-third strength in terms of manpower.[37] This was a sharp decline from the 1976 and 1977 peak manpower strength of about 750,000 in Soviet Asia. The PLA enjoyed about a four-to-one troop strength advantage in terms of units deployed facing those of the Red Army. The proportion of the Soviet budget devoted to defense also declined between 1976 and 1982.[38] The real growth of the Soviet military was only 2 percent per year during that period. Meanwhile, the PRC had developed ICBM and SLBM systems, which strengthened its nuclear-deterrent against both superpowers.[39]

Third, Beijing had already successfully played its "American card" in the sense that Moscow was still concerned about the potential emergence of an anti-Soviet entente consisting of the PRC, the United States, and Japan. Under those circumstances, the Soviets might prove willing negotiators.

Moscow's Concessions to Beijing

In August 1981, the USSR officially proposed to the Chinese Foreign
Ministry the adoption of mutual "confidence building measures" in the Far
East.[40] The PRC had already announced a cessation of ideological polemics
with the USSR in 1979. In 1982, Brezhnev affirmed that a "socialist social
system" existed in China.[41] In June, the USSR pledged never to be the first
to use nuclear weapons. That meant far more to China, with its relatively
weak nuclear deterrent and lack of a tactical nuclear capability, than it did to
the United States. About a month later, Brezhnev made a conciliatory speech
and suggested negotiations with China without preconditions. In response,
the PRC dropped its previous demands that the Soviets "reduce their influence" in Mongolia, Afghanistan, and Indochina, and pull their troops back
from the border prior to general bilateral negotiations.[42] Talks were begun in
October without notable results. Beijing provided an incentive to continue
the negotiations in 1983. In January, as a precondition for a general border
settlement, the PRC dropped its 1964 demand that the USSR acknowledge
the nineteenth-century border treaties as "unequal."[43]

   Sino-Soviet trade possibilities were also involved in the ending of the
Sino-US strategic alignment. Almost 70 percent of the machine tools in
China's factories were of Soviet and Eastern European origin and dated from
the 1950s and early 1960s.[44] Expanded trade with the USSR would enable
the PRC to renovate much of that aging equipment and at much lower costs
than buying new items from Japan and the West. The PRC was also in need
of more intermediate technology, not the forte of the industrialized West nor
Japan. The Soviet Union and Eastern Europe could prove to be valuable suppliers to the labor-intensive sectors of Chinese industry. The renewed Sino-
Soviet negotiations quickly resulted in a 1982 agreement to open frontier
trade, which grew rapidly through the mid-1980s, especially between
Heilongjiang Province and Siberia. The frontier trade is conducted on a
barter basis, thus saving scarce foreign exchange. At the national level as
well, Eastern Europe and the USSR offer far more opportunities for barter
agreements than do the Western nations and Japan.

   The PRC had its own internal political reasons to stabilize relations with
Moscow. The 1981 documents of the 6th Plenary Session of the 11th Party
Congress revealed a new awareness on the part of the Chinese leadership that
the Sino-Soviet dispute had deleterious domestic effects in China: "Normal
differences among comrades inside the party came to be regarded as manifes-
tations of the revisionist line or of the struggle between the two lines."[45]

   There were a number of additional factors involved in Beijing's decision
to distance itself from Washington, some of which related to China's foreign
policy toward the Third World. The PRC had been too hostile to Third World
nations receiving substantial assistance from the USSR. This hurt Beijing's

favorable relationship with the nonaligned movement and in the United Nations. For example, it was not until January 1983 that diplomatic relations were established between Angola and the PRC, and it was only then that the PRC recognized the African National Congress and the Southwest African People's Organization. These groups had long had the firm backing of virtually all of the nonaligned nations in the struggle against apartheid. The only reason the PRC had delayed the inevitable was the degree of Soviet influence present. On the other side of the coin, Beijing was seen as too friendly with repressive regimes (such as that of Chile) simply because they were anti-Soviet. Good relations with Third World nations were important to China economically as well; a favorable balance of trade with those countries netted over $2 billion in foreign exchange in 1982.[46] That surplus was much appreciated at a time when the PRC faced severe trade deficits with the industrialized nations, especially Japan.

Initial Limits of Sino-Soviet Détente

China's policy reorientation between 1981 and 1985 could only go so far. The so-called "independent" strategy was limited by several factors. First, the PRC still required access to Western technology and investments in order to succeed in its four modernizations, a plan that remained the top national priority of the Deng Xiaoping leadership. If the PRC appeared to be on the way to a rapprochement with Moscow, access to Western and Japanese technology and investments would be imperiled.

Second, the Soviets refused to yield on any of the "three big obstacles (Afghanistan, Kampuchea, and the militarization of the northern border regions). Still worse, Moscow deployed additional SS-20 IRBMs east of the Ural Mountains. In early 1986 when Mikhail Gorbachev stopped the SS-20 deployment, the Asian total was over one hundred missiles, each MIRVed with three warheads. In 1984, the Soviets offered India production rights on the highly advanced MiG-29, an aircraft that at that time had not been introduced into the air forces of the Warsaw Pact allies.[47] Soviet naval and air elements in Vietnam grew steadily throughout the first half of the 1980s. Thus, Moscow's actions and military potential still posed threats to the PRC's national survival. The United States posed a threat only to Beijing's revanchism.

Third, Beijing had to reassess the political situation in the United States beginning in 1984. Secretary of State Haig had resigned, and his East Asia assistant secretary, John Holdridge, had been politely removed from Washington through his appointment as ambassador to Djakarta. Those two figures had been the strongest advocates for maintaining good relations with the PRC. A new and alarming viewpoint began to take hold in Washington under the State Department leadership of George Shultz and his Assistant Secretary for East Asia Paul Wolfowitz.[48] They did not think China required any special consideration. It was too militarily weak to play a major international role, yet so vast as to cause a continuous problem to the Soviets just by being there. Its modern diplomatic history showed it to be an unreliable partner. Therefore, Washington need not make any unusual concessions to Beijing; a policy of "benign neglect" would suffice. With this new view prevalent in the State Department, Beijing could no longer take for granted US support on global strategic issues. Equally important to the policy-makers in the PRC, all indications were that Ronald Reagan would be re-elected president in 1984, so there was little prospect of a more malleable US leadership in the near future.

In the mid-1980s, Beijing found the fulcrum point on the teeter-totter between Moscow and Washington. It continued to improve state-to-state relations with the USSR and had reestablished party-to-party relations with most other Eastern European countries by late 1987. After retrenching on imports in 1981 and 1982, Deng Xiaoping's "open door" policy began to take effect, stimulating renewed Western and Japanese investments. Trade grew steadily with Western Europe, Japan, the United States, and especially Hong Kong. In 1987, Beijing reverted to a long-term strategy to regain Taiwan. It welcomed reporters from the ROC and hailed Taipei's decision to allow indirect travel to the mainland (ostensibly for the humanitarian purpose of visiting long-separated relatives). In the mid-1980s, indirect trade between Taiwan and the mainland developed through the entrepôt of Hong Kong, with Beijing's blessing.

Enter Mikhail Gorbachev: The Scene Changes

A priority ranking of Soviet foreign policy concerns in the 1980s would probably place the United States and the arms race as first. European diplomacy (both Eastern and Western Europe) was accorded second place. Afghanistan, China, the Middle East, and the Persian Gulf would follow in roughly that order. This was a sharp change from the early 1970s when Moscow was obsessed with the China problem, and it goes far to explain the 1982 initiatives of Brezhnev. A stabilized relationship with the PRC would enable Moscow to concentrate on more important current objectives. Unfortunately, the direct bilateral negotiations of 1982 to 1985 were disappointing except in terms of economic relations.

In Vladivostok on July 28, 1986, Secretary General Mikhail Gorbachev delivered a major policy statement on Asia. The world had already come to expect innovative ideas from this leader, and he did not disappoint his audience. For the region as a whole, he called for an Asian equivalent to the

Helsinki Conference of 1975. Such a conference would reinforce and legitimize the status quo. There is, however, little likelihood of a Soviet-sponsored "Asian security conference" convening in the foreseeable future. A number of regional conflicts are too intense. Even India, as the closest noncommunist Asian nation to Moscow, has so far refused to support the conference concept.[49]

On bilateral relations with the PRC, Gorbachev raised the likelihood of withdrawing "a substantial part" of the Soviet forces stationed in Mongolia, without seeking a quid pro quo from Beijing. Some 10,000 troops were withdrawn the next year, although four divisions remained.[50] A few months prior to his speech, he froze the level of SS-20s deployed east of the Ural Mountains. While neither of these measures affected the military balance, they served as tangible signals to Beijing that Moscow would rely less on coercive diplomacy and more on positive linkages in dealing with Beijing. In bilateral negotiations, the Soviets increasingly sought mutual benefit and accommodation.

Gorbachev's own words best describe the sharp break from the past:

> The USSR is prepared, at any time and at any level, to discuss with China questions of additional measures for creating an atmosphere of good neighborliness. We hope that the border dividing (I would prefer to say linking) us will become a line of peace and friendship in the near future. . . . We do not want the Amur River to be viewed as a "water obstacle." Let the basin of this mighty river unite the efforts of the Chinese and the Soviet peoples in using for mutual benefit the rich resources available there and for building water-management projects. An inter-governmental agreement on this account is being jointly worked out. And the official border might run along the main shipping channel. . . . In the northwest region the Soviet government is preparing a positive reply in respect to the issue of assistance in building a railway to connect the Xinjiang Uygur Autonomous Region with Kazakhstan.
>
> The Soviet people's attitude to the objective advance by the Communist Party of China—to modernize the country and build in the future a socialist society worthy of a great people—is that of understanding and respect. As far as it is possible to judge, we have similar priorities to those of China, i.e., accelerating social and economic development. Why not support each other, why not cooperate in implementing our plans wherever this will clearly benefit both sides? The better the relations, the more we shall be able to exchange our experiences. We note with satisfaction that a positive shift has become visible in economic ties. We are convinced that the historically established complementarity between the Soviet and Chinese economies gives great opportunities for expanding these ties. . . .
>
> The USSR attaches much importance to radical reduction of armed forces and conventional armaments in Asia to the limits of reasonable sufficiency. We realize that this problem should be tackled gradually, stage-by-

stage, by starting from some one district, say the Far East. In this context the USSR is prepared to discuss with the PRC concrete steps aimed at proportionate lowering of the level of ground forces.[51]

Gorbachev also suggested that "the moment was right" to "resume comradely dialogue and to remove unnecessary suspicion and mistrust" between Hanoi and Beijing. However, Gorbachev was careful not to commit his Vietnamese allies to anything concrete. He merely expressed a desire to see "the border between these two socialist states again become a border of peace and good neighborly relations."

In terms of bilateral Sino-Soviet relations and the long-simmering border confrontation, Gorbachev clearly sought to find an accommodation with Beijing. No mention was made of the one large block of territory in dispute (the Pamir Mountain range), but neither did he assert nonnegotiable claims upon the region. His mention of assistance in completing the Chinese portion of the Xinjiang-Kazakhstan rail link was quite a good omen for stability in the bilateral relations. In 1964, the PRC unilaterally canceled construction plans for the last link in the line, fearing that the USSR might use it as a means to foment separatism among the Uygurs. Beijing recommenced construction on the line in 1985 and expected it to be completed to the Soviet border by about 1990. The Chinese have even raised the possibility of double-tracking the rail line across Northwest China to make it an Eurasian complement to the Trans-Siberian Line.

At the very least, the completed track will facilitate trade with the USSR. Beijing claims that Xinjiang is an agricultural surplus region, but it is so distant from major Chinese markets that such perishable commodities as melons and vegetables often rot in the fields. Neighboring Soviet territories provide a natural market.[52] The completed rail line will also serve as further evidence that the positive aspects of the Sino-Soviet relations outweigh the threat perceptions. This is especially significant in a minority region that China has had difficulty controlling in the past.

On Vietnam, Deng Xiaoping indirectly responded to Gorbachev's olive branch by telling reporters that the most important thing would be for the USSR to stop supporting Vietnam's occupation of Kampuchea. Deng dropped his earlier demands for the withdrawal of Soviet military presence from Vietnam. He implicitly accepted the Soviet-Vietnamese alliance. He also stated on another occasion that real progress on any one of the "three big obstacles" would be sufficient to put Sino-Soviet relations on a new footing. Beijing would be willing to discuss a "general settlement" with Moscow at that time. However, Beijing rebuffed Gorbachev's January 1988 call for a Sino-Soviet summit meeting on the grounds of the Indochina problem.[53] Two years earlier, Deng described the Vietnamese occupation of Kampuchea as "the main obstacle in Sino-Soviet relations."[54] In 1988, with gains already made on the border and Afghan issues, Beijing seemed intent on obtaining significant Soviet concessions regarding Vietnam. Deng Xiaoping apparently decided to extract full value from China's "pivot position" in the strategic triangle.

As the tone of this discussion indicates, Gorbachev's initiatives are still in the preliminary stages of negotiation and it remains to be seen whether he will be successful in reducing Western and Japanese leverage in Beijing.

Notes

1. Gerald Segal, "China and the Great Power Triangle," *China Quarterly,* No. 83, Sept. 1980, pp. 499-505.

2. The US position, known as the "zero option," called for the elimination of all land-based MRBMs and IRBMs from Europe. This was flatly rejected by Brezhnev, but eventually accepted by Mikhail Gorbachev.

3. The Reagan strategy of "raising the costs" elicited a Soviet response. Brezhnev successfully stimulated a mass peace movement in Europe, causing President Reagan to be seen as virtually a war monger by many citizens of NATO nations. The United States eventually felt compelled to resume serious arms-control negotiations, and Gorbachev took the initiative by accepting arms-limitation agreements on US terms. By the end of the 1980s, he will probably have significantly reduced the Soviet military budget.

4. *Asiaweek*, Jan. 22, 1988, p. 11.

5. One notable exception to the policy of confrontation and nonnegotiation was Reagan's decision to lift the grain embargo imposed by Carter after the invasion of Afghanistan. The effectiveness of the embargo was questionable since a number of other suppliers helped fill the breach, and it had definitely hurt US farm income.

6. Kim went to Moscow in 1984, his first trip to the Soviet capital in twenty-three years.

7. The Soviet Pacific Fleet is using Wonsan and/or the adjacent port of Hongwon; it may also have port-of-call privileges at Najin. All facilities are on Korea's eastern seaboard. Kim Yu-Nam, "Soviet Strategic Objectives on the Korean Peninsula," in Ray Cline, James Miller, and Roger Kanet, eds., *Asia in Soviet Global Strategy,* p. 87. See also *The Economist,* Dec. 27, 1987, p. 39.

8. *Far Eastern Economic Review,* June 18, 1987, p. 82.

9. Seoul/Beijing two-way trade was about $2 billion in 1987 and was expected to continue to grow due to the high value of the Japanese yen, causing Japanese exports to be more costly. *Asiaweek*, Feb. 5, 1988, p. 47.

10. From an interview with an official of the PRC embassy in Washington, D.C. Mar. 1988.

11. North Korea broke relations with Vietnam as a result of the latter's invasion of Kampuchea in 1978.

12. Bilateral trade jumped from a paltry $308 million in 1982 to $647 million in 1983. In 1985, the two-way total was approximately $2.75 billion, or four times the 1982 level. State-to-state trade leveled off thereafter; the 1987 total was $2.6 billion,

but cross-border barter trade continued to grow rapidly in the late 1980s. Figures are from the International Trade Administration of the US Dept. of Commerce, *China's Economy and Foreign Trade, 1981-85,* Washington D.C., US Government Printing Office, 1984. See also *Far Eastern Economic Review,* July 25, 1985, p. 12, and *Newsweek,* April 11, 1988, p. 53.

13. Deng made the announcement at the 12th CCP Congress, Sept. 1, 1982.

14. Xinhua in *Beijing Review,* June 17, 1981, cited in Robert Sutter, "Realities of International Power and China's 'Independence' in Foreign Affairs," *Journal of Northeast Asian Studies,* Vol. III, No. 4, Winter 1984, p. 9.

15. Ashok Kapur, *Pakistan's Nuclear Development,* Appendix 2, p. 244.

16. Kapur, *Pakistan's Nuclear Development,* pp. 245-248, and *The Tampa Tribune,* Nov. 27, 1987, citing an unnamed US military intelligence official.

17. *Far Eastern Economic Review,* Jan. 26, 1984, p. 49.

18. United Press International, *Tampa Tribune,* April 24, 1988, p. 9-A.

19. Kenneth Walz, *The Spread of Nuclear Weapons: More May Be Better,* Adelphi Papers, No. 171, London, International Institute of Strategic Studies, 1981.

20. "People of the World Unite," Beijing, Foreign Languages Press, Aug. 15, 1963, cited in Leo Yueh-yun Liu, *China as a Nuclear Power,* p. 31.

21. Tatsumi Okabe, "Japan's Relations with China in the 1980s," in G. Sigur and Y. C. Kim, *Japanese and US Policies in Asia,* p. 103.

22. Gerald L. Curtis, "Japan's Foreign Policies," in Susan Shirk, ed., *The Challenge of China and Japan,* New York, Praeger, 1985, p. 481, from an article originally published in *Foreign Affairs,* Spring 1981.

23. *The Economist,* June 5, 1982, p. 61.

24. From 1972 to 1987, Japan accounted for only 8.7 percent of the cumulative foreign investment in the PRC. *Far Eastern Economic Review,* Sept. 8, 1988, p. 117.

25. Zhou Zhinian, "The Resurgence of Japan," in Harish Kapur, ed. *As China Sees the World,* p. 79.

26. "National treatment" provides that the Japanese firms in China have the same access to cheap raw materials, labor, and bank loans as Chinese concerns. *Far Eastern Economic Review,* Sept. 8, 1988, p. 117.

27. In the first half of 1988, the PRC enjoyed at $500 million trade surplus. *Far Eastern Economic Review,* Sept. 8, 1988, p. 117.

28. *Renmin Ribao,* Feb. 11, 1987.

29. Robert Scalapino, *Major Power Relations in Northeast Asia,* p. 63.

30. Allen Whiting, "The Politics of Sino-Japanese Relations," a conference paper presented in Aug. 1987. In the published book chapter, Whiting rephrased his assessment of Sino-Japanese relations: "Sino-Japanese friendship . . . is not realizable in this century." In J. Dreyer, ed., *Chinese Defense and Foreign Policy,* p. 161.

31. Pi Ying-hsien, "Normalization of Peking-Moscow Relations: The Process and Prospects," *Issues and Studies,* Vol. 21, No. 8, Aug. 1985. See especially the Russian-language publication references on p. 111.

32. A. Doak Barnett, "China's International Posture: Signs of Change," in S. Shirk, ed., *The Challenge of China and Japan,* pp. 446, 454.

33. C. G. Jacobsen, *Sino-Soviet Relations Since Mao,* p. 84.

34. Sutter, "Realities of International Power," *Journal of Northeast Asian Studies,* p. 11.

35. Monte Bullard was the US Army attaché in Beijing during this period. Based on numerous conversations with military leaders, he found that the Chinese were quite confident both of their ability to deal with a conventional Soviet invasion and their nuclear "second strike" deterrent. See Bullard, *China's Political-Military Evolution: The Party and the Military in the PRC, 1960-1984*, p. 21.

36. Osamu Miyoshi, "Soviet Collective Security Pacts," in R. Cline, et. al., *Asia in Soviet Global Strategy*, p. 26.

37. Allen Whiting, *Siberian Development and East Asia*, p. 93.

38. Scalapino, *Major Power Relations in Northeast Asia*, p. 57.

39. As of 1988, two nuclear-powered missile-launching subs had been produced, each carrying twelve missiles with a 1,200-mile range. Four more are scheduled to be completed by the early 1990s. John Lewis and Litai Xue, "Strategic Weapons and Chinese Power," *CQ*, No. 112, Dec. 1987, pp. 553-554.

40. Sutter, "Realities of International Power," p. 14.

41. Sutter, "Realities of International Power," p. 14.

42. *Far Eastern Economic Review,* May 28, 1982, p. 12.

43. *Far Eastern Economic Review,* Mar. 31, 1983, pp. 23-24.

44. Laurence Freedman, "Sino-Soviet Economic and Technological Factors," in Douglas Stuart and William T. Tow, eds., *China, The Soviet Union and the West*, p. 80.

45. *Far Eastern Economic Review,* May 28, 1982, p. 38.

46. Sutter, "Realities of International Power," p. 17.

47. *Far Eastern Economic Review,* Aug. 16, 1984, p. 24.

48. Sutter, "Realities of International Power," p. 18.

49. Liang Jiejun, "The South Asian Crises," H. Kapur, *As China Sees the World,* p. 144.

50. *Far Eastern Economic Review,* December 8, 1988, p. 30.

51. Foreign Broadcast Information Service, *Daily Report, Soviet Union,* July 29, 1986, pp. R14-19. A polished translation is contained in Novosti Press Agency, Moscow, "Mikhail Gorbachev: New Soviet Peace Initiatives," Dec. 1986.

52. *China Pictorial*, Nov. 1987, p. 33.

53. *Beijing Review,* Vol 31 No. 5, Feb. 1-7, 1988, p. 17.

54. Pi Ying-hsien, "Peking-Moscow Relations Since Gorbachev," *Issues and Studies,* Vol. 23, No. 11, Nov. 1987, p. 106.

10

Whither the Sino-Soviet Dispute?

As a major factor in international relations, the Sino-Soviet dispute is over. Bilateral relations from 1982 to 1988 combined threat reduction with growing connections of mutual benefit. The border will remain armed for the indefinite future, but the sense of military confrontation has virtually disappeared. Cross-border barter trade provides a peaceful routine along those portions of the border where towns and transportation routes are located. Geopolitical rivalry, especially in Asia, will also continue, but the competition is muted by more communications, coordination and, in some cases, cooperation. Sino-Soviet relations reflect the sorts of strains one might expect between a superpower and a major regional power not part of a common alliance system. Party-to-party ties, severed since 1966, are not yet reestablished and remain as the major political symbol of the Sino-Soviet rift. Those uniquely communist relations might be resumed once the terms of an Indochina settlement have been determined, or as a result of the 1989 Deng-Gorbachev summit meeting.

One approach to surveying the current status and future prospects for Sino-Soviet relations is to evaluate progress on what Deng Xiaoping dubbed the "three big obstacles" that have troubled their bilateral ties. Beijing generally listed them as the militarization of the northern border, Afghanistan, and Indochina. The PRC confronted the USSR with these demands when bilateral talks were re-instituted in 1982, and they initially served as major barriers to progress. A subtle change took place in the role of the "obstacles" beginning about 1985. They had symbolized Soviet bad faith and justified China's uncompromising hostility. Deng began to reshape them into a negotiating agenda, enabling the two nations to reach an accord on the relative power distribution in Asia in which both China and the USSR will acknowledge each other's interests and status.[1] Each of the three obstacles merits examination in terms of the current situation and future potential.

Border Talks: Current Status and Prospects

While the border dispute per se is not one of the three obstacles, it was the proximate cause of the military confrontation in the 1960s and 1970s. Border agreements will be a precondition to additional progress in reducing the military tension between the two nations.

The riverine boundary separating Manchuria and Siberia is probably the most difficult border problem. None of the historical treaties between Russia and China dealt with the issue of the riverine islands. The 1860 Treaty of Beijing simply specified that the Amur and Ussuri rivers were to serve as the eastern boundary between China and Russia. Since they flow north, ice blocks the access to the sea until late spring, causing an annual inundation of almost all of the upstream islands, rendering them unfit for habitation.

The only important inhabited island is situated at the confluence of the Ussuri and Amur rivers. Translated into English it is known as Bear Island—Heixiazi Dao on the accompanying map.[2] While poorly drained, Bear Island is sizable, being about twenty-five miles long and ten miles wide at its southwestern base. The island has been under Soviet control since Moscow consolidated its revolution in Siberia in the early 1920s. There is a small permanent population, and a number of weekend cottages are owned by citizens of nearby Khabarovsk. It rests on the Chinese side of the main channels of both the Ussuri and Amur rivers. Since Mikhail Gorbachev conceded that the thalweg, in principle, should be the method for settling the riverine islands dispute, the PRC claim is much strengthened. If the island is to remain in Soviet hands, Beijing would have to "grant" its ownership to the USSR.

The Soviets claim that the island should remain under their control due to the long period of occupancy and the proximity to Khabarovsk. The Chinese claim that the island should be turned over to them; in return they promise to preserve Soviet access and respect the property rights of the Soviets owning homes on the island. The PRC also has offered to keep the island demilitarized so as to avoid any threat to Khabarovsk. Both sides have agreed to disagree on these points. So, the border talks were stalled until the autumn of 1988. However, both Chinese and Soviet officials emphasized that the talks were being carried out in a professional manner and without polemics.[3] Both sides also emphasized that there is no sense of "threat" or crisis on the border. Navigation matters are being routinely handled, and barter trade is flourishing. A Chinese spokesman suggested that the very absence of threat or crisis will probably mean that the talks are apt to drag on for a considerable length of time. However, in early November 1988, following a round of talks in Moscow, the "Manchurian borders" were declared to be nearly settled.

Another area of the border that has not yet been addressed by negotia-

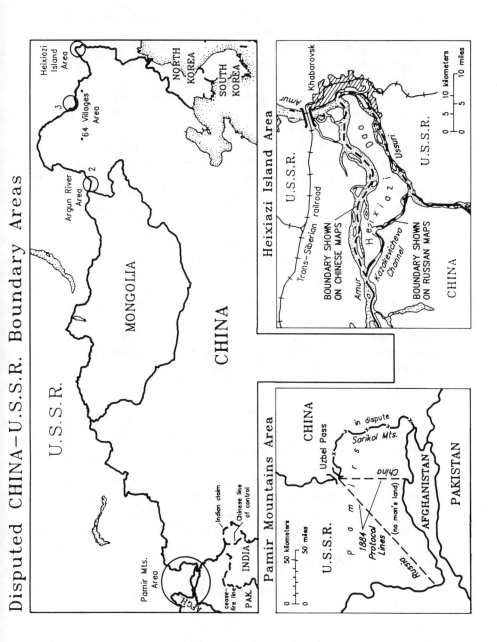

Disputed CHINA–U.S.S.R. Boundary Areas

tions is a sizable region claimed by China in the Pamir Mountains just north of the current Afghanistan-China border. At the suggestion of the USSR, negotiations on this sector were delayed until the eastern boundaries could be resolved. Nineteenth century treaties are of little use due to severe ambiguities in the language. Furthermore, the region had not been surveyed at that time, thus rendering the maps an exercise in cartographic imagination.[4] The area, which is very lightly populated, is at such a high elevation that there is no soil; only mountain peaks and valleys strewn with glacial moraine are to be found there. The current line of occupation runs along the east-west watershed in the region and thus serves as a natural boundary.

The Soviets argue that no change should be made in the de facto Pamir boundary. Their bargaining position is strengthened by a treaty signed with China in 1924. Both parties agreed that the then-current border positions would continue until such time as the boundary could be "re-demarcated." The Soviets point out that to re-demarcate is not the equivalent to redrawing the border. Rather it consists of checking that markers are where they are supposed to be.[5] The 1924 treaty would be of limited value to the Soviets on the riverine border talks, where the thalweg can be used to re-demarcate, but it would be more relevant to the Pamirs, where the boundary has been occupied by Russia for almost a century and already follows the east-west watershed. When the western-sector border discussions eventually begin, the Soviets could argue that what remains to be done is only a technical survey and the installation of markers. One Chinese official suggested that Beijing would be willing to drop its claims to this region if the Soviets would turn over Bear Island to the PRC.[6]

In June 1981, some eighteen months after the Soviet invasion of Afghanistan, a new border treaty was signed between those nations. The PRC protested the agreement, claiming that Moscow had annexed the Wakhan Corridor, which serves as the only point of contact between the PRC and Afghanistan. According to the Office of the Geographer, US State Department, such claims were alarmist.[7] The treaty apparently called for a new delineation of the existing border, but it would not affect the PRC except that some of the territory involved lies in the Chinese-claimed western Pamir Mountains, a claim that Beijing was not likely to obtain in any case. However, regardless of treaty status, the Wakhan Corridor has been under firm Soviet control since 1978, a year before the occupation of Afghanistan's capital. Most of the local Kirgiz herdsmen (some 1,300) were driven south into Pakistan, and the remaining Wakhi population has tended to favor the Soviet-supported Kabul regime. One reason for such support may be Moscow's improvement of the main east-west road, an improvement that allowed easier access and better economic opportunities for the populace in that remote region.[8] It remains to be seen whether the Soviets will withdraw totally from the Wakhan Corridor as their forces leave the rest of Afghanistan.

The Force Levels Issue

Regarding the military balance, Gorbachev offered in 1986 to negotiate mutual force reductions on a sector-by-sector basis that could commence in any area where territory is not in dispute. However, the degree of troop reduction would not be large; over the past decade, the Soviets have unilaterally reduced their ground-force troop strength by almost half. Moreover, too many benefits accrue to the USSR by maintaining a strong military presence in Soviet Asia. The USSR would most likely "mothball" whatever units might be removed from the Sino-Soviet border in order to reduce the bloated defense budget. There are about 180 divisions in the Soviet ground forces, more than any rational peacetime defense need could justify. Indeed, the budget savings benefit is probably one major reason why Gorbachev initially made the mutual force reduction offer to the PRC.[9]

When Beijing fully defines the three big obstacles, it specifies the Soviet military presence in Mongolia as an integral part of the first obstacle. Indeed, Mongolia constitutes probably the most sensitive of the border sectors. Not only does it provide the best invasion corridor into northern China, but it also involves more political issues than any other sector. There are limits on what Gorbachev can offer the Chinese. In 1983, the leadership of the Mongolian People's Republic (MPR), concerned that Sino-Soviet détente might be made at its expense, launched a virulent anti-China campaign that saw the expulsion of thousands of Han Chinese.[10] Continued Soviet influence in the MPR is conditioned upon Moscow's ability to defend Ulan Bator against Chinese power. Gorbachev is in no position to meet the Chinese demand that all Soviet forces be removed from the MPR. The PRC leadership probably realizes this, but cannot acknowledge it without admitting that China is perceived as dangerous by its smaller northern neighbor. Gorbachev did authorize the withdrawal of about 10,000 troops in 1986, but four divisions remain. Further deep cuts in the Soviet military presence were announced in March 1989.

Afghanistan

The second of the three obstacles moved toward a resolution in 1988. Afghanistan was a dilemma for Moscow. Moscow wanted out but could not find a way that would insure that Kabul would not become a hostile nation, linked with Iran, and potentially adding to the restiveness of millions of Soviet Moslems. While this threat potential has been much exaggerated in the Western press, Moslem fundamentalism still could strengthen ethnic nationalist demands.[11] Meanwhile, Pakistan obtained major benefits from the United States and the Moslem world for supporting the mujahedeen. China

stood by its Pakistani ally and would not help the Soviets extricate themselves from the Afghanistan morass unless some quid pro quo could be
found.

In January 1988, Moscow made clear its intention to withdraw from
Afghanistan beginning that calendar year. Gorbachev's only precondition
was a US cutoff of military aid to the mujahedeen. In March, Washington
proved unwilling to meet that condition unless the Soviets ceased supplying
the puppet government in Kabul as well.

Pakistan further muddied the waters by demanding that a coalition government be formed prior to the Soviet withdrawal. When Gorbachev was
asked by Western journalists what role the USSR would play in setting up a
coalition government, he replied:

> When it is suggested to us that the USSR should take part in talks on the
> issue of a coalition government, or even talk to third countries, our answer
> is firm and clear: don't expect us to do it; it is none of our business. Or
> yours, for that matter.[12]

From Moscow's standpoint, if it cannot have a communist Afghanistan,
the second best outcome is to have a weak and divided neighbor. If the seven
major groups of mujahedeen fall out among themselves and are unable to
agree on a central government, the situation would then allow for "warlord
politics" and a continued influential role for the USSR as an arms supplier if
nothing else. Thus Gorbachev's refusal to participate in the creation of an
coalition government for Kabul need not be attributed to concern for
Afghanistan's sovereignty.

Preparations for the withdrawal continued despite the absence of international cooperation. The initial method adopted was to seek a series of local
agreements with Afghan chieftains allowing Soviet forces to pull out peacefully from the various regions. By mid-January 1988, the Soviets claimed to
have an armistice in effect with 40,000 resistance fighters and pending cease-
fire agreements with an additional 114,000.[13] As the major supplier of the
mujahedeen, the United States, agreed to reduce arms supplies in proportion
to the Soviet withdrawal. Washington also agreed to allow Afghan
Communist party participation in a future coalition government that would
include mujahedeen representatives and possibly be led by the former king,
Zahair Shah. Those initial agreements broke down in March 1988, but that
breakdown did not affect Soviet determination to leave. The pullout began in
mid-May and was completed in February 1989.

Preventing the development of close ties between Afghanistan and Iran
is now in the mutual interest of the United States and USSR, but even with
superpower cooperation, the military and political situation remains volatile.
Future domestic stability for the Afghans remains clouded. Internecine war-

fare could easily break out within the mujahedeen. There are an estimated 200,000 communist party members in Afghanistan who face a future fraught with danger. The USSR may have to make provisions for resettling Afghans, just as the United States had to accommodate many Vietnamese.[14] The Soviets may also attempt to convert provinces bordering the USSR into bastions of communist strength, supplied and supported from bases on Soviet territory.

It has been estimated that about one-third of all villages in Afghanistan have been destroyed or badly damaged in the eight years of fighting and extensive aerial bombing. There are over three million refugees currently living in Pakistan. The regeneration of Afghanistan's agrarian economy will require a large-scale and expensive multinational effort.

Indochina

Progress also marks the third of the three big obstacles, but the nature of the final resolution is very unclear (even more so than the resolutions to the first two issues). Hanoi initially announced that it would pull its military forces out of Kampuchea by the end of 1990, a claim that was widely disbelieved. The SRV did withdraw about 20,000 troops in November 1987; it announced in June 1988 that an additional 50,000 troops would be withdrawn by the end of the year.[15] That would have left only about 70,000 Vietnamese troops in the country. In June, the Vietnamese military command was removed and the remaining military forces were placed under the control of the Phnom Penh government. In mid-1988, Hanoi announced that it had speeded up its withdrawal schedule and would have none of its troops in Kampuchea after the summer of 1989. However, at the close of 1988, it seemed that the troop reductions were behind schedule. The initial Vietnamese troop reductions set off a scramble to find some political solution for Cambodia's twenty years of war and death. It may be that some of the powers involved would like to see the Vietnamese remain a bit longer, providing time to strengthen the power base of Prince Norodom Sihanouk.

In the 1988 negotiations, all parties involved agreed that Kampuchea should be independent and neutral.[16] All endorsed a four-part coalition government led by Prince Sihanouk.[17] The PRC finally came around to agreeing that the Khmer Rouge must not be allowed to play a dominant role in a new government, although Beijing continued to insist that the leadership had reformed and that the hated Pol Pot was no longer influential.[18]

The major remaining obstacle is the timing and methods to be used to weaken the military clout of the Khmer Rouge. That obstacle is intricately linked to the Vietnamese withdrawal. Beijing insists that all Vietnamese forces leave Kampuchea, after which time Chinese military support to the communist insurgents would be cutback or eliminated. A Sino-Vietnamese agreement was reportedly reached in late January 1989 calling for final Vietnamese military pull-out from Kampuchea in September. During the interim, the Chinese would eliminate their assistance to the Khmer Rouge.

Meanwhile, the thirty thousand-man army of the Khmer Rouge has stockpiled arms against just such a contingency. In the autumn of 1988, the Khmer Rouge began forcing refugees to move from the Thai border camps to new locations inside Kampuchea. Though Khmer Rouge do not control all the camps, they do dominate the majority. Meanwhile, the United States began a program of supplying Prince Sihanouk with the wherewithal to build an armed force.[19] The aim was to allow the prince and his noncommunist rival, Son Sann, to develop armed forces sufficient to guarantee their political viability. The logistics have required that such support be funneled through Thailand; therefore the Thai government will play a critical role in determining the balance of forces in Kampuchea. The Thais favor a weak and divided Kampuchean leadership in order to maximize their influence in the region.

Whatever the eventual solution, Moscow will have played a major role in Vietnam's decision to withdraw from Kampuchea. Hanoi is totally dependent on Soviet military and economic assistance. Gorbachev doubled the previous level of Soviet assistance to Vietnam in its 1986-1990 Five Year Plan to $5 billion for the total period.[20] Including military assistance, Vietnam is costing Moscow as much as $8 million daily, but that is a manageable outlay for a major power, and the benefits derived are perhaps worth the cost. The first benefit to the Soviet Union resulting from the military aid is that Cam Ranh Bay provides the only major port for the Soviet Pacific fleet between Vladivostok and the Indian Ocean. Second, it ties down Chinese ground forces far from the Soviet border, and, finally, it provides aerial reconnaissance as far as the Philippines.[21] The Soviets are not about to leave Indochina.

Deng Xiaoping stated that a fully normalized Sino-Soviet relationship depended on Moscow's assistance in getting Vietnam out of Kampuchea.[22] The PRC made it clear that the Vietnamese occupation is the issue. Beijing does not demand that the Soviets remove their military presence from Vietnam, much less abrogate their 1978 alliance. In January 1989, progress was sufficient to enable a PRC agreement to a Gorbachev-Deng summit in May 1989.

The Soviets almost certainly did pressure Hanoi to begin its troop reduction in Kampuchea. After five years of refusing to negotiate with China on the Kampuchean issue, Sino-Soviet talks were held in Beijing in August 1988 without the presence of Vietnam. Hanoi's regional ambitions were increasingly interfering with Gorbachev's Asian strategy of improving relations with the PRC, the ASEAN nations and Japan. However, Moscow must tread carefully lest it endanger its position and privileges in Vietnam. For years, the United States attempted to use the Soviet Union to deliver a suitable peace to the Vietnam War. Moscow could not do so. Vietnam is now more dependent on the USSR than it was in the 1960s, but there are limits to the Kremlin's political leverage.

Prospects for Sino-Soviet Détente

Progress has been made on all three major stumbling blocks to improved bilateral relations, and additional progress can be expected. But what if there is a continued stalemate in Indochina, or even unexpected reverses in improving the border situation, or new levels of violence in Afghanistan? Happily, none of the three issues entail crisis diplomacy. None threaten to escalate into broader conflicts imperiling Deng's priority attention to domestic economic development and modernization. None of the three require significant new defense expenditures for the PRC. Thus, Beijing is prepared to wait.

Triangular relations have also entered a relatively stable period. Since, Beijing has taken the pivot position with both Washington and Moscow competing for influence, there are currently no reasons for China to move significantly closer to either superpower. There are, however, a number of compelling reasons why it should not. A true rapprochement with Moscow would destroy the close economic relations with the West thereby grievously damaging the "four modernizations." Economic development and modernization of the PRC is China's top national priority; it must be protected at all costs. The so-called "independent" stance between the superpowers seems best suited for that purpose, as long as the policy retains its current Western tilt.

There is no reason for Beijing to again seek a strategic alignment with the United States, since the direct Soviet military threat is diminishing. In all likelihood, a true entente with the United States would create new Soviet military pressures against the PRC. It would certainly end the mutual confidence-building measures now underway between Beijing and Moscow. Using its favorable position in the strategic triangle, the PRC is currently able to obtain virtually all it can afford in military technology and weapons systems from the United States and Western Europe. In 1986, an agreement was signed with Washington to provide $500 million in avionics for Chinese fighter-interceptor aircraft. The package included sophisticated target acquisition and fire-control radars from the F-16. Also in 1986, the United States pulled ahead of Japan as the second largest foreign investor in the PRC (behind Hong Kong). The PRC has about 30,000 students in the United States, a major source of technology transfer, the majority of whom are receiving financial aid from the universities involved and from other public and private US sources.

From its pivot position, Beijing is able to wrest similar concessions from

Moscow. In bilateral negotiations during 1987, the Soviets offered free assistance in updating 156 industrial plants dating from the 1950s. The Soviets also promised cooperation in developing the Chinese nuclear-power industry.[23] All SS-20 IRBMs based in Soviet Asia are to be removed and destroyed as part of the 1987 "zero option" agreement between Moscow and Washington. As discussed in Chapter 9, Gorbachev is also assisting the PRC complete its railway through Xinjiang to the border with Soviet Kazakhstan.

The Chinese stance in the strategic triangle is not one of equidistance; in his former capacity as premier, Zhao Ziyang affirmed that in 1986.[24] Beijing's economic ties to the West and Japan are much stronger than its economic relationship with the Soviet bloc (in trade alone, the 1986 figures were $25 billion compared to $3 billion, respectively).[25] Issues do separate the PRC from the West, and particularly the United States. Beijing is sharply critical of "Star Wars" and Washington's Central American and Middle East policies. It refused to condemn the USSR for shooting down Korean Air Lines Flight 007 in 1983. In the UN, China votes with the Third World nations against the industrialized West. Taiwan and Korea remain unresolved issues dangerously close to home.

Collectively, those divisive problems are small when compared to the conflicts separating Beijing and Moscow. It is only the USSR that poses a major military threat to the PRC. Its alliances with Vietnam and Mongolia are inherently anti-Chinese, and the friendship treaty with India is partially intended to contain Chinese power and influence. The best that can be hoped for is that Beijing and Moscow will continue to manage their rivalry.

The Sino-Soviet dispute accumulated a great deal of momentum over the past three decades. Policies implemented during the height of the rift still carry on and have assumed their own internal logic. Foremost among these was the Soviet military buildup in East Asia:

> Moscow obtains immense benefits from the mere stationing of strong military forces in Siberia and the Soviet Far East. Because the Soviets have almost no other effective political instruments, the Kremlin has found the Asian components of the Red Army its key to enhanced influence in Asia. The Soviet military presence in Vietnam, in Afghanistan, on the northern islands off Japan and in the sea and air of the Western Pacific is based on the more or less permanent placement of those 51 divisions adjacent to China.
>
> For another thing, the Soviets have found the Siberian force a convenient means of influencing distant events from inside their own border. Since Vietnamese security from further Chinese attack depends on the Soviet threat to Xinjiang and Manchuria, so Soviet naval and air rights at Cam Ranh Bay and Danang are purchased by Moscow's anti-Chinese military capabilities. India is protected, like Vietnam, not merely by a security treaty with the Soviet Union, but also by Soviet divisions east of Tashkent. . . . Finally,

Soviet influence in Pyongyang, such as it is, is based on Soviet military capabilities in the Primorskaya.[26]

Thus, while this chapter opened with the assertion that the Sino-Soviet dispute had faded from the attention of policy-makers, the Chinese struggle against Soviet "hegemonism" in Asia has not ended, nor will Gorbachev suggest carrying forward the troop reductions to the point of demilitarizing the Sino-Soviet border.

Since the adoption of the "independent" foreign policy position at the 12th Party Congress in 1982, Beijing has been able to improve its political and economic relations with both Washington and Moscow. The PRC would undoubtedly like to perpetuate its current favorable position in the strategic triangle. In order to do so with the United States, Beijing will have to carefully manage the Taiwan problem, prevent the worsening of Sino-Japanese relations, and keep a close watch over the mercurial North Korean leadership. In order to protect its favorable position vis-à-vis the Soviets, Beijing will have to negotiate in good faith on the border issues and avoid renewed military attacks on Vietnam. In June 1988, Chinese naval forces shelled Vietnamese boats in the disputed Spratly Islands. Managing restraint with the SRV seems to be more difficult for Beijing than avoiding direct provocations with the USSR. The PRC apparently retains some of the historical Chinese hegemonistic attitudes toward its Southeast Asian neighbors.

Fortunately, there is nothing on the international horizon that poses a grave peril to the current stasis in the strategic triangle. Chinese arms sales to Iran and Iraq (needed to generate convertible currency) proved troublesome to the United States. However, France's sale of Exocet missiles to Iraq preceded by almost five years the Chinese "Silkworm" missiles to Iran. Washington's own hands are far from clean. The Iran-Contra fiasco resulted in Iran obtaining approximately 4,000 anti-tank missiles. The issue was seemingly laid to rest in November 1987 when the United States obtained a *nolo contendere* agreement from Beijing; without admitting to selling missiles to Iran, the PRC said that it would stop doing so. New concerns arose in March 1988 with the discovery that Saudi Arabia had purchased a number of IRBMs from the PRC. Without nuclear or chemical/biological warheads, such weapons have little military value due to their poor accuracy. Moreover, Saudi Arabia made a no-first-use pledge and promised not to transfer the missiles to any third party. Finally, Saudi Arabia is not Iran. Thus the Saudi missile crisis swiftly faded from news headlines.

Continuing troubles can be anticipated as a result of differing perspectives regarding human rights. In 1987, the United States focused its criticism on the Chinese handling of dissidence in Tibet. The Reagan administration also sharply criticized abortion practices in the PRC. These issues are not apt to become serious obstacles in bilateral relations, but they do provide ongoing justification for Beijing's independent foreign policy stance.

Notes

1. Richard Nations, *Far Eastern Economic Review,* Mar. 20, 1986, p. 66.

2. The Chinese refer to it as "Blind Man's Island" (Heixiase Dao), and the Soviets more accurately give it two names since it is more than one island, Big Ussuri (or Chimnaya Island) and Tarabarovskiy Island, separated by narrow channels.

3. Interviews were conducted with officials of the Chinese and Soviet embassies in Washington.

4. John Garver, "The Sino-Soviet Territorial Dispute in the Pamir Mountains Region," *CQ* No. 85, Mar. 1981, pp. 107-118.

5. Novosti Press Agency, *Fact and Fantasy: On the Question of a Sino-Soviet Border Settlement,* Moscow, 1982, p. 32.

6. Author's interview at PRC embassy, March 1988.

7. Conversation with Sandra Shaw, Office of the Geographer, US State Department.

8. *Asiaweek,* June 10, 1988, p. 16.

9. Thomas Robinson, "The New Era in Sino-Soviet Relations," *Current History,* Sept. 1987 p. 243.

10. William Heaton, "Mongolia in 1983: Mixed Signals," *Asian Survey,* January 1984.

11. In 1987, *Literaturnaya Gazeta* published a series of articles that claimed that a parallel Islamic infrastructure existed and flourished alongside the Soviet system in central Asia (Martin Walker, "Fundamental Problems in Soviet Islamic Republics," *The Manchester Guardian,* Apr. 24, 1988, p. 10). However, Walker also points out that most of the "Islamic problem" is indigenously generated within the USSR. An Iranian-sponsored fundamentalist threat that spread through Afghanistan to the Moslem republics of the USSR was an exaggeration accepted by some Western analysts and probably a few leaders in the Kremlin as well.

12. *Manchester Guardian,* Feb. 14, 1988, p. 7.

13. United Press International, *Tampa Tribune,* Jan. 17, p. 8A.

14. *Asiaweek,* Jan. 22, 1988, p. 11.

15. *Asiaweek,* June 10, 1988, p. 10.

16. The nations directly and indirectly involved in seeking a solution for Kampuchea include the United States, USSR, PRC, Vietnam, and the ASEAN bloc, (featuring Thailand and Indonesia as its major negotiators).

17. The four-part coalition would consist of the Vietnamese-supported government in Phnom Penh, Sihanouk's own group, a faction led by former Premier Son Sann (with an armed force of several thousand), and the Khmer Rouge.

18. A false rumor circulated, perhaps inspired by Beijing, that Pol Pot was terminally ill and in a Chinese hospital. Later the PRC conceded that he should not be part of any future government, and offered the PRC as a site for his permanent political asylum.

19. *Far Eastern Economic Review,* Oct. 27, 1988, p. 17.

20. Richard Nations in the *Far Eastern Economic Review,* Mar. 20, 1986, p. 69.

21. *The Economist,* July 14, 1984, p. 29.

22. R. Nations, *Far Eastern Economic Review,* Mar. 20, 1986, p. 66.

23. Donald Zagoria, "China and the Superpowers: Recent Trends in the Strategic Triangle," a conference paper to be published in a forthcoming book on Chinese foreign relations edited by Robert Scalapino.

24. *Washington Post,* Jan. 12, 1984, p. A30.

25. Zagoria, "China and the Superpowers."

26. Thomas Robinson, *Far Eastern Economic Review,* Apr. 4, 1982, p. 32.

11

The Moral of the Story

Pessimists have described history as the endless chronicle of human folly. To some extent, this book supports that view. Mistaken perceptions, hostility, racism, exploitation, and the deaths of well over a million people characterize the relationships among Moscow, Beijing, and Washington since 1950. On the other hand, general war has been averted, and the prospects for stability among the three powers look bright.

There are also observations to be drawn concerning the nature of power relations per se. The first is the political importance of nuclear weapons in a situation where one power has a first-strike potential against another. It could be argued that US nuclear dominance was a sufficient cause of the Sino-Soviet rift. Yet once the USSR achieved a second-strike capacity in the mid-1960s, Moscow felt free to play a global role and involve itself in regional conflicts far from its borders. Once China achieved a "proportional nuclear deterrent" in the late 1960s, combined with Sino-American détente, it had an underlying sense of security in the face of the Soviet military threat. As Mao put it, "Once I have six atomic bombs, no one can bomb my cities."[1]

The twenty years since the end of the 1960s saw a sharp decline in coercive nuclear diplomacy. According to a Chinese count, the United States threatened to use nuclear weapons on nineteen occasions between January 1946 and December 1975.[2] It is difficult to identify a single case of nuclear coercion by any nation since then, unless one considers the Carter Doctrine for the protection of the Persian Gulf as an indirect nuclear threat.

The declining political role of nuclear weapons was initially due to the rise of US-Soviet parity, combined with the emergence of triangular relations with China and a "German solution" in Europe. The severity of the crises among the major powers has also lessened. Arms control assumed a much more important role than in previous years, but it should be understood to be a mutual attempt to minimize the importance of nuclear weapons in power relations. Successful arms-control negotiations reflect and prolong a relative power balance among the actors involved. The PRC will begin to play a role in such talks. It was already an actor in the 1987 decision to abolish all Soviet and US missiles in the 300- to 3,500-mile range. The strong voices of Beijing and Tokyo helped convince the USSR to include its Asian-based SS-20s as well as its European ones.

The second concluding observation concerns the preeminence of national-security considerations in determining the political behavior of major nations. To some extent, this viewpoint was foreordained by the evidence selected for discussion herein. Only marginal attention has been devoted to economic and ideological aspects of the international relations examined in this book. Yet Khrushchev's blatant economic warfare against China between 1959 and 1961 was totally ineffectual. His earlier use of economic carrots to cement the Sino-Soviet alliance in the mid-1950s also failed once the Maoist leadership realized that a dependent relationship was developing. Much of the ideological polemics disguised conflicting national-security objectives. When Beijing and Moscow began to seek areas of mutual accommodation in the 1980s, the ideological issues largely vanished.

National-security perspectives are best able to explain the twists and turns of the Sino-Soviet dispute. Moscow's security "leverage" over Beijing gradually weakened in the 1950s. Stalin was able to bring Mao to heel during the Korean War. Khrushchev was able to maintain Soviet leverage by using the carrot of nuclear sharing, though only for one or two years. After the Taiwan Straits crisis, the USSR was never able to regain control of its junior partner in the alliance. Brezhnev's militarization of the dispute was no more successful than Khrushchev's economic warfare.

There is an important corollary to the centrality of national-security perceptions. Threats are hazardous, especially in relations among major powers. Threats often occur when a nation attempts to convert military superiority into political advantage over a major rival. The intimidation almost always provokes countermeasures, some of which may be worse than the condition that prompted the threat in the first place. From the US side, the threat to Manchuria posed by the invasion of North Korea resulted in immensely increased war costs both in human and material terms. The US threat of "massive retaliation" and the nuclear "brinksmanship" of the Eisenhower era resulted in nuclear proliferation (Soviet nuclear assistance to the PRC). Kennedy's rapid buildup of ICBMs led to the Cuban missile crisis and the later massive deployment of Soviet ICBMs. In the Nixon and Carter administrations, US-supported efforts to win Afghanistan over to a pro-West posture led to the Soviet backing of a dangerous coup d'état and later intervention. The Soviet conventional and nuclear military threats to China in the late 1960s led directly to US/PRC détente. Finally, Beijing's threats to Vietnam were the major factor in the formation of the Vietnamese-Soviet military alliance.

In the absence of foreign threats and with confidence in one's own deterrence, international relations can function routinely based on the pursuit of economic and political self-interest. Nuclear weapons are then remote and without political impact; under such circumstances, they become the paper tiger that Mao asserted them to be in 1948.[3] The world is closer to that halcyon state in the late 1980s than it was in the first three decades of the atomic age, but the barriers to progress loom large. In the future, the concern may be less with US-Soviet relations and the strategic triangle involving China. Increasingly, the threat potential to international stability seems likely to come from new nuclear actors who have yet to stabilize the rules of the game with their regional enemies.

Notes

1. The quotation comes from a conversation with Andre Malraux circa 1965, cited in Richard M. Nixon, *Memoirs*, p. 557.

2. Wang Qianqi, "Nuclear Weapons and International Security," in Harish Kapur ed., *As China Sees the World*, p. 44.

3. It is arguable that there has been no successful use of coercive nuclear diplomacy since the Cuban missile crisis of 1962, and the US participants have since downplayed the nuclear role even in that case. The 1973 Kissinger-instigated nuclear alert in the latter stages of the Yom Kippur War was a much stronger measure than was needed to deter a Soviet initiative for a joint US-Soviet peacekeeping force on the Sinai. For a different viewpoint, which poses at least the continuing potential for coercive nuclear diplomacy, especially by the United States, see Richard Betts, *Nuclear Blackmail and Nuclear Balance*.

Bibliography

Government Journals and Documentary Collections

Beijing Review, Beijing.
China Pictorial, Beijing.
International Relations, Moscow.
Novosti Press Agency. *Fact and Fantasy: On the Question of a Sino-Soviet Border Settlement,* Moscow, 1982.
University Publications of America: Research Collections, *CIA Research Reports—China, 1946-76.* Frederick Mary., 1981.
———*CIA Research Reports—the Soviet Union,* 1946-76.
———*Documents of the National Security Council, 1947-77.* Four "Supplements" accompany this collection, the latest of which was released in 1987.
———*Top Secret Hearings by the US Senate Committee on Foreign Relations, 1959-66.*
US Central Intelligence Agency, National Foreign Assessments Center, *Chinese Defense Spending, 1965-79,* Washington D. C., 1980.

Books and Monographs

Ambroz, Anton. *Realignment of World Power,* Vols. I & II. N.Y., Robert Speller & Sons, 1972.
Amstutz, J. Bruce. *Afghanistan: The First Five Years of Soviet Occupation.* Washington, D.C., National Defense University Press, 1986.
An, Tai-sung. *The Sino-Soviet Territorial Dispute.* Philadelphia, Westminster Press, 1973.
Armstrong, J.D. *Revolutionary Diplomacy: Chinese Foreign Policy and the United Front Doctrine.* Berkeley, University of California Press, 1977.
Barnds, William J. *India, Pakistan and the Great Powers.* N.Y., Praeger Publishers, 1972.
Betts, Richard K. *Nuclear Blackmail and Nuclear Balance.* Washington, D. C., Brookings Institution, 1987.
Bloomfield, Lincoln, et al. *Khrushchev and the Arms Race: Soviet Interests in Arms Control and Disarmament.* Cambridge Mass., M.I.T. Press, 1966.
Bobrow, D., Chan, S., and Kringen, J. A. *Understanding Foreign Policy Decisions: The Chinese Case.* N.Y., Free Press, 1979.
Bottome, Edgar. *The Balance of Terror: Nuclear Weapons and the Illusion of Security, 1945-85.* Boston, Beacon Press, 1986.
Bradsher, Henry. *Afghanistan and the USSR.* Durham, N.C., Duke University Press, 1985.
Breslaur, George. *Khrushchev and Brezhnev as Leaders.* Boston, George Allen & Unwin, 1982.
Brodie, Bernard. *War and Politics.* N.Y., Macmillan, 1973.
Brown, Harrison, ed. *China Among the Nations of the Pacific.* Boulder, Colo., Westview, 1982.

Brumberg, Abraham, ed. *Russia Under Khrushchev.* N.Y., Praeger Press, 1962.

Bullard, Monte. *China's Political-Military Evolution: The Party and the Military in the PRC, 1960-84.* Boulder, Colo., Westview, 1985.

Burrows, William E. *Deep Black: Space Espionage and National Security.* N.Y., Random House, 1986.

Buszynski, Leszek. *Soviet Foreign Policy and Southeast Asia.* N.Y., St. Martin's Press, 1986.

Camilleri, Joseph. *Chinese Foreign Policy.* Seattle, University of Washington Press, 1983.

Chen, King C. *China's War With Vietnam, 1979.* Stanford, Calif., Hoover Institution Press, 1987.

Cheng Chu-yuan. *Economic Relations Between Peking and Moscow, 1949-63.* N.Y., Praeger Press, 1964.

Clemens, Walter C. *The Arms Race and Sino-Soviet Relations.* Stanford, Calif., Hoover Institution on War, Revolution and Peace, 1968.

Cohen, Raymond. *Threat Perception in International Crisis.* Madison, University of Wisconsin Press, 1979.

Conquest, Robert. *Power and Policy in the USSR.* N.Y., Harper and Row, 1967.

Corson, William. *The Armies of Ignorance.* N.Y., Dial Press, 1977.

Cumings, Bruce, ed. *Child of Conflict: The Korean-American Relationship, 1943-53.* Seattle, University of Washington Press, 1983.

Dallin, David J. *Soviet Foreign Policy After Stalin.* Philadelphia, Lippincott, 1961.

Day, Alan J., ed. *China and the Soviet Union, 1949-1984.* N.Y., Longman, 1985.

Deutscher, Isaac. *Russia, China and the West.* N.Y., Oxford University Press, 1970.

Dial, R. L., ed. *Advancing and Contending Approaches to the Study of Chinese Foreign Policy.* Halifax, Center for Foreign Policy Studies, Dalhousie University, 1974.

Dutt, Subimal. *With Nehru in the Foreign Office.* Columbia, Missouri, South Asian Books, 1977.

Dyson, Freeman. *Weapons and Hope.* N.Y., Harper & Row, 1984.

Edmonds, Robin. *Soviet Foreign Policy: The Brezhnev Years.* N.Y., Oxford University Press, 1983.

Elliot, David W. P. *The Third Indo-China Conflict.* Boulder, Colo., Westview, 1981.

Ellison, Herbert J., ed. *The Sino-Soviet Conflict: A Global Perspective.* Seattle, University of Washington Press, 1982.

Ford, Gerald. *A Time to Heal.* N.Y., Harper & Row, 1979.

Freedman, Robert Owen. *Economic Warfare in the Communist Bloc.* N.Y., Praeger Publishers, 1970.

Garthoff, Raymond. *Détente and Confrontation: American-Soviet Relations from Nixon to Reagan.* Washington, D.C., Brookings Institution, 1985.

———ed. *Sino-Soviet Military Relations.* N.Y., Praeger Press, 1966.

Gelman, Harry. *The Soviet Far East Buildup and Soviet Risk Taking Against China.* Santa Monica, RAND Corp. (R2943-AF) 1982.

George, Alexander,and Smoke, Richard. *Deterrence in American Foreign Policy: Theory and Practice.* N.Y., Columbia University Press, 1974.

Gibert, Stephen P. *Soviet Images of America.* N.Y., Crane Russak Co., 1977.

Gittings, John. *Survey of the Sino-Soviet Dispute.* N.Y., Oxford University Press, 1968.

Gottlieb, Thomas M. *Chinese Foreign Policy Factionalism and the Origins of the Strategic Triangle.* Santa Monica, RAND (R-1902-NA), 1977.

Goure, Leon, Kohler, Foy, and Harvey, Mose. *The Role of Nuclear Forces in Current*

Soviet Strategy. Miami, Center for Advanced International Studies, University of
Miami, 1974.

Griffith, William E. *Sino-Soviet Relations, 1964-65.* Cambridge, Mass., M.I.T. Press,
1967.

————ed. *The Soviet Empire: Expansion and Détente.* Lexington, Mass., Lexington
Books, 1976.

Gurtov, Melvin, and Hwang, Byong-Moo. *China Under Threat: The Politics of
Strategy and Diplomacy.* Baltimore, Johns Hopkins University Press, 1980.

Halperin, Morton H. *China and the Bomb.* N.Y., Praeger Press, 1965.

————*The 1958 Taiwan Straits Crisis: A Documented History.* Santa Monica, RAND
Corporation (RA4900-ISA) 1966.

————ed. *Sino-Soviet Relations and Arms Control.* Cambridge Mass., M.I.T. Press,
1967.

Hardgrave, Robert L. *India Under Pressure: Prospects for Political Stability.* Boulder,
Colo., Westview, 1984.

Hart, Thomas G. *Sino-Soviet Relations: Re-examining the Prospects for
Normalization.* Aldershot, England, Gower Press, 1987.

Haselkorn, Avigdor. *The Evolution of Soviet Security Strategy, 1965-75.* N.Y., Crane
Russak Co., 1978.

Hiniker, P. J. *Revolutionary Ideology and Chinese Reality.* Beverly Hills, Calif., Sage
Publishing Co., 1977.

Hinton, Harold. *China's Turbulent Quest.* Bloomington, Indiana University Press,
1972.

————*Three and One-half Powers: The New Balance in Asia.* Bloomington, Indiana
University, 1975.

Hoffmann, Erik, and Fleron, Frederic, eds. *The Conduct of Soviet Foreign Policy.*
London, Butterworth & Co., 1971.

Holloway, David. *The Soviet Union and the Arms Race.* New Haven, Yale University
Press, 1984.

Horelick, Arnold L., and Rush, Myron. *Strategic Power and Soviet Foreign Policy.*
Chicago, University of Chicago Press, 1966.

Hosmer, Steven T., and Wolfe, Thomas W. *Soviet Policy and Practice Toward Third
World Conflicts.* Santa Monica, RAND Corporation, 1983 (later republished by
Lexington Books, Lexington, Mass.).

Hsieh, Alice Langley. *Communist China's Strategy in the Nuclear Era.* Englewood
Cliffs, N.J., Prentice-Hall, 1962.

Hsiung, James C., ed. *Beyond China's Independent Foreign Policy: Challenge for
the US and Its Asian Allies.* N.Y., Praeger, 1985.

Hsiung, James C., and Kim, Samuel, eds. *China in the Global Community.* N.Y.,
Praeger, 1980.

Hsueh Chun-tu, ed. *China's Foreign Relations: New Perspectives.* N.Y., Praeger,
1982.

Isenberg, Irwin. *The Russian-Chinese Rift: Its Impact on World Affairs.* N.Y., H.
Wilson Co., 1966.

Jacobsen, C.G. *Sino-Soviet Relations since Mao: The Chairman's Legacy.* N.Y.,
Praeger, 1981.

Johnson, Chalmers. *Autopsy on People's War.* Berkeley, University of California
Press, 1973.

Johnson, Lyndon. *The Vantage Point.* N.Y., Holt, Rinehart & Winston, 1971.

Johnson, Stuart E., and Yager, Joseph A. *The Military Equation in Northeast Asia.*
Washington, D.C., Brookings Institution, 1979.

Jones, David R., ed. *Soviet Armed Forces Review Annual* (1978 issue cited in footnote). Gulf Breeze, Fla., Academic International Press.

Jukes, Geoffrey. *The Soviet Union in Asia*. Berkeley, University of California Press, 1972.

Kalicki, J.H. *The Pattern of Sino-American Crises*. N.Y., Cambridge University Press, 1975.

Kaplan, Steven S., ed. *Diplomacy of Power: Soviet Armed Forces as a Political Instrument*. Washington, D.C., Brookings Institution, 1981.

Kapur, Ashok. *Pakistan's Nuclear Development*. N.Y., Croom Helm, 1987.

Kapur, Harish, ed. *As China Sees the World: Perceptions of Chinese Scholars*. N.Y., St. Martin's Press, 1987.

Kelman, Herbert C., ed. *International Behovior: A Social-Psychological Analysis*. N.Y., Holt, Rinehart and Winston, 1965.

Kim, Ilpyong J., ed. *The Strategic Triangle: China, the United States and the Soviet Union*. N.Y., Paragon House, 1987.

Kintner, William R., and Scott, Harriet F. *The Nuclear Revolution in Soviet Military Affairs*. Norman, University of Oklahoma Press, 1968.

Kissinger, Henry. *The White House Years*. Boston, Little, Brown, 1979.

———*Years of Upheaval*. Boston, Little, Brown, 1979.

Laird, Robin, and Herspring, Dale. *The Soviet Union and Strategic Arms*. Boulder Colo., Westview Press, 1984.

Larson, Thomas B. *Soviet-American Rivalry*. N.Y., W. W. Norton, 1978.

Lawson, Eugene K. *The Sino-Vietnamese Conflict*. N.Y., Praeger, 1984.

Ledovsky, Andrei. *The USSR, the USA and the People's Revolution in China*. Moscow, Progress Publishers, 1982.

Legault, Albert, and Lindsay, George. *The Dynamics of the Nuclear Balance*. Ithica, N.Y., Cornell University Press, 1976 (2nd edition).

Lieberthal, Kenneth. *Sino-Soviet Conflict in the 1970s: Its Evolution and Implications for the Strategic Triangle*. Santa Monica, RAND Corp. (R2342-NA), 1978.

Liu, Leo Yueh-yun. *China as a Nuclear Power in World Politics*. N.Y., Taplinger Publishing Co. 1972.

Louis, Victor. *The Coming Decline of the Chinese Empire*. N.Y., New York Times Books, 1979.

Low, Alfred. *The Sino-Soviet Confrontation Since Mao Zedong*. Boulder, Colo., Social Science Monographs, 1987.

Mackintosh, J.M. *Strategy and Tactics of Soviet Foreign Policy*. N.Y., Oxford University Press, 1962.

MacLane, Charles. *Soviet Policy and the Chinese Communists, 1931-46*. N.Y., Columbia University Press, 1958.

Mao Zedong. *Selected Works of Mao Tse-tung*. Vol. IV, Beijing, Foreign Languages Press, 1961.

Mayers, David A. *Cracking the Monolith: US Policy Against the Sino-Soviet Alliance, 1949-55*. Baton Rouge, Louisiana University Press, 1986.

Medvedev, Roy. *China and the Superpowers*. N.Y.C., Basil Blackwell Inc., 1986.

———*Khrushchev*. Garden City, N.Y., Anchor, 1983.

Myers, Ramon H., ed. *A US Foreign Policy for Asia: the 1980s and Beyond*. Stanford, Calif., Hoover Institution Press, 1982.

Nixon, Richard M. *The Real War*. N.Y., Warner Books, 1980.

———*Memoirs*. N.Y., Grosset & Dunlap, 1978.

O'Leary, Greg. *The Shaping of Chinese Foreign Policy*. N.Y., St. Martin's Press, 1980.

Olsen, Edward. *US Japan Strategic Reciprocity.* Stanford, Hoover Institution, 1985.

Papp, Daniel S. *Vietnam: The View from Moscow, Peking, Washington.* Jefferson, N.C., McFarland & Co., 1981.

Pollack, Jonathan D. *Perception and Action in Chinese Foreign Policy.* Ph.D. dissertation, University of Michigan, 1976.

———*Security, Strategy and the Logic of Chinese Foreign Policy.* Berkeley, University of California, Institute of East Asian Studies, 1981.

———*The Sino-Soviet Rivalry and Chinese Security Debate.* Santa Monica, RAND Corp. (R2907-AF), 1982.

Powers, Thomas. *The Man Who Kept the Secrets.* N.Y., Alfred Knopf, 1979.

Prados, John. *The Presidents' Secret Wars.* N.Y., William Morrow & Co., 1986.

———*The Soviet Estimate.* N.Y., Dial Press, 1982.

Radvanyi, Janos. *Delusion and Reality: Gambits, Hoaxes and Diplomatic One-upmanship in Vietnam.* South Bend, Indiana, Gateway Editions, 1978.

Rais, Rasul, B. *The Indian Ocean and the Superpowers.* Totowa, N.J., Barnes and Noble, 1987.

Ray, Hemen. *China's Vietnam War.* New Delhi, Radiant, 1983.

Reardon-Anderson, James. *Yenan and the Great Powers: The Origins of Chinese Communist Foreign Policy, 1944-46.* N.Y., Columbia University Press, 1980.

Roseneau, James, ed. *Domestic Sources of Foreign Policy.* N.Y., Free Press, 1967.

Rupen, Robert A., and Farrell, Robert, eds. *Vietnam and the Sino-Soviet Dispute.* N.Y., Praeger Publishers, 1967.

Rybakov, Vladimir. *The Burden.* London, Hutchinson, 1984.

Scalapino, Robert A. *Major Power Relations in Northeast Asia.* Lanham, Md., University Press of America, 1987.

Schelling, Thomas. *Arms and Influence.* New Haven, Yale University Press, 1969.

Schram, Stuart. *Chairman Mao Talks to the People.* N.Y., Random House, 1974.

Schurmann, Franz. *The Logic of World Power.* N.Y., Pantheon Books, 1974.

Schwartz, Harry. *Tsars, Mandarins and Commissars.* N.Y., Doubleday, 1973.

Segal, Gerald, ed. *The China Factor: Peking and the Superpowers.* N.Y., Holmes and Meier, 1982.

———*The Great Power Triangle.* N.Y., St. Martin's Press, 1982.

Shevchenko, Arkady N. *Breaking With Moscow.* N.Y., Alfred Knopf Co., 1985.

Short, Philip. *The Dragon and the Bear: Inside Russia and China Today.* N.Y., William Morrow, 1982.

Shub, Anatole. *An Empire Loses Hope: The Return of Stalin's Ghost.* N.Y., W. W. Norton & Co., 1977.

Shulman, Marshall D. *Stalin's Foreign Policy Reappraised.* Cambridge, Harvard University Press, 1963.

Simmonds, J. D. *China's World: The Foreign Policy of a Developing State.* N.Y., Columbia University Press, 1970.

Simmons, Robert R. *The Strained Alliance: Peking, Pyongyang, Moscow and the Politics of the Korean Civil War.* N.Y., Free Press, 1979.

Snyder, Glenn H. *Deterrence and Defense.* Princeton, N.J., Princeton University Press, 1961.

Solomon, Richard, and Kosaka, Masataka, eds. *The Soviet Far East Build-up: Nuclear Dilemmas and Asian Security.* Dover Mass., 1986.

Stuart, Douglas, and Tow, William T., eds. *China, the Soviet Union and the West.* Boulder Colo., Westview Press, 1982.

Stueck, William. *The Road to Confrontation: American Policy Toward China and Korea, 1947-50.* Chapel Hill, University of North Carolina Press, 1981.

Sutter, Robert A. *The China Quandry: Domestic Determinants of US China Policy, 1972-82*. Boulder, Colo., Westview Press, 1983.
———*Chinese Foreign Policy After the Cultural Revolution, 1966-77*. Boulder, Colo., Westview Press, 1978.
Talbott, Strobe, ed., *Khrushchev Remembers: The Last Testament*. Boston, Little, Brown & Co. 1974.
Taylor, Jay. *China and Southeast Asia*. N.Y., Praeger, 1974.
Thornton, Richard. *Soviet Asian Strategy in the Brezhnev Era and Beyond*. Washington, D.C., Washington Institute for Values in Public Policy, 1985.
Triska, Jan, and Finley, David. *Soviet Foreign Policy*. London, Macmillan Co., 1968.
Tsou, Tang. *China in Crisis* (Vol. II): *China's Policies in Asia and America's Alternatives*. Chicago, University of Chicago Press, 1968.
Tucker, Nancy Bernkopf. *Patterns in the Dust: Chinese-American Relations and the Recognition Controversy, 1949-50*. N.Y., Columbia University Press, 1983.
Ulam, Adam. *Expansion and Coexistence: Soviet Foreign Policy, 1917-73*. N.Y., Praeger Publishers, 1974 (2nd edition).
———*Dangerous Relations: The Soviet Union in World Politics, 1970-82*. N.Y., Oxford University Press, 1983.
Vernon, Graham, ed. *Soviet Perceptions of War and Peace*. Washington, D.C., National Defense University Press, 1981.
Wedeman, Andrew H. *The East Wind Subsides: Chinese Foreign Policy and the Origins of the Cultural Revolution*. Washington, D.C., Washington Institute Press, 1987.
Whiting, Allen S. *The Chinese Calculus of Deterrence*. Ann Arbor, University of Michigan Press, 1975.
———*Siberian Development and East Asia*. Stanford, Stanford University Press, 1981.
———and Sheng Shih-tsai. *Sinkiang, Pawn or Pivot*. East Lansing, Michigan State University Press, 1958.
Wich, Richard. *Sino-Soviet Crisis Politics: A Study of Political Change and Communication*. Cambridge, Mass., Harvard University Press, 1980.
Wilson, Dick. *The Neutralization of Southeast Asia*. N.Y., Praeger, 1975.
Wirsing, Giselher. *The Indian Experiment: Key to Asia's Future*. New Delhi, Orient/Longman, 1972.
Wong-Fraser, S.Y. *The Political Utility of Nuclear Weapons*. Lanham, Md., University Press of America, 1980.
Yahuda, Michael. *China's Role in World Affairs*. N.Y., St. Martin's Press, 1978.
Yao Ming-le. *The Conspiracy and Death of Lin Biao*. N.Y., Alfred Knopf, 1983.
Zagoria, Donald S., ed. *Soviet Policy in East Asia*. New Haven, Yale University Press, 1982.
———*Vietnam Triangle: Moscow, Peking, Hanoi*. N.Y., Pegasus, 1967.
Zimmerman, William. *Soviet Perspectives on International Relations 1956-67*. Princeton, N.J., Princeton Univesity Press, 1969.

Articles and Book Chapters

Barnett, A. Doak. "China's International Posture: Signs of Change," in Shirk, Susan, ed. *The Challenge of China and Japan*. N.Y., Praeger, 1985.
Berbrich, John. "Growth of Soviet Military Power in Asia," in Cline, R. S., Miller, J.

A., and Kanet, R. E. *Asia in Soviet Global Strategy.* Boulder, Colo., Westview, 1987.

Bernstein, Thomas P., and Nathan, Andrew J. "The Soviet Union, China and Korea," *Journal of Asian Studies,* Vol. 25, No. 1, 1982, pp. 67-110.

Bridgham, Philip, Cohen, Arthur, and Jaffe, Leonard. "Mao's Road and Sino-Soviet Relations: a View from Washington, 1953," *The China Quarterly,* No. 52, Oct.-Dec. 1972.

Curtis, Gerald L. "Japan's Foreign Policies," *Foreign Affairs,* Spring 1981.

Garrett, Banning. "China Policy and the Constraints of Triangular Logic," in Oye, K. A., Leiber, R., J. and Rothchild, D. *Eagle Defiant,* Boston, Little, Brown & Co., 1983.

Gelman, H. "The Communist Party of India: Sino-Soviet Battleground," Barnett, A. Doak, *Communist Strategies in Asia,* N.Y., Praeger Press, 1963.

Glaubitz, Joachim. "Aspects of Recent Soviet Policies Toward Asia," in Whetter, Lawrence L.,ed. *The Political Implications of Soviet Military Power.* London, McDonald and Jones, 1977.

Heaton, William. "Mongolia in 1983: Mixed Signals," *Asian Survey,* January 1984.

Hsieh, Alice L. "The Sino-Soviet Nuclear Dialogue," *Bulletin of Atomic Scientists,* Jan. 1965.

Jencks, Harlan. "China's Punitive War on Vietnam," *Asian Survey,* Vol. 19, No. 8, Aug. 1979.

Johnson, Alister I. "Chinese Nuclear Force Modernization: Implications for Arms Control," *Journal of Northeast Asian Studies,* Vol. 2, No. 2, June 1983.

Kimura, Hiroshi. "Soviet and Japanese Negotiating Behavior," *Orbis,* Vol. 24, No. 1, Spring 1980.

Lee, Edmund (pseudonym). "Beijing's Balancing Act," *Foreign Policy,* Summer 1983.

Lewis, John Wilson, and Xue Litai. "Strategic Weapons and Chinese Power: The Formative Years," *CQ* #112, December 1987.

Menon, M. Rajan. "The Military and Security Dimensions of Soviet-Indian Relations," in Donaldson, Robert H., *The Soviet Union in the Third World: Successes and Failures.* Boulder Colo., Westview Press, 1981.

Mitchell, R. J. "A New Brezhnev Doctrine: The Restructuring of International Relations," *World Politics,* Vol. 30, No. 3, 1978.

Miyoshi, Osamu. "Basic Soviet Strategy Toward Japan," in Cline, R. S., Miller, J. A., and Kanet, R. E. *Asia in Soviet Global Strategy.* Boulder, Colo., Westview, 1987.

Naughton, Barry. "The Third Front: Defense Industrialization in the Chinese Interior," *CQ* #115, September 1988.

Nelsen, Harvey. "Strategic Weapons in the Sino-Soviet Dispute," *Issues and Studies,* Nov. 1985.

Noorzoy, M. Siddieq. "Soviet Economic Interests in Afghanistan," *Problems of Commumism,* May-June, 1987.

Okabe, Tatsume. "Japan's Relations with China in the 1980s," in Kim, Y. C., ed. *Japanese and US Policies in Asia.* N.Y., Praeger, 1982.

Pi Ying-hsien. "Peking-Moscow Relations Since Gorbachev," *Issues and Studies,* Vol. 23, No. 11, November 1987.

Ra'annan, Uri. "Peking's Foreign Policy Debate," in Tang Tsou, ed. *China in Crisis,* Vol. II, Chicago, Chicago University Press, 1968.

Robinson, Thomas. "The Sino-Soviet Border Dispute," *The American Political Science Review,* Vol. 66, No. 4, Dec. 1972.

Scalapino, Robert. "China and Northeast Asia," in Richard H. Solomon, ed. *The*

China Factor: Sino-American Relations & the Global Scene. Englewood Cliffs, N.J., Prentice Hall, 1981.

Segal, Gerald. "China and the Great Power Triangle," *China Quarterly,* No. 83, Sept. 1980.

———"China's Strategic Posture and the Great Power Triangle," *Pacific Affairs,* Vol. 53, No. 4, Winter 1980-81.

———"The Soviet Threat at China's Gates," *Conflict Studies,* No. 143, London, Institute for the Study of Conflict, 1983.

Stern, Lewis. The Vietnamese Expulsion of the Overseas Chinese," *Issues and Studies* (Taipei), Vol. 23, No. 7, July 1987.

Sutter, Robert G. Realities of International Power and China's 'Independence' in Foreign Affairs," *Journal of Northeast Asian Studies,* Vol. III, No. 4, Winter 1984.

Tretiak, Daniel. "China's Vietnam War and Its Consequences," *The China Quarterly,* No. 80, Dec. 1979.

Walker, Martin. "Fundamental Problems in Soviet Islamic Republics," *Manchester Guardian,* Vol. 138, No. 17, Apr. 24, 1988.

Walz, Kenneth. "The Spread of Nuclear Weapons; More May Be Better," *Adelphi Papers* No. 171, London, Institute of Strategic Studies, 1981.

Whiting, Allen. "Quemoy in 1958: Mao's Miscalculations," *China Quarterly* No. 62, June 1975. See also the brief amending note by Whiting in *CQ* No. 63.

Index